THE GREAT BETRAYAL

D0416215

The Author

For two decades, John Drennan was the most feared scribe in Leinster House. Some politicians loved him, most hated him, but all agreed that he was the wiliest, the most accurate, the most independent and the most sagacious chronicler of the Dáil soap-opera.

Then, in a move that stunned the political establishment, he left Ireland's largest newspaper, *The Sunday Independent*, to join a struggling fledgling party called Renua. He may be a spinner now, but in his writing that independent voice and inquiring eye continues to shines through.

John lives in Portlaoise with his wife and two sons.

Praise for John Drennan

'There is a fierce intelligence and fierce independence at work here. No one escapes his gimlet eye, and he brings to the whole bizarre ecosystem of the Dáil a unique perspective: that of the insider who remains resolutely outside.'

BRENDAN O'CONNOR, *The Sunday Independent*

'John Drennan has a David Attenborough-like fascination with the unique traits and curious customs of pond life, though his creatures dwell in Leinster House. His storytelling style is stage Irish, and like a culchie Cicero, he laces his brilliance with bile. It is the politics of Paddy and in the tradition of Hall's Pictorial Weekly via Craggy Island.'

GERARD HOWLIN, *The Sunday Times*

'If Paddy really wants to know the story, generally he asks Drennan first.'

LISE HAND, *Irish Independent*

'Drennan is one of the best pundits in Ireland. He has an understanding of politics that is both instinctive and intellectual.'

PAT LEAHY, *The Sunday Business Post*

'[Drennan] reads the political game like the sort of bookie who always leaves Cheltenham with a full satchel.'

IVAN YATES, *Newstalk*

THE GREAT BETRAYAL

How the Government with
the Largest Majority in the
History of the Irish State
Lost its People

John Drennan

Gill & Macmillan

Gill & Macmillan
Hume Avenue
Park West
Dublin 12
www.gillmacmillanbooks.ie

© John Drennan 2015

978 07171 6875 0

Print origination by O'K Graphic Design, Dublin
Printed and bound by ScandBook AB, Sweden

'This Be the Verse' taken from *The Complete Poems* © Estate of Philip Larkin and
reprinted by permission of Faber and Faber Limited

This book is typeset in 12/17 pt Minion
Chapter heads are typeset in 48 pt Machine Regular

*The paper used in this book comes from the wood pulp of managed forests.
For every tree felled, at least one tree is planted, thereby renewing natural
resources.*

A CIP catalogue record for this book is available from the British Library.

5 4 3 2 1

ACKNOWLEDGEMENTS

This book would not have been possible without the unique Gill & Macmillan team, who have provided me with such an expert platform for my wandering thoughts for a number of years.

Thanks are especially owed to Fergal Tobin, Conor Nagle, D Rennison Kunz, Catherine Gough, Ruth Mahony and Teresa Daly, who are role models for all publishers in their expertise and patience.

I would also like to thank former journalistic colleagues such as Ronald Quinlan, Miriam Lord, Niall, Philip, the EFL brigade, Darren, Lise Hand, Eileen Brophy, Anne Harris, Eoghan Harris, Liam Collins, John, Tony and all of the rest for the help support and fun they provided in difficult times.

Also, of course, John Lee, whose willingness to talk about anything other than politics made writing about politics bearable.

There are many others in the world of politics I could thank for all their help, but they wisely would prefer if I didn't.

So I won't.

Finally, to Ciara, Timothy, Micheál and Alice, thanks for giving me a reason to do these things.

CONTENTS

No question, now, what had happened to the faces of the pigs. The creatures outside looked from pig to man, and from man to pig, and from pig to man again; but already it was impossible to say which was which.

GEORGE ORWELL, *Animal Farm*

They fuck you up, your mum and dad.
They may not mean to, but they do.
They fill you with the faults they had
And add some extra, just for you.

But they were fucked up in their turn
By fools in old-style hats and coats,
Who half the time were soppy-stern
And half at one another's throats.

Man hands on misery to man.
It deepens like a coastal shelf.
Get out as early as you can,
And don't have any kids yourself.

PHILIP LARKIN, 'This Be The Verse'

THEY DO NOT MEAN TO, BUT THEY STILL DO

Who would have thought that a poem from the 1970s by the slightly balding poetic chronicler of the stilled dreams of middle England, Philip Larkin, would provide us with the most fitting description of the surreal madness of Irish politics in recent years? Then again, given that this is the story about faith grounded in nothing more permanent than the quicksand of hope, followed by a Great Betrayal that was all the worse for being clothed in such respectable garb, perhaps it is not quite so strange.

We were, prior to 2011, a nation that was resigned to the concept of betrayal. Bertie Ahern, that most loved of Taoisigh and the cutest and most cunning of them all, had betrayed us by flitting down the political foxhole of retirement just before the hounds had snapped his neck. Further betrayal, or rather a series of them, by his successor Cowen, inspired more by lassitude and carelessness rather than intent, had destroyed the independence of the Irish Republic. The word 'betrayal' might sound excessive to describe the mechanics of the bank bailout and the policies of austerity that followed. But this was more than an economic phenomenon. Recessions come and go, but they do not normally cost states their independence.

In our case, the bailout and the subsequent arrival of a Troika of governors from the European Union, the European Central Bank and the International Monetary Fund saw Ireland reduced to the status of an EU satrap. The fall back into a form of Home Rule created a psychologically scarred country that was fiscally and psychologically ravaged by the reparations imposed on its citizens as payment for the frolics of a small caste of bankers and developers. Ancestral vices like mass emigration and unemployment flooded back in, until finally the citizens got their chance.

In the coldest of springs, as part of a great national citizens' revolt, the perennially unloved Pious Protestors of Irish politics, Fine Gael and Labour, were elected to end all this. The voters did not list their requirements, but their core demand was clear. Such was the scale of the destruction of Fianna Fáil that it was clear that the voters were ready for a revolution in governance. And, via the largest majority in the history of the state, they had given the new Coalition the tools to just that.

It was a cheering prospect for our newly elected Coalition, but it contained one fatal danger. The serially cheated-upon Irish voters were used to political deceits but the 2011 election marked a definitive upswing in hope for change and reform. Were a government elected with the biggest majority in the history of the state to renege upon their mandate for change, truly this would be the greatest betrayal of all.

Larkin is apposite because the Great Betrayal by the Coalition Cartel of the Democratic Revolution we were promised in 2011 was a very English sort of affair. Quiet, polite, mannerly but, despite the astonishing absence of public turbulence, very, very real. Never before, not even in times of war, had an administration garnered such a huge majority. Never before had the public anticipated change with such hope. Never before, not even under Albert Reynolds, did an administration so comprehensively squander its mandate.

Larkin's vicious lines about the influence of parents apply to many Irish administrations of the past:

> They fuck you up, your mum and dad.
> They may not mean to, but they do.
> They fill you with the faults they had
> And add some extra, just for you.

The Coalition, however, and the potential for change it promised should have marked a new dawn for Irish politics, one without any 'fucking up' of the Irish public. To adapt a phrase made famous by Fianna Fáil's Ray Burke in another era, 'a line had been drawn in the sand'.

But as inevitably as the passing on of parenting mistakes from one generation to the next, the Coalition fulfilled the premise of Larkin's poem. Of course, like Larkin's mum and dad, Eamon and Enda never meant to fuck up the Democratic Revolution. But they still did. And like Larkin's mum and dad, the Coalition didn't just continue the faults we already had; instead, they spiced up the nature of Irish misgovernance with some extra faults just for us.

This was a pity, for when they started, both Enda and Eamon were well-intentioned. Mind you, it is hard to find an Irish politician who isn't. But unfortunately, the enervating leadership styles they adopted – Enda's swinging between the opposing poles of Bertie-Lite and Victorian Dad-style governing and Eamon Gilmore's Mrs Doubtfire-esque 'careful now' ethic – contributed further to the electorate's disillusion with the Irish political system, already devastated during the Celtic Tiger era of a self-interested politics of carelessness.

Perhaps we should not be too harsh with our political class. Given their veteran status, the Grumpy Old Men of our new Coalition had obviously been 'fucked up in their turn / By fools in old-style hats and coats'. The problem with handing on their own flaws to the new administration, in a continuation of the destructive cycle of political parenting that had dominated Irish politics since the Civil War, was that the Irish electorate had changed. As Lucinda Creighton noted after her departure from Fine Gael, the election of 2011 marked the death of Civil War politics. Paddy, as Enda declared on election night, had voted for a different way of doing things.

If Enda had actually paid heed to his own words, we might be writing a different tale. Instead, rather than inaugurating the democratic revolution the Irish voters were looking for, the Coalition's Grumpy Old Men, exhausted by the length of their political journeys to power and discouraged by the Augean state of the Ireland they inherited, turned their backs on reform. Instead, they set their aim at an easier task, that of imposing a veneer of order and civility on the discordant pyre of the failing Irish Republic. This fundamentally flawed decision fatally misunderstood the mood of Irish voters. By 2014, it was clear the Coalition's failure to generate the psychological healing of the Irish electorate via a moral and political revolution was, in the eyes of the voters, a betrayal too far.

Such a sequence would not have come as a surprise to our curmudgeon of a librarian poet. In Larkin's poem, despite the lightness of the rhythm, a truly dystopian tone enters his final chilling warning:

Man hands on misery to man.
It deepens like a coastal shelf.
Get out as early as you can,
And don't have any kids yourself.

Larkin's lines highlight the inexorability of the cycle of inherited flaws, whether in parenting or democratic politics. While his advice to 'get out' is straightforward when it comes to not having children, in the case of politics the choices are not as simple. The only easy way to 'get out' of democratic politics is to embrace the politics of the great dictator, and even the benevolent variants of that school of government tend, in the long run, to hand on even more misery to man.

This means our thin alternative is to hope, always hope, that in democratic politics the vicious cycle embodied by Larkin's parents can be broken. Sadly, the verdict is already in on the Coalition. We know it failed – not always for bad reasons, but it did. The question this book hopes to answer is how it failed and why, because only when that is known can we try to break the cycle.

CHAPTER 1

PADDY IS GOING TO HAVE A DEMOCRATIC REVOLUTION

The Coalition wears its brightest colours as a new dawn is promised

It is rare for Ireland's dusty old political soap-opera to experience a defining moment. For the most part, Irish politics struggles along like a marriage in which love has gone into hiding. While there may be occasional moments of passion, in general it is a thing of routine interspersed with occasional feverish bouts of bickering about things that are not important at all.

Over the course of Irish history, there have been a few defining moments, occasions where it seemed as though we were at the edges of a new dispensation. The revolutionary triumph of Eamon de

Valera and his post-Civil War *sans culottes* in 1932, the election of Seán Lemass in 1959 and Garret FitzGerald's tenure as Taoiseach in the 1980s were all junctures at which revolutionary change to Irish political life appeared to be possible. The accession of Charles Haughey to power, shrouded as it was in elemental fears and sepulchral prophecies, appeared to be a moment that signalled something too – although the problem was that nobody, including Haughey himself, appeared to know what that 'something' was, and by the close of his fantastical career, no-one, including Haughey, cared that much any more.

Election night 2011 certainly appeared to meet all of the requisite criteria for revolutionary change. The Fianna Fáil *ancien regime* had been massacred in a manner resembling the fall of Constantinople, where, according to myth, by the time the Turks finished their devastation of Constantinople, the body of the last Emperor was only recognisable by his purple imperial slippers. On election night 2011, the age-old war between the Fianna Fáil, the Cute Hoors of Irish politics, and their Pious Protestor counterparts in Fine Gael and Labour reached what appeared to be a similarly definitive conclusion. But was the reign of the Cute Hoors fully over? Or would the historical attraction of Ireland's politicians to bad behaviour colonise the austere ranks of our newly formed Coalition?

Certainly a huge transformation had occurred. Since 1997, the Cute Hoors of Fianna Fáil had, with the help of an astonishing variety of political side-kicks, held the whip hand over the luckless Pious Protestors of Fine Gael and Labour. This was nothing new, for, although the public face of the Cute Hoors was affable, Fianna Fáil had dominated the theatre of political combat with an iron fist since its formation in 1927. However, in the wake of Bertie Ahern's 2007 election triumph, a new spirit of despair had entered the ranks of the Pious Protestors. As Fianna Fáil snuggled up to their new and still somewhat astonished Green Party coalition partners,

Pat Rabbitte, the third Labour leader in a row to be declawed by Bertie's patented political technique of strangulation by affability, was moved to wonder whether Fianna Fáil would ever be removed from power again. Pat had a point, for even when the milk began to curdle in the court of Good King Bertie as the Taoiseach attempted to untangle himself from his tribunal travails, the imminent arrival by *force majeure* of Brian Cowen (affectionately or otherwise known as Biffo) as Taoiseach provided the despairing opposition with another classic example of Fianna Fáil's enduring capacity to change their appearance just as trouble comes trotting around the corner looking for them. Once again, the most ruthless political party in Europe had read the runes and realised that the chill winds that were stripping away the fool's gold of Bertie's Gatsby-style age meant a strong leader was required to fearlessly steer the ship of the Irish state through the dangerous currents ahead. However, the strong leader did not, as we know, work out in that manner and Fianna Fáil's invincibility was shaken. As disaster followed disaster over their final two years in government, it looked as though the Cute Hoors had used up their entire store of karma.

The eviction of Fianna Fáil made way for the incoming Coalition of Pious Protestors, a group of Grumpy Old Men (along with a couple of token women) who made for an unlikely set of iconoclasts, given the age, gender and political profile of its members. Its membership also included thoughtful and sometimes radical figures from the Labour Party such as Pat Rabbitte, Ruairi Quinn and Joan Burton, a couple of talented political brats such as Fine Gael's Leo Varadkar and some, like Fine Gael's Phil Hogan, who seemed amenable to practicing the dark arts on soft civil service mandarins. This varied team meant we really did dare to hope that, despite the shortness of time they had to make a mark, the knowledge they gleaned during their exile would give the Coalition the stomach to engage in real and substantive reform.

The belief that the new Coalition would lean towards the iconoclastic was fanned by the unlikely form of Enda. All Irish election victories attract at least one defining statement that summarises their import for the state. These can range from the delightfully casual 'another All-Ireland, Jack' by one Fianna Fáil TD as Jack Lynch backed his way into the Taoiseach's office to the high-octane 'flawed pedigree' oration by Garret FitzGerald that set the tone of political discourse in the Haughey era on an unchangeable course. On election night 2011, in spite of a galaxy of opinionated political and media stars fighting for the right to coin the defining summary of this strange election, it was Enda Kenny who, all on his own, caught the mood. In the RTÉ studios, on the night of the count, the soon-to-be Taoiseach promised that the incoming Coalition would not leave 'our people in the dark' because 'Paddy likes to know what the story is'. Kenny's eccentric phraseology and his use of the racially loaded term 'Paddy' came in for some stick from some overly sensitive commentators, but in one sentence the incoming Taoiseach had summarised the defining flaw of the chaotic government of Brian Cowen. The apparent core value of Cowen's ill-starred administration, whether influenced by fear or genuine paternalism, was that the Irish public did not have the right to do anything other than silently acquiesce to its decisions. This had, almost invisibly, been the most corrosive factor in the erosion of Fianna Fáil's grip on the Irish psyche. Fianna Fáil, who in the past had embraced the peasant society-style concept of tribal politics more comprehensively than any other party in Ireland, simply did not appear to understand that in a modern Republic the people believed they had the right to information.

Mr Kenny, our soon-to-be Dear Leader, also noted on that famous election night that what had happened was a veritable 'democratic revolution' in which the voters had not 'taken to the streets' but instead had 'wreaked vengeance on those who let them down' via the more conventional route of the ballot box. It was certainly a revolution in numbers and personnel. But although the St Patricks of the Pious Protestors had chased the snakes of the Fianna Fáil Cute Hoors to the very edge of the Irish political shoreline, one question still hung in the air. Were the Pious Protestors for real or did they only want to clothe themselves in the tattered old robes of the previous imperial crew?

As we begin on our journey to track the rise and fall of a government elected with the largest majority in the history of the state, it is worth remembering the mood of that first hopeful day on 26 February 2011. Often, tangible political messages become tangled up in a confusing narrative of programmes for government, infighting for cabinet plums and vast legislative plans. Straight after the 2011 election however, the dominant feeling was one of a genteel revivalist-style attitude of hope. The Irish electorate had, in what was an Irish Bastille Day minus the shootings and guillotines, metaphorically stormed the barricades of power and thrown the *ancien regime* into the gutter. In a clever piece of spin, the two TDs chosen to proclaim the elevation of Dear Leader Enda to Taoiseach were the youngest members of their respective parties. Labour's Ciara Conway promised that 'in the words of that programme written by Tom Johnson 92 years ago, our purpose must … be "to secure that no child shall suffer hunger or cold from lack of food, clothing or shelter" … and to provide the "care of the nation's aged and infirm, who shall not be regarded as a burden but rather entitled to the nation's gratitude and consideration"'. It was, as we would find out over the Coalition's lifespan, a statement that was utterly incompatible with the *Realpolitik* of austerity. Meanwhile, for Fine Gael, Simon Harris proudly declared that 'today, the period of mourning is over for Ireland'. It was, he said, time for us to 'hang out our brightest colours and together, under Deputy Kenny's leadership … move forwards yet again as a nation'. Back in March 2011, this seemed charming, albeit in a school-boyish sort of fashion.

Inevitably all eyes were on Enda Kenny. In retrospect, it might seem strange but although he had been the Fine Gael leader for just under a decade, very little was known about the man. For most of us, he was a riddle hiding behind the enigma of a nod hiding behind a wink that was hiding behind a nudge to the ribs. In truth, had we paused to consider it, we would surely have noticed far too much hiding going on for comfort, but of course we didn't. Instead, in a classic example of the immaturity of our political discourse, the great and the not-so-good confidently sermonised on why there was no need to worry about Mr Kenny's enigmatic nature. This was, they proclaimed, because when one becomes Taoiseach, the office makes the man. Although a commonly-held view, sadly this is a school of belief as accurate about the nature of governance as old beliefs in the divine right of kings. The real truth about Taoisigh is that the capacity of the man defines the reputation of the office.

It should have been more unnerving that this purportedly great age of democratic revolution was founded on talk was of how the Taoiseach would accommodate himself to and be moulded by the very institutions of the state that had failed so comprehensively. Still, the Taoiseach-centred nature of Irish political discourse meant we had to overlook the elliptical nature of the man himself to try and discern meaning from his public pronouncements in order to predict how he, and our brand new Coalition, would get on. So although it was expressed in a somewhat odd fashion, Enda's declaration of Paddy's Bill of Rights offered us some hopeful prospects for the consummation of the Democratic Revolution.

On the opening day of the 31st Dáil, the incoming Taoiseach certainly struck a more elevated tone than his Paddy comment on election night when he claimed that the country stood 'on the threshold of fundamental change'. Given that Enda had been hanging affably around the Dáil club for four decades without making much of a run at any radical reforms, some eyes were raised at his promise that the central theme of his administration would be a 'renewal of what political leadership in Ireland should be about'. Still, even in Irish politics, Damascene conversions are theoretically possible. And to our innocent and hopeful eyes, even if only for the sake of his own political health, our Dear Leader Enda had to be serious about his 'democratic revolution' promise.

The incoming Taoiseach even incorporated a touch of Arthurian high sentiment with his pledge to 'enter into a covenant with the Irish people' that 'honesty is not alone our best policy, but our only policy'. His use of the word 'covenant', whether accidental or intentional, was particularly loaded. Irish voters are used to their politicians making promises and have come to expect that they will be broken; indeed, many voters would almost be disappointed if they were kept. A covenant, however, is much more binding. If Mr Kenny has any understanding of English at all – and what politician doesn't?– he would have known a covenant is an oath of fealty. This particular covenant with the Irish people was all the more significant because it was not been made under the barrel of an electoral gun; by this stage, the Coalition was home, hosed and installed in Dáil Eireann.

You could hardly blame us for thinking, 'Good Lord, the man is serious!' At the very least, we tried to convince ourselves this might be the case, out of the mannerly pleasantness that is the Irish curse.

All this stuff about covenants was indeed a long way from the old Biffo 'we are where we are, now shut your traps and stop complaining' school of non-governance. In the most emotionally intuitive line of his speech, Mr Kenny expressed his genuine belief that 'the old ways of politics damaged us not alone financially, but emotionally, psychologically and spiritually'. It was not easy for us to adjust to the concept of a Taoiseach who might possess the virtue of emotional empathy. Again, whether by accident or intent, Mr Kenny had tapped into something profoundly important to the Irish electorate, for the damage done by the recession and subsequent austerity measures was not merely fiscal. Something greater was eating away at the core of a citizenry that had seen the hard-won independence of the Irish Republic so flightily discarded.

As part of his appointment as Taoiseach, Mr Kenny also pledged to 'introduce the most ambitious ever programme for reform since the foundation of the State'. A key element of this would include, 'with the people's approval', the abolition of Seanad Éireann. This was a promise that sent a shiver running across the spines of the plump unfeathered Seanad hens. It was difficult to see how our dusty old senators could resist a government with the largest majority in the history of the Irish state. For now however, the Taoiseach was uninterested in the specifics. Instead, he implored us to once again 'believe in our future ... let us lift up our heads, turn our faces to the sun and ... hang out our brightest colours'. It was a fitting conclusion to his maiden speech as Taoiseach, cleverly crafted with language that consistently conjured up images of light bursting out of dark. Now all Mr Kenny had to do was to deliver this sunrise.

Of course, even at this point there were doubters. But it was surely not too unreasonable to hope that, although his Coalition was immediately confronted with the problems of an Irish Republic that had collapsed in upon itself, Mr Kenny would not turn out to be like so many others, full of piss and wind and very little else, like the infamous barber's cat. For that day at least, it was enough that, after the carefully cultivated imbecility of Bertie and the bureaucratese of Mr Cowen, our new Taoiseach was offering us a different register of thought, one that contained at least a drizzle of the American theory of progress, renewal and optimism. To a country devastated by EU-imposed austerity and used to the 'we are where we are' approach to politics, the American Dream ideology, which relies on change, reform and responsibility, was especially necessary. After the materialistic excesses of the Celtic Tiger era, in which the citizens of

Ireland had almost become sickened by surfeit, and the thin famine
of recession and austerity that followed, we could surely be forgiven
for hoping that a prophet who understood the electorate's need for
nutrition of an emotional, spiritual and psychological variety had
emerged.

Eamon Gilmore, whose Labour Party had scraped into
government in a similar manner to the last Americans leaving
Saigon at the end of the Vietnam conflagration, also caught the
millenarian mood, observing that 'we have been conscious of the
hope and goodwill of the people. Many people have stopped me
in the street or called out from a passing car to simply say "Good
luck".' In claiming that this would be a 'national government', the
Tánaiste, like Mr Kenny, was specifically asserting that this was no
ordinary come-day-go-day administration. The responsibilities
the Coalition set for themselves and our resultant expectations
were therefore significantly higher. But even as Gilmore piously
observed 'hope is never a burden', there was one lacuna within
all the chatter. Although there was much emotion and chat about
morality, tangible plans were thin. Traditionally Irish politics has
been far too often the politics of sentiment. The original 'man with
a plan', Seán Lemass, characterised the verbal rodomontade of
Irish politics as 'that school of dying for Ireland' rhetoric. If you
were of a somewhat more riotous mindset, you might compare
the rhetorical capacities of Irish politicians to the scene in *Blazing
Saddles* in which Hedley Lamarr, the evil villain, summarises his
latest diabolical scheme while in the bath having his back scrubbed
by his sidekick Taggart. Lamarr declares that his mind is 'a raging
torrent, flooded with rivulets of thought cascading into a waterfall
of creative alternatives'. After a brief moment of silence, an awed
Taggart responds, 'God darnit, Mr Taggart you use your tongue
prettier than a twenty-dollar whore'.

We had certainly experienced a surfeit of the politics of the twenty-dollar whore. But after the high-blown sentiment of Enda and Eamon, who could believe that Paddy was not going to have his Democratic Revolution? The historians among us pointed out that governments with excessive majorities fared poorly. In 1977, Fianna Fáil's Jack Lynch and his 84 TDs had talked warily of the dangers of 'carrying a full jug' and although much was written about the Brobdingnagian scale of the incoming administration, its majority was not that much larger than that of the ill-fated Fianna Fáil–Labour coalition of 1992. It had more than a hundred TDs and yet it collapsed in flames less than three years after it was elected. Still, this time would surely be better. After all, Jack had been something of an old woman past his prime, constantly being hand-tripped by the spectre of Charlie Haughey. And the Fianna Fáil–Labour administration of Albert Reynolds and Dick Spring was essentially an accidental creation, and one dogged by a perceived sense of betrayal on the part of an electorate that had been intent on voting Fianna Fáil out of office.

When it came to doubters of the new Coalition and its programme for the Democratic Revolution, they were indeed sparse – well, at least during that first sacred debate of the 31st Dáil. Sinn Féin's Mary Lou McDonald noted that we should be 'honest enough to say that the current programme for government, regardless of how it is dressed up, is essentially Fianna Fáil-Lite'. At this point, few were inclined at this point to surrender to that or to Micheál Martin's prophecy that politicians such as Mr Gilmore would swiftly learn that 'it is not 'Labour's way or Frankfurt's way' and he will learn that Mr Trichet [President of the ECB] is more than a "mere civil servant"'. Instead we hoped that Fine Gael's Peter Mathews would be prophetic rather than idealistic in his belief that, 'in the words and thoughts of Edmund Burke, we are not just delegates for the people who elected us here. We are trustees for them'. The tale of Peter's time in 31st Dáil would in time evolve into a real judgement on that particular dream. For now though, the somewhat less idealistic among us emerged from the great galaxy of political sentiment, blinking and confused by the darting lights. We wondered what on earth had we just done, while still hoping that somehow, just maybe, it would all work out for the best.

In retrospect, the prophecy of the Socialist Party's Joe Higgins was far more accurate than the hopeful fallacies we peddled. In a finely judged speech, Higgins warned that 'the *Oxford Dictionary* defines "revolution" as the overthrow of a government or social order in favour of a new system'. If this definition was correct, he said, then 'the programme presented by Deputy Kenny is a grotesque betrayal of that revolution because it proposes almost to the letter to continue the reactionary programme of the old order of the late and unlamented regime of Fianna Fáil and the Green Party, a regime that was rightly reviled, rejected and sent to oblivion by the Irish people for its economic and political crimes'. Fine Gael backbenchers, who were utterly unused to anything harsher than the deification of Dear Leader Enda, went into shock as Higgins said, 'this is not the first time the Irish political elite responded to an Irish and Europe-wide crisis by sacrificing its people. Nearly one hundred years ago, the forebears of today's speculating EU financiers ... plunged into war in a vicious competition for markets raw materials and profits. The Irish Parliamentary Party of the day will be forever remembered in infamy for its campaign to dragoon a generation of youth to feed the insatiable appetite of the imperial war makers'. Higgins made it clear that when it came to a willingness to sacriface 'our people, our services and our youth to feed the equally insatiable appetite of the ... European and world financial markets', Fine Gael and Labour would play 'an equally shameful role' to Fianna Fáil.

Sinn Féin's Gerry Adams confined himself to noting 'it is appropriate that we gather here at the beginning of Lent, given what is coming for the citizens of the State'. It was in truth one of his more accurate prognostications. Independent TD Shane Ross was even closer to the mark when he warned us that 'we do not know exactly what is being promised at all, except that the Labour Party and Fine Gael will be the government over the next few years and will stick together, come hell or high water'. Ross presciently hoped that 'the Fianna Fáil version of cronyism is not replaced by a Fine Gael–Labour version of cronyism'. And he also warned that he feared that, 'because of the parameters and restrictions of the economy, the government will almost inevitably yield to the temptation to be a government so similar to the previous one ... that it will be indistinguishable from it'.

Not many people listened to Joe, Shane and the rest of the naysayers. Instead, in what unfortunately was to become an ongoing trend, the chirruping rooks of the Fine Gael backbenchers, after they recovered from their initial shock, broke into a disapproving chorus. And truthfully, in the immediate afterglow of the execution of Fianna Fáil, we were too entranced by the numbers secured by the Coalition of the Grumpy Old Men to pay attention to voices of dissent. Shane Ross's prediction hung eerily in the air, but surely after all the Coalition's lofty speech-making and promises, we would not end up back in Biffo's 'we are where we are' land. If the Coalition of all the Grumpy Old Men and the cawing rooks of the Fine Gael backbenchers needed incentives for courage, all they had to do was look straight in front of them and witness the horrors that political failure had inflicted on Fianna Fáil. In 2007, Fianna Fáil had been elected on the subterranean fears of the electorate that the boom was over and the somewhat contradictory hope that Bertie might be able to weave his economic alchemy a final time. Even then, it felt as if securing the self-interested trust of the Irish electorate was a dangerous prize for Fianna Fáil to celebrate. Now all that was left was the bitterest of dregs.

Of course, we now know the Coalition would slip slowly and

inexorably towards that very place in which Biffo the Unready had
left Fianna Fáil. But how did it happen? After all, we had experienced
our fairy-tale ending with the triumph of the Fine Gael–Labour
Pious Protestors. This fairy tale's official narrative was that good
had defeated, if not evil, then certainly sloth and self-indulgence.
Ahead of us, the fairy tale said, there would be purification and
repentance for some but ultimately everything would end well. The
problem, alas, with using fairy tales to describe the real world is
that in the real world, things don't always tie up as neatly. In the
real world, fairy-tale scenarios can take unexpected and capricious
Gothic turns. Sometimes in the real world, the fairy-tale Prince gets
barbecued by the dragon. Sometimes, despite the best of advice,
Hansel and Gretel end up being boiled in the cauldron.

In our case, there were a number of problems with the fairy tale
our new government of Pious Protestors constructed in March
2011. It wasn't just that the group of white knights who arrived to
slay the Fianna Fáil dragon were gentlemen of a somewhat elderly
hue, riding donkeys rather than noble steeds. The drama of their
rescue mission was also somewhat compromised by the fact that by
the time our motley knights arrived, the aged dragon had run out
of flames some years earlier, fallen into a deep sleep and could not
be roused into battle. Mind you, when it came to our Grumpy Old
Don Quixotes, there was no excessive banging of shields. Instead,
after a couple of timorous shouts, mostly from the Labour knights-
errant, our heroic Pious Protestors glided gently away from the
mangy form that was far smaller than the mythical creature they
had been planning to bravely take on.

Furthermore, the unavoidable fact remained that the damsel in
distress our heroes had rescued was a woman of loose morals who
had enjoyed plenty of good times with the poor dragon before he
ran out of puff – and, more importantly, cash. Still, as our Grumpy
Old Men delicately slipped away from the declawed dragon with a

less than impressed damsel, who was only going with them in the absence of anything better, they could not be criticised too harshly for the failure to deliver a perfect fairy-tale ending. After all, even in fairy tales you can only work with the material you are given. And for all of the sulkiness of the damsel in distress, no-one else was exactly queuing up to rescue her. But before we chronicle the adventures and misfortunes that our Grumpy Old political adventurers went on to encounter, it should be noted that at this early stage a happy ending was not impossible. The stars may have been set against our Grumpy Old Men and, as a few prescient speakers on the opening day of the 31st Dáil pointed out to deaf ears, there was scant evidence they were journeying towards a land of milk, honey, peace, prosperity and bread, let alone towards the promised Democratic Revolution, whatever that might be. But we had Enda and we had Enda's speech and we had a Vatican choir of sincerely voiced fine intentions and public faith and a record Dáil majority – have we mentioned that? – to back up the fine sentiments. Surely that would be enough for some form of transformation. March 2011 was not the time for the fairy-tale dream to be shattered, for no-one, including our rescued damsel, was in the mood for listening to doubts. That was a story that would change.

CHAPTER 2

EMBALMED RADICALS

Fianna Fáil turns away from its palace of desolation

Sometimes, to escape from where you are, you have to go back to the past before you can go forwards. So if we are to understand how the Democratic Revolution arrived at the desert it found itself in by the close of 2014, we must first return to the location a horrified Fianna Fáil found themselves in 2011. In the days of Lemass and de Valera, they had been the great radicals of Irish politics. Though they had since veered between the poles of aristocracy and populism, they had still retained a veneer of radicalism. That day now appeared to be over. Back in that strange post-election time, there were many indignities to be endured, but perhaps the cruellest example of Fianna Fáil's new standing as the Embalmed Radicals of Irish politics was their eviction from their old party rooms on the fifth floor of Leinster House. The political symbolism was stark: the fifth floor is reserved for the biggest party in Dáil Eireann and the biggest party, since 1932, had always been

Fianna Fáil. In March 2011, it was time for all the dusty old portraits of de Valera, Lemass, Lynch, Haughey and the rest to experience the indignity of being taken down so the new Fine Gael bosses could occupy the fifth floor rooms.

This was only one example of how absence and exile would become the defining narrative of Ireland's traditional governing party. We are more used to it now but back in the heady post-election days of March 2011, the upheaval of the traditional order of Irish politics was quite a shock. Fianna Fáil had always been political giants. Like their political predecessors in the Irish Parliamentary Party, who faded into obscurity after the Easter Rising, and the Whigs, a party of British Liberals who, having created and governed an Empire for three hundred years, floated out of Irish politics after the First World War as lightly as spores in a summer breeze, Fianna Fáil had become our natural governing class. Then suddenly they were peripheral.

Such was the scale of the Fianna Fáil defeat that, for the first time since 1927, it was incapable of mustering a candidate for the Taoiseach's office. As the parliamentary party's shrunken last remnants gathered together like the defeated remnants of Napoleon's Russian army, the party of de Valera and Lemass, the nation-builders who had fought in 1916, of Lynch, a leader more beloved even than Daniel O'Connell, of the sulphurous Haughey and of Bertie, a leader more loved even than Lynch, they instead were a sideshow. All the captains and the kings, the dynasties, the ministerial marshals, the cavaliers and the puritans – all had fallen, and a fair few foot-soldiers had been hacked up in the aftershock too. The sting of Fianna Fáil's loss was accentuated all the more by what surrounded them. It was bad enough to see Fine Gael on the government benches aping Fianna Fáil but Fianna Fáil themselves were now no bigger than the Independent Motley Crew, the oddest group of deputies to enter the house since those that made up the nether regions of Jack Lynch's triumph in 1979, which had brought such exotic Fianna Fáil blooms as Pee Flynn into Irish life. Now Fianna Fáil's long-established politicians were seated among all manner of eccentricity, from Mattie McGrath, the scattergun former Fianna Fáil Independent TD who took out Haughey's masterful mandarin Martin Mansergh, to iconoclastic 'new' TDs such as Shane Ross, whose newness was compromised for some by his three-decade-long standing as a senator. By contrast, Luke 'Ming the Merciless' Flanagan was a true Dáil debutant, a cannabis activist transformed into a turf-cutting advocate. On his first attempt at election, Flanagan was destroyed by his then landlord, Fianna Fáil TD Frank Fahey, by a margin of roughly 100 to one in the voting stakes. In the 2011 election, Frank lost his seat and 'Ming' topped the poll.

That wasn't the worst of it for Fianna Fáil either. Michael Wallace, a bottle-blonde building developer with a taste for pink, had topped the poll in Wexford and was now the owner of a Dáil seat from which to gaze around vacantly. Mr Wallace would swiftly achieve much notoriety over his tax affairs and over an inept comparison of a Fine Gael female backbench TD and Miss Piggy. Those Fianna Fáilers who believed in the virtues of Dáil dress etiquette could only stare in horror at the donkey-jacketed membership of the United Left Alliance which included Richard Boyd Barrett, who was for once in a public space without the comfort blanket of his trusty loud-hailer. In the most unique Dáil, in terms of personnel at least, since that of 1922, even the Sinn Féin ranks contained curious new members, including, for the first time, its leader Gerry Adams, whose wooden performances and general air of dislocated unease swiftly saw him being caricatured as 'an idiot abroad'.

It took the Embalmed Radicals of Fianna Fáil some time to recover from their great fall. Indeed, some would argue that they have never fully regained their health after that seismic shock. It has not helped that, such were the extent of the wounds the party experienced, Fianna Fáil has not yet been able to face them. Fianna Fáil's great turning away from the reasons behind their defeat in March 2011 was most starkly evident in their failure to conduct a structured inquiry into the election. There was no Fianna Fáil equivalent to Fine Gael's 2002 Flannery Inquiry into the then state of Fine Gael. In many ways, that was understandable. Unlike Fianna Fáil, Fine Gael was used to defeat and was ready to learn from it. By contrast, Fianna Fáil went from being a great political monolith to a party as small and vulnerable as the Labour Party. But this turning away was a cataclysmic oversight by Fianna Fáil, for even a physician cannot heal themselves without at least a preliminary diagnosis.

Fianna Fáil's new condition was epitomised by their first shivering post-election party gatherings at a variety of small dark Dublin hotels. They were brittle-mannered affairs not unlike James Joyce's 'The Dead' – although in the Fianna Fáil version of story, the delicate individual dying of political consumption in an icy landscape was the party itself. These palsied party gatherings revealed a party lost in the moral maze created by its past, seeking a better future via nice sentiments about political reform and the invention of a strange political child known as a Local Area Representative (shadow county councillors, apparently). Fianna Fáil was experiencing as existential a crisis as the country that had despatched it almost as far as the grave. As the party lay in the political settle-bed, coughing occasionally as it tried to rise before sinking back, we were treated to the spectacle of Fianna Fáil trying to rebrand themselves as 'good' with Micheál Martin repeatedly listing out all the progressive legislation our dispossessed Cute Hoors were producing. Of course, we understood why Fianna Fáil wanted to appear progressive on issues such as same-sex marriage and bicycle lanes, but by focusing on soft issues of political correctness rather than on the earthy social policies of previous years, Fianna Fáil's platform seemed to dissolve into a homage to harmlessness. In bowing to the ethos of the queer studies wing of some amorphous British Polytechnic, Fianna Fáil appeared inauthentic.

Fianna Fáil was, of course, in denial about this. They will not, even now, talk about it. But they need to learn the lesson of Lionel Shriver's novel *We Need to Talk About Kevin*: even at this belated stage, Fianna Fáil need to talk about Fianna Fáil if they are to ever recover. Back in 2011, Fianna Fáil were understandably less than keen with such a prospect; to do it then, they would have had to open the party's coffin lid and engage with the legacy of Bertie. And worse still, they would have to face a second sarcophagus to have a chat with Biffo too. The Fianna Fáil of 2015 complains and bleats about how they have already done this, and in truth they are partially right. In the classic Irish way, we and Fianna Fáil have talked incessantly about that toxic Fianna Fáil duo. But, as is so often the case in Irish politics, it has all been talk and nothing else. It has consisted of babble, caricature and playing the blame game. But this only examines the surface of things. The gathering normalisation of our country should not disguise two simple truths: that this is a country where something went terribly wrong and that Fianna Fáil was intimately connected to the going wrong. But they were not alone in that regard. And in fact, maybe by finding out what went wrong with Fianna Fáil, we might discover what ailed the state, for in many ways Fianna Fáil were the mere facilitators of what were ingrained national characteristics.

In this conversation, all roads inevitably lead to Bertie. You have to wonder sometimes how Bertie Ahern thought this retirement thing would work out. He certainly approached it with a level of reluctance that suggested he wasn't at all enthused by the prospect. Still, the ex-Taoiseach must have expected better than being chased around his allotment by photographers; indeed, he also probably expected to have more to do with his post-politics life than to go pottering around his allotment. Of course, after all his messing with tribunals, even Bertie realised that when he left, we were gone well past his strange zenith, when the European Union was on its knees pleading for Mr Ahern to be its President. But although his desires were more modest than they might once have been, Mr Ahern surely must have hoped for some of the usual comforts of former Taoisigh: the quiet dignity of a ghost-written column in *The Irish Times*, the occasional honorary degree, some company directorships or even, at the worst, a lecturing career as a Yeatsian public man. It was not to be. Instead Ahern found himself being coursed to the end by that nemesis called Flood, leading a tribunal he had set up under pressure from his Progressive Democrat coalition footstools. Bertie claimed, after the ropey Flood Tribunal report, that he bore 'the members of the tribunal no ill-will.' Even by the diversionary standards Mr Ahern had mastered, this was a statement that could only inspire a plea of 'pull the other one, Bertie, so we can hear the bells again'. This was the very tribunal that forced Bertie's resignation from Fianna Fáil just before a posse led by his successor as Fianna Fáil leader, Micheál Martin, arrived bearing a motion calling for poor Bertie's expulsion on the grounds of 'conduct unbecoming'. Deep in his heart, Bertie must have mused over the contrast between the utter reluctance with which he had cast Charlie Haughey into the wilderness and the speed with which Micheál moved to despatch Fianna Fáil's previously most loved son.

Of course, as was so often the case with Bertie, nothing was quite as it appeared and the fall of Bertie was a complex and morally loaded affair. One of the most intriguing events in this saga was an apparently harmless *News of the World* ad that ultimately may have enraged the Irish public even more than Bertie's alleged corruption. In the advertisement, broadcast just after Mr Ahern became a sports columnist for the newspaper, a house-owner in the middle of making breakfast is startled, upon opening a cupboard, to find the former

Taoiseach sitting inside it and drinking a cup of tea. Mr Ahern then looks up in a woebegone way and mutters 'I never thought I'd end up here but I have the latest on the big match'. The subsequent national angst is more understandable than it might seem from this distance. One of the most genuinely felt comfort blankets the electorate erect around our political leaders is the perception of their dignity. Our politicians may be incapable or corrupt and sometimes even both. The least that we ask is that they are not undignified, that they do not embarrass us. Even in the roughest hours of his life when he was seen to be an old fraud, Haughey maintained his dignity. By contrast, with his ill-thought-out *News of the World* ad, Bertie was seen to have cheapened himself, his office and, by extension, us.

Bertie's post-Taoiseach loss of dignity was all the more hurtful for us because of his particular position in the story of Fianna Fáil and Irish political life. Bertie Ahern was the Irish Narcissus. Like the original Narcissus, Bertie attracted unprecedented levels of rapt admiration and uncritical love. Like Narcissus too, Bertie's pride was his nemesis, for it was the Taoiseach's belief in his own perfection that diverted him from the realities of the collapse of the Tiger he had built in his own reflection.

Of course, when the crash came, the intensity of our affair with Bertie, and more critically our shared guilt, meant the break-up was all the more ferocious. The viciousness of the schism was intensified by the revelation that Bertie, our great shape-shifting leader, was also our very own Dorian Gray. We should surely have known all along, for Mr Ahern's political persona had always been based on being the image of that which we ourselves wanted to be. He was the great Irish totem who, as long as he appeared to be ageless, eternally seductive and always young, would keep us in a similar condition. Then the Flood Tribunal thrust us up to the political attic to see the real state of the man and, by extension, ourselves – and the screaming began. Or rather it should have, but in fact there was no screaming at all. Instead, a chilly silence descended over Mr Ahern's very existence. It was almost as though George Orwell's famous memory hole in *1984* had been re-invented specifically for the man formerly known as 'our Bertie'. We might not have *1984*'s infamous Ministry of Truth where old newspaper articles and photographs were revised in order to serve the propaganda interests of the government but the erasing of Mr Ahern from the records of the state has been equally comprehensive. In fact, the only thing that has not occurred is the revocation of his honorary degrees.

At the time it seemed to be for the best that Mr Ahern became the designated national scarecrow to shake at a quivering Fianna Fáil. Like an Irish Guy Fawkes, Bertie's example was held up to put manners on Fianna Fáil TDs and to convince the Irish electorate that Bertie, rather than Paddy, was responsible for the bit of fine mess we found ourselves in. But in acting this way, we were cheating ourselves.

Ironically, the prototype for this kind of historical erasure was set by Bertie's mentor Charlie Haughey, for we engaged in the same process with him, turning the former Taoiseach into a national roué without examining our own complicity in his storied times. Indeed had we looked more closely at how we facilitated the Gatsby-style follies of Mr Haughey and the collapse of his theatre of illusion built on credit and lies, we might have seen in Haughey's tale a dry run for the Celtic Tiger. But we did not and with the departure of Bertie, we ended up in Biffo's 'we are where we are' land. Meanwhile, Bertie, like all scapegoats, took on the status of 'the guilty one' and freed us of having to look too closely into the mirror.

If Bertie was the Irish Narcissus, his successor Brian Cowen was a far different creature. They do, however share one similarity: both have been exiled from Irish political life. In the case of Mr Cowen, his laudable status as the antithesis of Bertie is best epitomised by that unfortunate 'Biffo' moniker. There was, surprisingly in retrospect, a brief time where the term was almost used affectionately. By the close of Biffo's government career though, it was more an angry epithet than a fond nickname. It was a thing spat out with contempt rather than affection, signifying alienation and anger. Nothing captured the great decline of Biffo after his fall from power than the spectacle of the Obamas' homecoming in Moneygall, Co. Offaly, Mr Cowen's own home turf. The Coalition's great triumph in bringing the Obamas to Ireland was in full flow by the time we remembered to wonder where Biffo was. Then, out of the corner of an eye, we spotted a dishevelled Cowen. The man, who only two years earlier had supped in the White House and somewhat embarrassingly read the wrong speech, stood lost in the crowd as the stardust of Barack and Michelle swept by. They never even saw the poor abandoned tramp of Clara, who had been left politically homeless by Ireland's angry electorate. And really, it could hardly be expected they would. The Obamas are winners. Still, it all seemed a little ungracious that even in his heartland, poor old Biffo would be so blatantly sidelined.

In fairness, Mr Cowen does not attract the same vitriol as Bertie Ahern. Instead, we tend to view our Mr Cowen in the same light as those bad girls in the 1950s who had to be packed off to a Mother and Baby Home until all the embarrassment died down. However, his erasure is as curious as that of Bertie, for although his span as Taoiseach was shorter, Mr Cowen dominated the consciousness of the Irish public in a similar manner to Ahern. Indeed, some would argue that, when it came to media coverage and public attention, Mr Cowen actually surpassed our Bertie. That, alas, was not a good thing at all. Biffo was no captivating Narcissus like Bertie. Instead, poor Biffo was the original Celtic Tiger piñata. But while sweets had always rained down from Bertie's piñata, as the nation swayed around Biffo blindly, swinging wildly like children at a birthday party and generally connecting with the big swaying lump, we were rewarded with wasps.

Although we are in the process of doing a very fine job of forgetting him, we should actually remember poor Biffo provided us with the defining line of the Gethsemane-style garden of fiscal and economic sorrows. During his time of in government, thousands of acres of newsprint were devoted to covering the extent of the Irish financial crisis, to reporting the flowing rhetoric of the opposition and to publishing fine analytical pieces from economists about how the crash they had failed to predict was inevitable. Despite many complaints about the absence of any fine rhetoric from Mr Cowen, there was no excess of national gratitude when the Taoiseach finally did speak. The nation was ready for Mr Cowen to explain how we had arrived at this pass and, more importantly, how on earth we might find a soft way out. Instead, we were treated to the blunt directness of Mr Cowen's famous 'we are where we are' summation, which summed up where we, ahem, were.

What left the Irish public particularly cold was that Mr Cowen never defined what the land of 'where we are' actually was. It is not as though such a definition wasn't necessary. Back in the age of Biffo, we were living in a completely unique space beyond conventional description. In theory, the Ireland of 2008 was technically experiencing a 'recession', but a recession is ultimately just a cold assortment of facts with explainable causes and outcomes, predetermined by previous and future actions. We, by contrast, seemed to be experiencing something more fundamental, something unprecedented, something that bore a closer resemblance to those Greek myths about hubris in which excessive pride is always the gateway drug to catastrophic punishment by distant angry gods who are never wrong.

Ironically, despite our complaints, Mr Cowen's declaration actually represented a moment of perfect illumination. 'We are where we are' was an implicit confession of the total impotence of Irish politicians and it offered us no illusions. There was nothing in it to suggest a plan was on the way to help us escape. Instead, with almost casual insouciance, Biffo was confessing that neither he nor anyone else had a clue how we had gotten ourselves into this unprecedented situation. The worst aspect of 'we are where we are' was that it represented an implicit admission that poor Biffo and his generals could think of no roadmap out of this space in which the Irish public was being compressed beyond endurance. 'We are where we are' was a confession that Fianna Fáil had, at the greatest time of crisis for the Irish state since the Second World War, run out of ideas. Instead, the most they could suggest was that we wait it out, lying still like the wounded fox who hides, shocked by the pain, in a defeated huddle in the hope that its immobility might spare it from the chasing pack of dogs. Fianna Fáil in the age of Biffo seemed to think that the only response to the recession available to the Irish public was passive acquiescence in our inevitable decline, mingled with an occasional self-pitying bleat about the unfairness of our status as the passive, piteous victims of execrable fate. 'Twas a long way we had gone from being the 'uncrowned kings of Europe'.

Mr Cowen became the most visible symbol of our failings in other key areas. This meant that, unlike Bertie, we could never warm to him, for Biffo was the public representative of the frailer side of our character. The problem with Biffo was that secretly Paddy feared that this poor national (and sometimes international) clown was one of us. Like us, he was sloppy. Like us, Biffo saw life and business as something you conducted on the wing. Like us, he reacted with utter incomprehension when doing this led to tragedy. Like Bertie, the excision of Mr Cowen from public life was total, as the Obamas' visit to Moneygall so cruelly displayed. And as with Bertie, his exile was our absolution. It showed that the calamitous state of the country was the fault of the fates and of Bertie and Biffo, rather than Paddy.

There was of course a third public face of Fianna Fáil before their catastrophic fall from grace: Brian Lenihan. In what was perhaps a vivid example of the party's chaotic state in 2010, a dying man appeared to represent their best future for many in Fianna Fáil. Fianna Fáil's attraction to Brian Lenihan is fitting, as it encompasses the ongoing attachment of Irish people to tragic heroes. Lenihan was a Finance Minister who lost his duels with the ECB and Jean-Claude Trichet and who was, along with Biffo, rolled over by the Irish banks in a manner that a Reynolds, a Haughey, a MacSharry, possibly a Quinn and maybe even a Bertie would not have been. But he was charming and he was a romantic figure – he was the sympathetic leader the Irish public were looking for. Indeed, such was the intensity of emotion surrounding his death that as swifts and swallows flitted through the dying light on the chilly spring evening of his funeral and the old Fianna Fáil capos and consiglieres shuffled past his coffin, it was almost as though the funeral of Brian Lenihan was the funeral of Fianna Fáil itself.

In a radio interview with Miriam O'Callaghan in 2009, Brian Lenihan spoke poignantly about the death of his younger brother from leukaemia. He recalled one Christmas in particular, when his dying little brother's disinterest in the galaxy of Christmas gifts he had received was a warning to the young Brian that the things of this world were no longer for his brother. By contrast, up to the end, Lenihan continued to be fascinated by the world he lived in. On one of the last evenings he spent in Leinster House as outgoing Finance Minister, Lenihan mischievously noted that he had left a few landmines for the incoming Coalition to deal with. It was hard to believe, despite his emaciated state, he was a dying man. But a few weeks later, like Bede's sparrow flying from the light of a banquet hall in winter, he was gone. Lenihan was not perfect. But any analysis of Lenihan's flaws should be tempered by his broader influence. As *The Irish Times* said of another Irish political icon, Noël Browne, 'if he goes, something clean, something pure, something rare will go too'.

When Lenihan died, something rare left. And we still wonder if his death was the prologue to the passing away of Fianna Fáil, a party that now seems to have nothing left to pique the interest of Irish voters. That is strange, because up to a decade ago one of Fianna Fáil's main strengths was its capacity to re-invent itself to meet the needs of the age. Far before the era of focus groups, they managed to secure a perfect symbiosis with the psyche of the voters. The apogee of the Fianna Fáil brand was, of course, reached under Bertie. Under Bertie, Fianna Fáil was, when compared to the Pious Protestors of Fine Gael and Labour, a party of winners. More importantly, Fianna Fáil was, even when it danced with billionaires, seen as the party on the side of the small man. By contrast, Fine Gael, were the political representatives of frigid elites such as large farmers, hospital consultants and the bar library. Like the Tories under Margaret Thatcher, Fianna Fáil was the party that understood the small man in the white van. All of that is now gone. The Fianna Fáil brand is now associated with apologies, absence, peripherality, the swift exit of female senators and desolation. At the advent of the Pious Protestors' Democratic Revolution, the three faces of a failing Fianna Fáil were Bertie, the deceitful Dorian Grey; Biffo, a paragon of wistful impotence; and Brian Lenihan, a ghostly dead hero. The dominant theme of Fianna Fáil suddenly became one of absence. After watching the steady decline of Fianna Fáil from power to exile, the triumphant Coalition could hardly be criticised for pointing and sneering at these poor Embalmed Radicals trapped in the aspic of their own history.

But when it came to the Coalition, who appeared to be too proud of their as yet unsecured triumph for ease, a question simmered in the background. Were they laughing at that which they might yet become if they failed? The great error Fianna Fáil committed under Bertie Narcissus was that they never appealed to our better selves. Instead they took the clever cynical decision to simply reflect our baser desires in everything from economics, politics, regulation, the public sector and the environment. Under Biffo, this error was accentuated by a sense of intellectual lassitude, which meant that Fianna Fáil was unable to even attempt the arduous process of building a new Republic out of the ashes of the Tiger. Still, the good news for our new Coalition was that so long as these fundamental errors were dodged, they were sure to avoid becoming the new Fianna Fáil.

CHAPTER 3

THE GRUMPY OLD MEN TAKE OVER

Men from the past take charge of a young country's future

I n 2014, three years after he had finally been appointed to thefull cabinet, two decades after being elected as a TD, just as the end of his ministerial career began to beckon ever more urgently, Pat Rabbitte ruefully noted that fine words about foreign policy triumphs were buttering no parsnips amongst an increasingly chilly domestic electorate. It was, by then, all too, too late to re-capture the electorate. By that stage, the Coalition, and in particular its cabinet of Grumpy Old Men, were like Al Pacino's character in the final scene of *Carlito's Way*, who, when fatally wounded, declares, 'sorry, boys, all the stitches in the world cannot sew me together again'.

In truth, with hindsight, it was probably too late for the Coalition from the start. The fine words and felicitous sentiments of the Dáil's first day were no sooner over than a new-born government of balding, or at best grey-haired, men emerged out of the beautiful chrysalis of Enda's rhetoric. Whether they liked it or not, it was written in the stars: they were from the start and would eternally be known as the Coalition of the Grumpy Old Men. Of course, there were exceptions but they were essentially peripheral. The children of the Coalition, such as Fine Gael's Leo Varadkar and Simon Coveney, busied themselves keeping out of harm's way as they laid plans for their future dreams. There were even women: Labour's Joan Burton, the then Minister for Social Protection, may have been of a similar vintage to the Grumpy Old Men, but she was of an entirely different disposition. Joan was so cheerful and solicitous that, were it she rather than her namesake Joan of Arc that stood on a pile of burning faggots in medieval France, she would be concerned that the smoke was irritating the eyes of her English captors.

Joan and the frisky young Fine Gael ministers were a minority group. Still, it was remarkable how quickly the moral exultation of that first day of Dáil speechifying, where we were all in it together, disappeared. In fairness, it should be noted the tide was definitely set against our Grumpy Old Men. After fourteen years in opposition wilderness, they marched triumphantly into the Department of Finance, bringing with them the biggest mandate in the history of the state only to find a desert winking back at them. In the initial brief meeting, the department's civil servants took that mandate and gently placed it into a shredder and with that, turned everything, every small dream and big promise, to dust. Normally, new governments take over countries with luxuries such as a functioning civil service, money to pay the bills, a budget, the capacity to borrow and international allies. The Grumpy Old Men had none of these delights. Far from gaining their long-hoped-for state, they had instead inherited a basket case wrapped up in a crisis. They were terracotta warriors guarding a dead Republic, rather than rulers initiating a democratic revolution.

That is not to say that they turned away or that their spirit was broken, but the Coalition's innocence and hope was stripped away

from them before the new administration even began. If the Old
Men weren't Grumpy before getting into government – and in truth
many were – after their first few hours in power, they were heading
that way at a lick. Worse still, the two defining moods they adopted
in response to the governing dilemma that faced them were an
outrageous level of self-pity and a distressingly cautious political
ethic of 'careful now'. This wasn't, to put it mildly, the setting
required for a democratic revolution. However, we should not
blame the Grumps too much for their state of mind. In the midst of
the Great Disruption caused by Ireland's great economic class and
the austerity that followed, Mr Kenny and his cabinet had to deal
with a public sector debauched by the evils of social partnership, a
mandarin civil service elite debased by irresponsibility and ease, the
biggest collapse in wealth in the history of the Irish state, sovereign
bankruptcy, banking bankruptcy – and that's before considering
such European delights as the possibility of a two-tier Euro, credit
default, bank runs, political schisms, sovereign debt, banking debt,
the cross-fertilisation of sovereign and banking debt, the possibility
of domino-style economic collapse and the onrushing junk bond
status of the PIGS, Portugal, Italy, Greece and Spain.

Intriguingly, Pat Rabbitte appeared to be the Coalition member
most deeply affected. It is possible his political and analytical
sophistication grasped the import of the crisis they had inherited
more swiftly than most of his colleagues. However, the problem
with Pat was that although he was equipped to diagnose the
consequences of the crisis, he wasn't designed to map a route out of
that morass. As Minister for Communications, Energy and Natural
Resources, Pat was also stranded in the wrong department, one
that was essentially too small to be of real weight. He eventually
found himself playing the role of the guard dog – noisy enough to
irritate but not big enough to frighten. In a curious way, Pat was the
Eamon Ryan of the Coalition. This meant that, like his Green Party

predecessor, cross Pat spoke the most sense, but had the least clout to back it up.

Ironically, over time Enda evolved into the Grumpiest Old Man of all. For some, this was a surprising transformation. But hidden beneath his winking and his nodding and his increasingly awkward efforts at looking hip and down with the young people, a Grumpy Old Man has always lurked in Enda. The truth of the matter is that Enda is a child of the Irish 1960s. He was formed by the GAA, by 'The Riordans' (a popular agricultural soap-opera those under forty will never have heard of), by women working in the home and by deference to every pillar of a state that had so fundamentally betrayed its own citizenry. No matter how he tries to disguise it, Enda is a man living out of his time. Gay marriage puzzles him; abortion makes him nervous; well-heeled articulate women make him even more nervous; and smart phones confuse him. He is a creature of the dynastic school of Irish politics, of the era of the burning sod of turf rather than of the digital age. In a strange way, the child of Liam Cosgrave is the Cosgrave of his era, for while Mr Cosgrave may have been a greyer figure than Enda, the current Grumpy Old Taoiseach is as fatally detached from his society as Liam Cosgrave was.

In the early days of the Coalition, Enda managed to avoid being roped into the Grumpy Old Men set, but that would change. So too did the new Tánaiste and Minister for Foreign Affairs, Eamon Gilmore, although oddly enough this turned out not to be as good for Gilmore as it initially appeared. Instead of becoming another of the Coalition's Grumpy Old Men, Mr Gilmore swiftly evolved into its 'Invisible Man'. This evolution did not serve him too well, for the voters were as prepared to despise his absence as his presence. Indeed, as the Coalition's term progressed, the voters inclined towards using the invisibility of Mrs Doubtfire of Dún Laoghaire as a carpet-beater to whack him, if they could only have seen him.

Initially Fine Gael's James Reilly was so delighted to be a member of the Coalition that our new Health Minister didn't qualify for the Grumpy Old Man team. But as James's fatally dated 'my way or the highway' style of conducting business emerged, it quickly became evident that James belonged to the Grumpy Old Men wing of things. And, troublingly for the Coalition, James's Grumpy Old Man behaviour had one devastating counterpoint. As he became tangled up with difficulties in his personal finances and a cataclysmic series of squabbles with his Junior Minister, Labour's Róisín Shortall, Reilly's status as a buffoon blundering around the HSE's poorly designed China shop began to depress the electorate, even more than the rest of the Grumpy Old Men. In the case of Reilly, he was the one who made us grumpy!

Fine Gael's Richard Bruton, Minister for Jobs, Enterprise and Innovation, was not, in fairness, one of the Grumpy Old Men. Instead, like his Labour cabinet colleagues Ruairi Quinn (Education and Skills) and Brendan Howlin (Public Expenditure and Reform), he was more of a Grey Eminence. Given that such fine creatures are seen to possess more intelligence than is normally attributed to our politicians, that might not appear so bad. But in the vulgar public mind, the difference between a Grumpy Old Man and a Grey Eminence was essentially one of degree. The Grey Eminences Bruton, Quinn and Howlin might not have inspired as much opprobrium as their livelier colleagues. However, the reserved attitude of total separation from the voters that they adopted was equally inimical to the development of any form of dialogue with the country's citizens. This, allied to the sense that they belonged to a different era, meant the three Grey Eminences of the Coalition added to the sense of accelerated alienated disconnection sweeping through the voters.

Fine Gael's Phil Hogan was a somewhat different political creature. As he was only in his late fifties, it might have been assumed that a young fellow like Phil was too much of a child to be a Grumpy Old

Man. In fact, Phil became the most high profile Grumpy Old Man of them all. With his sharp tongue and an arrogant manner that fatally failed to disguise his political defects, Phil became the lightning rod for all of the Coalition's deficiencies. Phil's Grumpy status was understandable to some extent. As Minister for the Environment, Community and Local Government, a lot of hospital passes were thrown his way, from our farmers' uncertain relationship with sewage to the difficulties Dubliners have with property tax, and few of his Coalition colleagues, Michael Noonan excepted, stepped up to help Phil out. However, Phil's Grumpy Old Man standing stems from something more fundamental. The issue with Phil is that he came to power too late. After twenty-two years as an opposition TD, he was finally on the government benches – but the longer you spend in Leinster House, the more your political innocence and idealism are undermined. If you really want to reform the state, you had better get in between your tenth and twentieth years. After that, like Phil, you've become a dusty old pragmatist who at their very best does neither good nor bad.

Sadly, in the case of Phil, he was rarely at his best, for his main default was bad. As Minister for the Environment, Community and Local Government, his attempts at reform tended to be minimal. His abolition of a few hapless town councils was presented as the greatest revolution since the 19th century. In fact, it was about as dramatic as the government's 1922 decision to re-paint the old imperial-red post-boxes independence-green as a display of how radical the changes independence were. Phil also presided over the introduction of the property tax, a scheme threatened with collapse by a combination of Mr Hogan's department's endemic incompetence and his own blithe indifference to the concept of public consent. Eventually the grown-ups in Revenue rescued Phil, but the damage to the Irish public's view of the Coalition was already done. Jean-Baptiste Colbert, a 17th-century French finance minister, famously observed that the art of taxation is to extract the maximum of feathers from a goose with the minimum of hissing. Phil's approach seemed instead to be to give the goose a few slaps on the beak to get it good and agitated before he commenced the plucking.

Fine Gael's new Minister for Justice Alan Shatter's default setting of waspish arrogance exponentially increased the possibility of trouble. Rarely, if ever, has an Irish minister come into office bearing such a grandiloquent CV of awed testimonials from nervous colleagues about his brilliance. Alan's problem was that his capacities were that of a sole trader. Due to their inability to tolerate or work with lesser morals, sole traders can never be successfully brought into a company. Alan's ability to start a row in a Buddhist convention probably merits a chapter all of its own. Suffice it to say, Paddy, due to his colonial heritage, does not like to be talked down to and Alan, alas, liked to do little else.

Of course, being Grumpy Old Men, the Coalition railed against their designation as Grumpy Old Man. But being designated Grumpy Old Men was not the worst fate they could suffer. In fact, Grumpy Old Men are often viewed with affection – so long as you don't have to spend too much time in their company. Furthermore, Grumpy Old Men are regularly portrayed as truth-tellers in a land of spin. They are the aged equivalent of the child who, with an increasing decibel level, continues to proclaim the Emperor is naked, no matter how anxiously they are told to shush. Unfortunately, the Coalition's Grumpy Old Men were so obsessed with themselves they wouldn't have even noticed a naked Emperor. What was worse still, our Grumpy Old Men could never be convinced that life was not so bad, that maybe they should cheer up somewhat. They were all now where they always wanted to be, in government rather than opposition, but no amount of power, perks or thoughts of their future pensions could console them. Instead, having finally gone

one up in the match, all they did was complain about the ball, the grass, the line markings, the referee, the truculent nature of their opponents and the contrariness of the fans. There were, of course, a couple of exceptions: Michael Noonan for one, that old rogue, who retained a rare capacity to talk with rather than at the electorate. In that sense, our new Minister for Finance channelled a very American style of politics, combining folksy comments with a sense of serene inner stability, something sorely needed by the Coalition. Though he would in time become a bit of a Grump, at the beginning of the Coalition's time in government, Noonan posited himself as the nation's grandfather crossed with a few trace elements of Goldsmith's school-teacher in the famous 'Deserted Village'. Like Goldsmith's creation, Mr Noonan was severe and stern. But he also had a hidden lightness of being that meant the citizens, if they were not bold, might be told a few jokes that would allow them to laugh with real glee. Joan Burton was another exception, and in a different and far more verbose fashion she became the nation's grand-mum. They, however, were the exceptions to the Irish public's growing perception that the Coalition was a decaying *Politburo*, staffed by men with a tremble in their hands and a grumble in their voices.

We might have accommodated ourselves to the government of the Grumpy Old Men were it not for one fatal flaw. They might have been able to survive and even thrive in a functioning state, but Grumpy Old Man Syndrome was utterly ill-suited to deal with the current needs of the country's citizens. By 2011, after the madness of the previous three years, a shroud of depression had gathered over Irish life in a manner not seen since the 1950s. The despair of the Irish populace was entirely understandable, for the similarities to that wretched age were chilling. In the 1950s, de Valera's Fianna Fáil had gone from being the dominant political party in the state to a weakened, powerless group, just as Fianna Fáil in 2011 had faded from power and now bore the status of a failed experiment. In the

1950s, the opposition, like Fine Gael and Labour in 2011, had been granted a grudging mandate due to the absence of anything better. Just like the 1950s, an opposition who had inherited a country of vanishing youth became a gerontocracy that seemed fit only to manage decline in a bad-tempered fashion. Something different, something transformational, something involving the sort of regeneration that would lift the people was needed – something like the government of Seán Lemass. Instead, we got the Grumpy Old Men.

The Coalition's triumph was, it seemed, part of a strange ongoing process in which Irish politics was been taken over by politicians of a downbeat nature. Scarcely fifteen years previously, the Irish political psyche was defined by the chutzpah of Fianna Fáil's Charlie McCreevy. Bertie Ahern possessed the frolicsome charisma that surely suits the young leader of a young country. However, slowly over time, a snarling spirit of dour Puritanism invaded the mindset of subsequent Fianna Fáil governments, and ultimately the final Fianna Fáil government bore a far closer resemblance to a Fine Gael than a Fianna Fáil administration. Then, just when we needed the old Fianna Fáil spirit of confident enterprise to transfer itself to the new Coalition – well, again, we got the Grumpy Old Men.

In fairness, the Coalition's adoption of a position of unadulterated self-pity was entirely understandable. The precarious state of the government the Grumpy Old Men inherited resembled the one Winston Churchill inherited in 1941. However, unlike Churchill, who inspired a buckling citizenry, self-pity was the Coalition's default setting. As a result of their self-pitying stance, they were too spiteful, far too early, when tested for either their own or our good. From the start, they were ready to be needled by the slightest real, perceived or accidental insult. And indeed they often confused mere questioning with malice. So it was that the Coalition led with deaf ears, unwilling to engage for fear of criticism. From a fatally early point, a debilitating non-dialogue of the deaf emerged. The previous government had squandered our independence, won after 700 years of struggle and that lasted less than a century, to become a colony again. This meant that what the Ireland of March 2011 needed the sort of positive leadership only a Clinton or a Roosevelt can provide. Instead, our brand new government consisted of the Grumps, who never considered the simple question troubling the rest of the country: how could such a dispirited crew generate the rise of the confidence that the country needed to rediscover if we were to regain a sense of self-respect, let alone start to hope for the future and kickstart our recovery?

It was a failure that was all the more surprising in the wake of Enda's accession speech, which appeared to recognise the pressing need to develop a new national spirit. Instead, about the only thing the Grumpy Old Men did quickly was to decide the core value of their administration would be to continue the old administration's 'careful now' politics of European appeasement. There were occasional reports of shouting matches with the Troika. But they were always behind closed doors, and, understandably, after the age of Bertie, Paddy was always going to be a bit of a Doubting Thomas about victories the hand cannot feel or the eye cannot see. Besides, to put it mildly, this was hardly the open government we had been promised.

Our faith in the promised change was further compromised by the fact that once the Coalition took up office, they took up an attitude of abandoned obsequy to every schoolyard bully. There was, it seemed, very little the Coalition could do, given the fiscal straitjacket they were in, and so they decided to succumb to the inertia of the 'careful now' school of rule. In fairness, this positioning was understandable: we are a small peripheral country surrounded by hostile German-led enemies. However, though it brought a certain outward tranquillity, applying the politics of 'careful now' to internal vested interests or the cold disinterested Troika of accountants who were now running the state did not facilitate the happiness of our Grumpy Old Men. Instead, succumbing to the desiderata of inertia had the most curious and unwanted of side effects. Sometimes, the church's warning that securing what you desire is not necessarily a route to joy is correct. And so it was for our brand new Coalition. The choking emphysema of inertia accelerated their growing bitterness, which manifested itself in an intriguing variety of ways. Their snarly squabbling over trivia such as appointments to state boards, which occurred with increasing frequency, was a symptom of the Coalition's frustration at the erosion of their self-respect that the unceasing pursuit of appeasement brought in its train. Of course, their squabbling was also the consequence of having too much time to do too little, for beyond ticking the boxes sent out by the Troika, our brand new ministers had nothing to do. Government ministers must, however, fill their days with something so the futile personal battles of Leinster House started fill up the most vacant of days and minds.

Unsurprisingly, Paddy got fed up fairly swiftly with the Grumpy Old Men of the Coalition. Having endured the dubious delights of a Fianna Fáil government that had become embittered by success, we were none too enthusiastic about a set of successors who appeared to be embittered by years of failure. It all created a strange sense of unreality, as a young, struggling country found itself being governed by a complacent cabinet of grey men, a pension-age class of Venetian doges who, alarmingly, knew nothing about our lives. The separation between the Irish people and their new rulers, which was escalating at an unnerving pace, was informed by another serious flaw in the Coalition. A central weakness of Fianna Fáil seems to be an inability to stop being political, even when it damaged the state they nominally swore to serve. Fine Gael and Labour are the obverse side of the coin. Once in government, the Coalition seemed to undergo a form of ordination after which they thought they were no longer politicians. Instead, the Coalition appeared to think they were legislators or political architects. But we already had plenty of those. What was needed instead was for the Coalition's ministers and TDs to live up to their actual constitutional role as messengers of the people.

Too often the Grumpy Old Men were content to be the respectful servants of the mandarins who had guided the Republic to the rocks, something that was fatal in a country seeking a revolution. It is said that on taking power in a UK that was almost as distressed as Ireland is today, Margaret Thatcher gathered her top mandarins and berated them at such forcible length for their role in the misgoverning of the UK that a couple of them subsequently had to be helped out of the meeting room. The story may be an urban myth but it makes for an interesting contrast with the Coalition's response to the debacle they inherited. After a brief month of throwing shapes on the reform front, a number of the civil service's most senior mandarins departed with their shoulders bowed by the weight of their vast pensions. The reason for the Coalition's glaring failure to act is hard to comprehend. Perhaps the decades they had spent in opposition had softened their self-confidence to the point at which no amount of political Viagra could straighten it up. The journeys of these strange Magi to office had certainly been hard and arduous. Yet having got there, their absence of desire for change was obvious and therefore all the more curious. It was almost as though, exhausted by their voyage, once they arrived in the castle and met the willing princess, their sole desire was to take a nap on the couch. But if they thought they would be thanked for restricting their ambitions to being Europe's pliable servants with the sole aim of returning the country to where it had been a decade ago, they had gravely misread the zeitgeist. This misunderstanding of the public mood was particularly problematic for Labour. Elected on the implicit promise that they would be the watchdogs of Fine Gael, they instead became its nodding dog that did not bark, watching passively as the country was sliced up in service of austerity. And no farmer wants to keep a voiceless dog.

The sole exception to Labour's doleful voicelessness was Joan Burton, whose public squawking whenever Brendan Howlin came near her department would have put Colbert's goose to shame. However, because Joan was open and loquacious, she was swiftly sidelined by the Labour powers-that-be as a bold girl giving cheek to the ever-invisible Tánaiste Eamon Gilmore. The more general mood in the Labour hierarchy was summarised by one senior spin-doctor who proudly observed that the absence of a narrative about what the Coalition was doing represented one of its successes. Given what they were doing, he had a point. But the concept that a vacuum represented a triumph of communication was a huge departure from Enda's promise that the new government would not leave Paddy in the dark.

Increasingly in Ireland's political *Animal Farm*, it looked as though the only difference between our democratic revolutionaries and the Fianna Fáil pigs was that the Coalition were looking for praise over their efficiency in implementing the Fianna Fáil plan and feeling sorry for themselves when it was less than forthcoming. Our Grumpy Old Men were heading towards a dangerous space at quite the lick. After a mere matter of months, our Coalition chameleons had already shed their democratic revolutionary skin and turned themselves into a new political cartel. This was hardly unique, for under Fianna Fáil, a vast cartel had evolved between politicians, the public sector and various vested interests under the mysterious blanket term 'social partnership', under which the only people who were left out were the citizens. Then, incredibly, the Coalition's policies began to breathe new life into this old unholy union of self-interest. This fall was, in many ways, very understandable. When you have been so out in the cold for so many years, the interest of those who were previously so much more important than you is, despite all the anger caused by previous rejections, terribly seductive. Of course, this unfortunately does leave you open to accusation of hypocrisy but the sting fades after a while. But transforming themselves into a new political cartel had one hugely important side-effect. It showed that, within mere months of their accession, the Grumpy Old Men were doing a very fine job of squandering a mandate that was as equivocal as it was large.

CHAPTER 4

A STRANGE POINT OF LITE ARRIVES

Enda becomes master and commander – but for how long?

I t would be inaccurate to say that the Coalition was always in the bad books. During its first year at least, Dear Leader Enda operated as a strange point of light within an administration that was visibly failing to thrive in a dangerous number of arenas. In fact, Enda's successes had been predicted by those who tried to dispose of him in the infamous 2010 heave. Or at the very least, his successes justified the analysis of Leo Varadkar in that heated time that Enda could be one of the best Foreign Affairs ministers we have ever had, if he would but go. Leo was, in fairness, partially right, for one of the most intriguing aspects of the rise of Enda during the Coalition's early period of speckled grace was how well foreigners got on with a Taoiseach who was securing, at best, grudging acquiescence for his existence at home. Our sense of bafflement at Enda's success abroad was much like the wonderment of a spouse when they see someone flirting with the partner they merely tolerate – surprising only until the spouse realises that the stranger gazing fondly upon their disregarded partner has no idea what their partner is really like at all.

Enda's capacity to dazzle foreign politicians was evident from the very start of his regime when, less than a wet week in office, Mr Kenny went to Washington. If proof were needed of the metamorphic qualities that come with power, nothing epitomised this more than the transformation of Enda Kenny during that visit. For decades, at the Galway races – anywhere else for that matter – Fine Gael were outside the tent, hoping the warm liquid trickling down their necks was rain. It wasn't. But on this occasion, with the media corralled behind a rope in the White House and treated with the special contempt that the rich and powerful reserve for journalists, Fine Gael were for once standing contentedly on the red carpet side of things. They, rather than Fianna Fáil, were sitting at the top table with President Obama and mingling with *Bonfire of the Vanities*-style millionaires and billionaires, the American ward bosses and corporate lawyers who decide how the world lives.

Fine Gael could hardly believe their eyes. And, to be honest, we had difficulties with our own.

What was particularly astonishing was that, amidst the gold drapes and the chilly marble splendour of the last Western Empire and in the company of President Barack Obama and some of the world's most powerful people, Taoiseach Enda Kenny seemed right at home. In truth, his delight and shock at how he far he had come were evident. After his first meeting with Obama, Enda stood before the media, said 'I've just come out from the Oval Office', and stopped. His caesura was a momentary admission that even he could not believe where he had ended up. And really, who would ever have imagined that a dreamy boy from Mayo called Enda would visit the celebrated Oval Office to be congratulated on his 'historic win' by the first black President of the United States? No wonder he was staring at Obama with the adoring eyes of a pre-coital virgin bride.

At first glance, the US President's praise appeared excessive, but then we remembered we used to claim it would be far easier for a black man to become the President of America than for a Fine Gael TD from Mayo to become Taoiseach. The reason for Enda's doting glances was soon revealed when the US President offered him the boon of a Presidential visit to Ireland. Within a week of becoming Taoiseach, Enda had achieved what Brian Cowen had failed to. And Mr Kenny made plenty of other hay of the impending visit, noting that it was 'in this time of challenge ... a unique statement of confidence' in our country. Implied in his statement was a clear warning to Europe that Enda had more friends than Angela Merkel.

For Enda, his trip to Washington represented the zenith of his long journey that started on a day in 2001 when the ceiling of the Mansion House twinkled with a thousand points of light and Michael Noonan wowed the assembled media with promises of a new 'social contract'. In the middle of Noonan's performance, a pallid figure clad in a grey gabardine coat had walked in and sat down without causing a rustle in the indifferent media ranks. It was his defeated rival for the Fine Gael leadership, already yesterday's boy king to such an extent he hadn't been even deemed fit for that simulacrum of power known as an opposition front bench position. Ten years later, Kenny had finally arrived at the powerful place he had been looking for.

Mr Kenny's joy at being in America was understandable for another reason. No other Taoiseach had so defined his persona using the lexicon of American politics. This, in itself, represented a positive change, because Irish politicians had been extraordinarily insular up until then. With regard to the last two Taoisigh, one was totally immersed in a land called Drumcondra while the other struggled to believe anything worthwhile existed beyond Clara. Mr Kenny, however, appeared to at a deep level to understand the connections between Ireland and America. Mr Kenny's instinctive empathy with the American spirit was all the more serendipitous for Ireland, because the way in which America defines itself was the way in which Ireland needed to start thinking to get out of the muddle of recession and austerity we were in. One of the points of tension between the philosophies of Paddy and America has always been Paddy's scathing disregard for the gauche American dream of freedom, accountability and the capacity for re-invention. The fact that America and the American Dream mythology had seized Enda's imagination so totally meant we could hope that, when it came to his still not very clear but much needed theory of for reforming the Irish state, Mr Kenny's instincts would be progressive.

Ironically, in the first few years of his leadership of Fine Gael, Enda's very public love affair with American politics and the Kennedy myth in particular had actually hampered his career as a serious politician. Enda, the gallivanting dreamy Western playboy, might have been captivated by the glamorous Kennedy brothers. However, the Kennedys' Camelot was founded not just on their effortless good looks, but on steely ambition mingled with the sort of vicious infighting and corruption that would have even caused Charlie Haughey to cough. The contrast between Enda dozing in the bed as soft afternoon sunshine caressed his unlined face and the cruel but necessary strength of the Kennedys left Fine Gael's blonde new leader dangerously open to the charge of being a fake. But, inspired by the country that epitomised re-invention, Mr Kenny redefined his own persona through the eight years of trial and resilience. He suffered in the blood and sand of the crucible of Irish politics and, merely by surviving, was given the chance to shape his and our destiny.

Enda's success in America was helped by the fact that no nation loves the 'high steppin', highfalutin'' sentiment that is Enda's stock in trade more than America. While those of us at home may have winced at his florid rhetoric about 'our horizons are fluid, they travel with us as we go' and his tales about 'my grand-uncle, the lighthouse keeper on the Brazos River in Texas', America lapped it up. But Kenny also made it clear that Biffo era of the quiet death of government was over. The Coalition's government would undertake an Irish equivalent to *glasnost* and become a bright new government 'open for business' to all. Kenny was still no JFK and, like the rest of the world, he also could not match the cool-as-a-foot-long charisma of Obama. But seeing Kenny in the environs of the White House gave us the opportunity to belatedly understand who exactly Mr Kenny might be, for there was, it seemed, a touch of the Ronald Reagan about him. Some might be offended by the comparison but, in spite of the scorn poured on Reagan's Hollywood past, he was the President who brought the Soviet empire down. And, importantly, he made an America which had lost confidence in itself feel proud once again. The latter was certainly something we needed back in Ireland.

We could only hope when it came to our struggle against the stranglehold of bureaucrats and bankers that Mr Kenny would be like the fabled hedgehog, who knows the one important thing, rather than the fox, who gets lost in all the many things he knows. Reagan was such a hedgehog, who, after the uncertainty of the Carter era, knew his great task was to bring the sunlight back to America. Kenny's job in Ireland was similar and in that regard, though it is easy now to forget, the Taoiseach's foreign successes were not unimportant. Ireland's reputation abroad had been shredded to the point where Nicolas Sarkozy could contemptuously ruffle the hair of the democratically elected Irish Taoiseach without fear of a diplomatic incident and the twin terrors of Merkel and Sarkozy could confidently summon the Taoiseach to the equivalent of a police shakedown on the matter of Ireland's corporation tax.

Happily, when it came to rebuilding foreign alliances, the Obama affair was not a one-off. While it would probably be excessive to suggest that Enda Kenny's first meeting with David Cameron resembled the diplomatic equivalent of *When Harry Met Sally*, it was a damn close run thing. And intriguingly, given our respective places in the world, the majority of the loving came from the UK side of the table. In his Downing Street speech, Mr Kenny, who can rarely be accused of being circumspect in the company of foreign leaders, was almost modest in his claim that the Anglo-Irish 'relationship is at an unprecedented high level of co-operation'.

Our relief at the time that foreign leaders would treat us with respect seems strange now. But back then, when we were the second 'I' in the dreaded PIIGS group, our survival as an independent state was a matter of genuine contention. Given the depressed state of the citizenry and the delicate nature of Paddy's psychology, the Queen's historic visit to Ireland in May 2011, albeit an event more carried by the Queen than Enda, represented another critical evolution in the recovery of our busted morale – although it is worth remembering that such was the stricken state of the national finances, we had to engage in the fiscal equivalent of scrabbling beneath the sofa to secure the necessary funding for the Garda overtime.

In the early days of the Coalition, there were also successes beyond Mr Kenny's ability to shepherd a vast array of foreign dignitaries around Ireland with the learned bonhomie of a Dublin Tour Bus guide. The worst excesses of the bailout were subtly disentangled: the detritus of the Anglo Irish Bank was swept beneath the metaphorical carpet and the prize of extended rather than immediate reparations for the promissory note was secured. Criticism of the incomplete nature of these efforts was muted, for Paddy rarely has a problem with the politics of paying on the 'never never'. Most critically of all, when it came to the great wound of Anglo Irish Bank, Dear Leader Enda secured a 'seismic deal' on banking in 2012. The devilish details were somewhat absent but the acquiescence of the other countries,

and our German bosses in particular, were of some importance. To
the Irish population, the deal suggested some form of forgiveness
had been achieved for Ireland's sin. Atonement had been made. We
were no longer outlying PIIGS.

At the time, it looked as though a progressive linear narrative
could be built around Enda, one in which his apprenticeship in
leading the psychologically distraught Fine Gael of 2002 had been
the perfect training for the defiant cajoling, enthusing, nodding, and
joking needed to fulfil his self-proclaimed objective of state-building.
In many ways, courting voters in the small pubs of rural Ireland as a
member of the opposition was great training for staying alert at EU
summits that drag on after midnight as Sarkozy runs rampant and a
Greek guy with a loose tie starts to fall asleep. More intelligent men,
such as Pat Rabbitte, might have withered at the challenges Enda
faced. But as we saw all too clearly with Brian Cowen, the figurehead
of a bloated Celtic Tiger raddled by excess and fit for no purpose,
intelligence in a time of war can sometimes be more of a vice than a
virtue. By contrast, Enda stayed awake and secured a deal that would
reverse the Great Disruption and the dreaded austerity that followed,
healing the wounds inflicted on us by his failed Fianna Fáil precursors.
Now all that was needed was a brief tidying up of the paperwork and
we would be sorted. Or so we were told.

Sometimes Mr Kenny even surprised us with the unexpected.
The cleansing force of his speech on the Cloyne Report into the
cover-up of clerical abuse was a re-invention of our conservative
Taoiseach as a transformative prophet chasing out Ireland's clerical
snakes and their swishing soutanes into permanent exile alongside
Fianna Fáil's Cute Hoors. Groundbreaking speeches such as this
meant that for an all too brief period it looked as though it might
be possible for us to love our Dear Leader. Mr Kenny's *Ne Temere*
expulsion of the Fine Gael Rebel Five for their opposition to the
Coalition's abortion bill appeared to further solidify the Taoiseach's

position with the electorate. There were some murmurings about the dangers of an autocratic Enda, but Enda's friend Paddy was not always averse to the occasional smack of firm governance.

There were some clouds, alas, darkening the supposed eternal sunshine of King Enda's court. Opinion polls in 2013 revealed the universal unpopularity of all party leaders, including Enda, two years into the Coalition's reign. The fact that two-fifths of the electorate supported no party at all suggested that Irish politics was heading towards a great existential crisis. Suddenly, a possible gap in the market for a new political party was emerging, at the very time when there was no shortage of loose horses running around that could coalesce to form a new political stable-yard. In spite of this, Enda and Fine Gael continued to reside in a happy land of clouds and cuckoos. As far as the Dear Leader was concerned, his grip on the Fine Gael party and the cabinet and his ability to keep them in power was absolute to such an extent that even not-so-Cute Old Phil was starting to make a popular comeback, courtesy of Michael Noonan's help in rescuing Phil from the property tax debacle.

The strength of the Taoiseach's political influence was epitomised by the nature of his relationship with the once-feared media. The docility of certain elements of the press towards King Enda may not have reached the level of Haughey era, when the *Irish Press* would ring Charlie Haughey to ask on what page he would like his photograph to be placed, but it has, on occasions, not been too far off it. While Enda was, of course, vaguely aware he was not loved by the work-shy or the welfare classes, as long as Fine Gael continued to hold middle Ireland in the same firm grasp that nurses use on wavering children, this was the only minor hint of blight darkening the Taoiseach's pastoral political landscape.

Of course, there was Labour too, but the blue-blooded wing of Fine Gael appeared to have very few concerns about their Coalition partners' status. A few thinking members of Fine Gael were wise enough to realise that the debilitated status of their ailing Labour 'partners' should not be a source of celebration. They knew that in war there is nothing worse than a weak ally: it will either drag you down or, like a scorpion when cornered, it will sink its fangs into you in the hope of facilitating some escape. During the Coalition's first eighteen months, the Labour Croppy Boys' policy when faced by the barking Fine Gael dog and its media acolytes appeared to be one of lying down and taking it, in the hope that if they did not make too much of a fuss, maybe the Fine Gael dog wouldn't bite them. But the few more forward-thinking members of Fine Gael knew a policy change from the Croppy Boys could have far-reaching consequences.

However, in 2013, we were basking in the golden age of King Enda, in which the Taoiseach had become a strange point of light within the addled Coalition Cartel. This was still a bit of a surprise for many, but it could be rationalised. The curious thing about being the Taoiseach is that the role has no specific job description. If you are Minister for Finance, Foreign Affairs or Education, you know what your day-to-day tasks are. If you are Taoiseach, however, your desk is an empty space. Even an experienced a politician as Lemass initially found the isolation of a job that you must define through your own personality rather than by accepting orders from above to be dislocating while poor Cowen literally drowned under the absence of any structure.

By contrast, it was possible, for a while, to believe that a political chameleon like Enda was, like Bertie, suited to the inchoate nature of the Taoiseach's role. Though the posh elements of Fine Gael continued to find Enda as Bertie-Lite difficult to deal with, the reality was that Enda as Bertie was working, if only in a frail manner. More importantly, Enda was giving his mostly cleverer-than-he ministers their head. So long as Kenny remained aware of their existence, the Taoiseach's regularly touted weaknesses were his hidden strengths. You see, both we and Mr Kenny – except for those dangerous occasions when he is in master-of-the-universe mode – know that Enda is not particularly good at doing concrete things or ordering people around. Unlike clever little chaps such as Richard Bruton, he is simply not designed for interpreting flow charts or engaging in comparative statistical analyses. Enda is, to put it bluntly, better at opening Google and promoting the new digital economy than understanding it. So long as Enda realised his unique genius was perfectly qualified to engage in the critical task of raising the national spirit, rather than the complicated business of actually trying to govern the country, all would be fine. And, for a time, it was. Unlike Bertie, Enda didn't say 'ah, the hardy man, working hard' to every individual he saw, but he did appear to have adopted Mr Ahern's view that the most critical role of a Taoiseach is to act as a national and international cheerleader. It is perhaps easy to mock such an objective, but given the damage the frankly embarrassing figure Mr Cowen cut on the world stage caused to Ireland's international image, surely efforts to repair it were of critical importance to a state that is dangerously dependent on the kindness of suspicious strangers.

It was not always easy to follow the advice of Scottish poet Robert Burns and see Enda as others do. There were still so many niggling issues, such as the rather lengthy wait for the Democratic Revolution to emerge from the cabinet ante-room and Enda's speech at the Davos summit, in which he correctly admitted the cause of Ireland's crisis was that we all went mad borrowing and so caused a national furore, and then had to apologise and promise never to blame Paddy again. This meant that, while we were reasonably enamoured with the Coalition, we were for now reserving final judgement. Paddy knows that the leader of any peripheral, bankrupt state can do very little outside of 'spirit of the nation' stuff in what is a dangerous, self-interested and increasingly fissiparous world, and Enda was, at least, having a cut at things. Success in politics and national leadership is all about character and our accidental Taoiseach's core quality appeared to be the well-disguised grim determination that those who are ambitious and egotistical, but not immensely talented, need to succeed.

By the close of 2013, though, questions about Enda's leadership were beginning to gather. In particular, unease was growing over his transformation into something that far too closely resembled Bertie Ahern for comfort. His metamorphosis into Bertie-Lite was so complete that at a variety of GAA launches, footballers such as the great Kerryman Páidí Ó Sé posed for photographs with Enda, smiling as broadly as if he were with a genuine Fianna Fáil Taoiseach rather than an accidental Blueshirt one.

The Irish electorate had hoped our new Coalition would adopt a 'never waste a good crisis' philosophy and move quickly to undertake serious political reform. But as the Coalition began to evolve into a new political and administrative cartel, the central powers of Mr Kenny and Mr Noonan decided that that swift and serious reform was not, in fact, what the electorate wanted. Of course, they knew that in 2011 Paddy had said he was all for reform, but they concluded that 'what Paddy says he wants and Paddy actually wants are two different creatures'. Revolutions may happen in other countries but since Independence and through Civil Wars, Cold Wars and World Wars, the only thing Paddy has been unyielding about is his determination to take the safest route possible. Indeed, it was probable that the backwash from our thoroughly incautious adventures with the Celtic Tiger intensified our natural love affair with conservatism, just as the generation of politicians who came to power after the upheaval of the Civil War were the most conservative in the history of the state.

If Paddy wanted caution, Enda was certainly the man for that job. And initially, the opinion poll figures held sufficiently to suggest the Kenny–Noonan approach might be right. The idealists of the world had spent two years berating the Coalition for their list of abandoned promises, which was as long as the scattered remnants of Napoleon's retreat from Moscow. In spite of this, and contrary to the expectations of some of the more prescient of the Grumpy Old Men, the Coalition's support levels continued to tip the 40% barrier. By contrast, support for the forces of radicalism – if it is possible to use such a term for that collation of Sinn Féin and disparate Independents – after their initial surge, hit the invisible razor wire of Ireland's conservative centre. They managed to capture the mood of discontent of the eternally dispossessed and the newly dispossessed, which provided them with the support of a third of the electorate; oddly enough, however, the unique combination of 'Ming' Flanagan and Sinn Féin's Martin Ferris failed to build on that success to try to penetrate the hard shell of Ireland's insider classes.

As 2013 came to a close and the Troika exit winked at the Coalition in the manner of a loose woman flashing her garter, the Grumpy Old Men might have been tempted into thinking they might have gotten away with it after all. The Coalition had excised the dreaded Croke Park Agreement from public discourse, replacing it with the new Haddington Road Agreement – the same deal, yes, but with a different name. The €3 billion a year debilitating wound of the promissory note had also been exorcised – or, more accurately, delayed. Thanks mainly to the kindness of the Revenue, property taxes had been imposed without sparking mass riots. In circumstances such as these, the ghosts of the Rainbow Coalition were well entitled to claim 'our plan is working'. And an even more glittering political prize was now at hand for our Coalition, for predictions were beginning to emerge that the Irish deficit might be just over 4% by 2014. Were that to occur, the Grumpy Old Men might be able to declare in their October budgets of 2014 and 2015 that the iron age of austerity was over.

There were, though, two potential flies skimming across the surface of the Coalition's ointment. The first was the danger Enda poses to his colleagues on those rare occasions when the Dear Leader feels confident. Once Mr Kenny abandons the canny Cosgrave-style caution that is his defining political trait and adopts his 'I am a leader of steel' approach, Mayo's Mini-Putin, and his Coalition fellow-travellers, are on a collision course with the political ducking stool. His Coalition colleagues hoped that Enda might have finally learnt the lessons of past errors. But alas, Enda was always a bit of a political slow learner.

The second was whether the cautious Noonan–Kenny doctrine of abandoning reform in order to hold the conservative insider elites would actually work. Their 'careful now' policies divided the voters into the 'haves', who Fine Gael wanted as supporters, and the 'have nots', who the other parties could fight for, represented an act of pragmatic cynicism that would have caused even Fianna Fáil to gag. Of course, pragmatic cynicism has never been a barrier to political success in our post-colonial satrapy. There was, however, one basic flaw in the Grumpy Old Men's gamble: if the 2011 election results were Paddy's genuine attempt to initiate a democratic revolution, there could be trouble ahead.

CHAPTER 5

ICE-COLD FOR LABOUR IN MEATH EAST AND ALL THAT

Labour's love is truly lost

By spring 2013, sunlight was not a feature of Labour's life in government. After a bitingly cold March by-election in Meath East, which saw their vote slump to 4%, as Eoin Holmes, Labour's previously loquacious candidate (who subsequently lost his council seat too) fled the building, zipping past the media with scarcely a word, we were on the road to that point in time at which Independent TD Shane Ross could chuckle in late 2014 that he had more councillors locally than Labour had nationally.

The dark mood within Labour was summarised by one figure who warned 'people are whispering to each other with pale faces, asking what we are going to do. There's a real re-kindling of interest in Keaveney; he has acquired a new resonance among amidst the lukewarm and the restless who want a leadership challenge'. Exiled Labour TD Colm Keaveney was not the only darling of the gathering forces of dissent. Our spooked source also warned that plenty of TDs and Senators were also whispering to Keaveney's companion in exile, Róisín Shortall, on the side. As it happened, Mr Keaveney would take a slightly different route and decide a half-living Fianna Fáil represented a better future route than the dying Labour Party. Róisín Shorthall, after two years of debilitating infighting with that clawless Fine Gael bruiser James Reilly, decided meanwhile that departure form Labour and beginning the precarious life of an Independent represented the best road to a political future. Though Róisín is not known for her gaiety, she has not stopped smiling since.

Fine Gael were not quite yet 'shackled to a corpse' in their choice of Coalition partner. But Labour bleeding did bear a more than passing resemblance to the Austro-Hungarian front with Russia in the First World War – useless to Germany and constantly depleting essential war resources. Unfortunately for the Labour Party, Dear Leader Enda was neither designed nor inclined to give his forlorn allies a hand either. This had nothing to do with the weakening of his internal credit within Fine Gael, as Enda was quite oblivious to that. The real source of Mr Kenny's disinterest in his Coalition partners' travails was that Enda is instinctively a sole trader. Even within Fine Gael itself, his mission is all about maintaining the special nature of his own position. Why then would this most tribal of politicians save the Labour Party, merely his partners in government and who do not bear his own brand upon their political rumps?

For Labour, their great fear for the future really only began to emerge after the Meath East by-election. Like any horror movie, there had been occasional distant shrieks and howls prior to this. Bur until the unwelcome results of Meath East, the Labour Party, currently the second largest in Leinster House, had hoped that unwelcome murmurings about a Green Party-style meltdown were excessive. They knew they were in trouble, but when it came to Meath East, their objectives were summarised by one spin-doctor who hoped that, 'with a bit of luck, we might finish above Sinn Féin'. To outsiders, it seemed Labour would be lucky to finish above the Workers Party. As it happened, they finished above the Workers Party. The problem was they finished behind Direct Democracy Ireland. This was the political equivalent of trailing in behind the UK's Monster Raving Looney Party.

So as Fine Gael thrived, or at least survived, what was wrong with poor Labour? Well, perhaps their biggest issue was their complete lack of understanding of the problems they faced. Drowning under the electorate's designation of Labour as 'Labour – the party that broke all yer promises', Labour floundered in the aftermath of Meath East. Somewhat typically for a party that is always too obsessed with the media for its own good, their response to their woes was to blame the self-same media. The media, Labour claimed, was undermining Labour's attempts to woo those who had once voted Fianna Fáil and were now winking at Sinn Féin. Worse still, the ailing party's response to Meath East was to send out the Gilmore *apparatchik* Derek McDowell, whose most notable political achievement consisted of the loss of a safe Labour seat to independent TD Finian McGrath of all people, to pen a written response to the crisis in an attempt to steady the now very nervous troops.

However, party members were thoroughly unimpressed by McDowell's claim, in *The Irish Times* inevitably, that Labour hadn't broken its promises – 'or at least none that matter'. Oddly enough, Labour TDs on the canvas had discovered that slight things, like child benefit and even that extra euro on a bottle of wine, matter to those people who had voted for Labour to protect them from Fine Gael. They now believed that, rather than protecting their voters by mediating the worst of Fine Gael's policies, Labour was engaged in a process of appeasing their Fine Gael overlords. Derek is, of course, terribly good with words but the electorate, and the Labour TDs and councillors looking for their votes, speak in single transferable sentences. Sadly for Derek and for Labour, the STS that defined how Labour was viewed was now 'Labour – the party that broke all yer promises'.

The walls were closing in on the Labour leadership and its TDs were now openly expressing dissent. In the post-Meath East wilderness, it fell to a pleasant former Green Party *apparatchik* called Steve Rawson to diagnose Labour's woes and prescribe a course for recovery. Most political blogs are, to borrow a celebrated Jackie Healy-Rae phrase, as useful as 'tits on a bull'. Rawson's blog is the exception, as he, with much knowledge and great insight, explained precisely why Labour was in real danger of suffering a Green Party-style meltdown. Rawson noted, more in sorrow than in anger, that during the by-election Labour's leadership and campaign team's messaging and optics were out of touch with the general mood of the country. The Labour candidate, for example, was an impressively dressed film producer and restaurant owner, whose central campaign platform was the importance of same-sex marriage. The problem with this, alas, was that he was championing it at a time when property tax notices were dropping in the doors of home-owners, many of whom were genuinely wondering if they would even have a property to be taxed next year. A loquacious latte salesman in an expensive pink shirt was not going to secure their support.

Rawson's observed that the distinct 'cool Hibernia' feel to the campaign possessed equally grim implications for our Greens – apologies, Labour. In 2006 and 2007, the Green Party had been the kings of 'cool Hibernia'. During their time of modest glory, the Greens had been called the 'Italian kitchen' party of Irish politics, because their support peaked at roughly the same time as Paddy decided only Italian designer kitchens were good enough for him. Like the Italian kitchens with their posh islands, a vote for the

Greens was a daring signal by the Sancerre-sipping *petite bourgeoisie* of Sandymount that we were modern and evolved. Fianna Fáil, Fine Gael and Labour were no longer good enough for Paddy. Instead, it was the Greens or bust.

Sadly, when Mr Bust arrived and we were forced back to cash-and-carry country for our home-fittings, we jettisoned the poor Greens alongside our designer kitchens. Like the shot deer that doesn't realise it is dead even as it flees, the Greens did not know that they had passed from this political earth until sometime after their death had already occurred. During that time, they continued to operate like a still-living political party. In the aftermath of the Meath East by-election, Rawson claimed that Labour was at the same futile game. Labour's decision to stake their all on same-sex marriage, mainly because they had nothing else to trade with, resembled the time where the Greens eagerly promoted civil partnership and a Lord Mayor for Dublin during the worst economic meltdown since the foundation of the Irish state. The mood of a bewildered and angry electorate towards the Green Party was not improved by a series of further imbroglios about greyhounds, deer hunting and puppy dog tails. Although, ironically, the Greens were actually the last sane members of Biffo's bizarre cabinet, the public perception their strange but harmless obsessions created caused the Greens to fall far harder than might otherwise have been the case.

Now Labour was at the same losers' game. Mr Gilmore, to the horror of most of his own party, claimed same-sex marriage was the civil rights issue of this generation. Most people in Ireland, by contrast, thought houses and jobs should be somewhat higher up the pecking order. As Labour's failure to recognise this saw the party slide ever more swiftly down the greased pole of popular support, you may be left scratching your head and wondering how Fine Gael managed to survive the electorate's wrath. According to Rawson, it was in fact simple enough. The 2011 general election,

Rawson contended, was far from being a radical transformation. It was instead a simple shift of voters from one conservative Catholic nationalist party to another. Fine Gael, who had conducted a stealth take-over of Fianna Fáil, were sitting in a fine and dandy position because they were doing what a conservative Catholic nationalist party says on the tin. They were looking after the Ireland that was gainfully employed and riding out the recession. What Labour was achieving was not so clear.

By March 2013, the success of the Fine Gael toughs in chasing Labour out of government behind the closed doors of the cabinet had yet to be fully revealed. However, it was already becoming apparent the poor old sons of Gilmore were alarmingly peripheral when it came to the red in tooth-and-claw items of government, such as the economy and tax. Labour's absence from these seminal issues led them to fill their policy gap with the mother's apron of constitutional reform. But the doddering nature of all Grumpy Old Men meant even these measures fell way short. The Coalition Cartel may have proudly noted that the Dáil was sitting more often and for longer hours than at any time in their history. All Paddy saw was politicians talking a lot more but still achieving nothing. He was not too far wrong either.

To a certain extent, the panic after Meath East was a tad unfair. In the past, it would be almost normal for Labour to be an also-ran in a rural constituency. But this was the biggest Labour Party in the history of the state and one which had thieved the Presidency from Fine Gael. They were used to living a bit better than their previous hand-to-mouth election subsistence existence. Labour's new status as the second largest party in the state was about to start causing serious trouble for Mr Gilmore, for one, often unexpected reason. As Mr Gilmore was about to discover, big parties have big expectations. Worse still, they have lots of nervy TDs. And that is bad news for leaders who don't deliver.

After the debacle of Meath East, the Labour Party became a spectral party governed by a ghost. It did not help that one of the party's main problems before Meath East was that its leader was already an absentee, due to Mr Gilmore's Foreign Affairs commitments, but Mr Gilmore's unfortunate metamorphosis into the ghostly leader of Labour had in fact started long before the devastating by-election result; the Meath East result simply made this problem unavoidably obvious. Some say the die was cast from the moment Mr Gilmore won a place in government in the manner that brought the cruel phrase used about Jack Lynch where the former 'reluctant' Taoiseach was accused of winning the Fianna Fáil leadership while backing away to mind. In fact, the decline had begun well before that. After the peak of the Gilmore Gale in 2010, when one opinion poll put Labour ahead of Fine Gael, a worm had taken root in Mr Gilmore's political innards.

Some politicians blossom at the prospect of real power. For others, alas, it has a similar effect to the sprinkling of salt on a snail. And in the case of the Labour leader, the prospect of real power saw Mr Gilmore begin a march of the Seven Sorrows. The drachma-style decline of the Gilmore currency was illustrated by the fate of his 'Gilmore for Taoiseach' posters. The ever-thrifty Joan safely stored some of the unfortunate posters tidily in an outside shed but most of the others were blown off the poles by unseasonable weather and ground into mush by the indifferent stilettos of the few remaining post-crash commuters. Two pre-election strategies that damaged Gilmore and his party in a more tangible way were Ruairi Quinn's pledge not to increase third-level education fees and Labour's 'Every Little Hurts' adverts. The ad warned that Fine Gael on its own in government would increase car tax, cut child benefit, increase duty on wine, increase VAT and DIRT, and bring in water charges. Once in power alongside Fine Gael, Labour did all the aforementioned things. These two strategies therefore leapt above the previous primacy of Haughey's infamous

'Health Cuts Hurt the Old, the Sick and the Handicapped' campaign in the pantheon of broken electoral promises.

The impact of Gilmore's declining reputation was made abundantly clear by the glaring error he made straight after securing power when Mr Gilmore accepted five rather than six cabinet positions. Labour justified this climb down with the claim that Fine Gael's 76 seats would have allowed them to form a single-party government without a moderating left-wing attachment. In fact, they had bought Fine Gael's cunning double-bluff. Fine Gael were much happier with their Labour partners than they would have been holding power under the grace and favour of Ming the Merciless and his disparate collection of friends. Ultimately, there were seven little words Labour could have used in the Coalition negotiations that would have sent their Blueshirt counterparts running into Labour's folded arms. These were 'governing at the pleasure of Shane Ross'. But by folding to the demands of the Fine Gael toughs and accepting five ministries, Mr Gilmore's status as the beta male of the Coalition was set in stone. Nor was that the end of Gilmore's ministerial woes. Labour's timid acquiescence to five cabinet positions almost sparked a domestic war with its casual betrayal of Joan, who tripped gaily down the ministerial corridor expecting the Finance portfolio only to leave, dazed and confused, with the less-than-attractive Social Protection gig. The Grumpy Old Men had gazumped our heroine in favour of Brendan Howlin. Though Joan is too much of a moral Methodist to cause trouble in such affairs, Mr Gilmore was on his own from that point. Beyond occasional expressions of sorrowful incomprehension at the Tánaiste's acts, Ms Burton adhered to the wise old policy of treating the leadership in a similar manner to gathering apples in autumn: instead of throwing up sticks and inviting all the associated dangers that ensue, she waited for the apples to ripen and drop harmlessly into her waiting hand, which, eventually, it did.

It did not harm Joan's leadership hopes that Gilmore's lethal submissiveness gene continued to grow and grow. Even on such safe Labour ground as bishop-bashing, it was the Fine Gael Taoiseach rather than the Labour Tánaiste who opportunistically seized of the Cloyne Report to deliver a speech that captured the public mood, albeit one that had far less to it than met the eye – unless you count rhetoric as meaning. The more important feature of Enda's was that, when it came to Labour's traditional territory of anti-clericalism, Fine Gael had left nothing but political crumbs for poor Mr Gilmore. In a shining example of his uncertain political style, Gilmore's subsequent decision to close the Vatican embassy left him looking like the small dog that only barks after the bigger hound has finished.

As Labour began to look irrevocably destined to suffer the wretched fate of all junior coalition partners, from the Greens to the Progressive Democrats, more problems for Mr Gilmore became obvious. His ministers, it became clear, were essentially sole traders. It wasn't that they didn't respect Mr Gilmore. It was just that, rather like the rest of us, they didn't really notice him. There was another problem too, epitomised by Brendan Howlin, the Minister for Public Expenditure. In an eerily similar way to Mr Kenny, the former primary school-teacher Howlin always wants to be a good boy, which made him the perfect child of the Troika. If child benefits were required, he supplied them; if health insurances increases were requested, he provided them; if household charges, student charges and school transport fees were the order of the day, Howlin was happy to accommodate, for so long as the ledger balanced then Mr Howlin was, like his masters, happy. The problem with this, of course, was that Paddy is more of a lively lad than a teacher's pet and he didn't want a good boy to be in charge of him. He wanted someone like a Charlie Haughey who, in representing their own interest, might also sort out some of Paddy's woes. As the party's support began to slump, some innocent members within Labour took the view that their travails might be eased if, like ET, Mr Gilmore came home and took over a high-profile department. Such assertions were usually quashed when the naïve souls were asked which one he would be good at.

As Colm Keaveney, the then Chairman of the Labour Party, stalked the Leinster House plinth looking for journalistic ears to whisper his 'concerns' into and the rest of the parliamentary party took the more discreet route of the many hidden nooks and crannies of the Dáil's warren of corridors, the strangest claim of all was that Labour's apparent timorousness was part of a cunning strategy. Apparently, after the travails and spats that had bedevilled previous coalitions, Labour had decided to sign a pact of mutual non-aggression with Fine Gael whereby each party would not interfere in the other's business. This was, in theory, a good idea – except for two small flaws. The first was that Fine Gael was far more incompetent in government than Labour's good boys. The second was that Labour kept getting the public blame for the debacles of the Fine Gael dunces.

Gilmore's timorous refusal to differentiate himself from his partners did little to ease the fears of the many new TDs and senators, who worried that their careers would be as short as those in Dick Spring's class of 1992. It was also remarkably naïve, for although Enda is a grand fellow, he is also the sort of political operator who, when he puts an arm around your shoulders, should be watched all the more carefully lest his hand slide its way down towards your wallet. Further adding to Gilmore's woes was the fact that dealing with Fine Gael was only one of many problems. Like a wounded animal on the Serengeti, Labour was under attack on several fronts by every variant of political creature, from the Sinn Féin jackals to the Anti-Austerity Alliance hyenas and including every spectrum of Independent from former Fine Gaeler to Ming. Labour was surrounded on all sides. Even Fianna Fáil were circling the wounded party, looking to re-annex their public sector voters who had fled to Labour in the last weeks of the election campaign in the vain hope that Labour would protect them from the worst excesses of Fine Gael. What haunted Labour most of all, like the continual tick-tocking of the crocodile in *Peter Pan*, was the threat of Sinn Féin and their ambitions for Labour's public sector vote. Labour feared they were headed the way of Sinn Féin's former competitors up North, the SDLP: extinction.

Really though, the circling beasts of prey were of secondary importance. Labour's problem was far more intimate and fundamental. It wasn't just that their leader was invisible. The Labour Party as a whole was in the dock for the failures of the Coalition but they were unable to issue any exonerating evidence. Labour appeared only capable of putting together a negative narrative of what it hadn't done and what it had stopped those terrible Fine Gael ruffians from doing. Rather like Biffo-era Fianna Fáil, it appeared to be utterly unable to tell us what it actually was doing. In a country frozen by an ice age of personal debt, mortgage debt, banking debt and sovereign debt, this narrative of negatives was a thin sort of gruel to be trying to tickle the voter's palate with.

For Labour, the worst news was that they had been ensnared by the single transferable sentence of 'Labour – the party that broke all yer promises'. When it comes to what caused the Great Betrayal of the Irish Democratic Revolution, you could make a thousand lists. But politics, not that our politicians ever appear to know this, is not about lists. It is instead about mood and tempo and about capturing and directing the sentiment of the public. And damningly for Labour, if the Great Betrayal were a court case, then that single sentence alone sufficed to carry the charge and convict the party. And before the trial even began, it was more than enough to condemn them to ongoing political impotence, where nothing they could say or do could turn the mindset of the country's citizens. Worse still, within the power game of the Coalition, the collapse of their public support had reduced them to the status of mere ciphers, for in fairness how could Fine Gael take any threats from a Labour party that was listlessly waiting to be annihilated should it say 'hello' to the Irish people with the slightest degree of seriousness?

One of the more intriguing features of the Labour fall was how much the party struggled to actually comprehend the reality of its decaying position. From the start, the Coalition was an administration that deluded itself into believing it was greatly welcomed, despite its actual status as a creature of necessity bred by the absence of anything much better to elect. Ultimately, the best measure of the imaginative failure at the heart of Labour was that it took a septuagenarian President to illustrate where the party had gone wrong. At a particularly beleaguered time in our history, it was Michael D. who led the beginnings of a revolt against the evils of austerity. Ireland has had no shortage of moral civil wars over issues that rivalled the great question of how many angels can dance on the head of a pin in terms of obscurity. Now, when the Coalition-backed policy of austerity generated the greatest moral split since 1922, Labour decided to embrace the politics of the three wise monkeys.

The great mistake politicians and economists made about the philosophy of austerity was to believe that it was a mere book-balancing exercise. Austerity, a word and a policy that came dominate our lives, was never just that. It was instead the great moral issue of our age in which a cabal of bankers, with the assistance of intellectually under-gunned and morally cowardly politicians, enslaved the citizens of a continent, not just our small, woebegone Ireland, in order to pay off their gambling debts. Reparations are generally imposed on the guilty, who normally, coincidentally, are the losers. With austerity, the tariff was imposed upon the innocent.

The consequences of this new economics of 'dumb austerity' for the people were profound. Occasional austerity is sometimes necessary for governments, who, although they would like to, cannot spend without restraint in order to ensure their own re-election. This was not what we were experiencing. Instead, what we were undergoing was a form of dumb austerity of the kind last seen when the Allies imposed reparations on Germany after the end of the First World War. After that particular decision, the economist J.M. Keynes famously warned in *The Economic Consequences of the Peace* that 'the policy of reducing Germany to servitude for a generation, of degrading the lives of millions of human beings, and of depriving a whole nation of happiness should be abhorrent and detestable ... even if it did not sow the decay of the whole civilised life of Europe'.

The new economics of dumb austerity represented an equivalent form of psychological oppression, one that colonised with an abacus rather than the threat of a tank. In fairness, we expected little better from Fine Gael than obedience to the abacus. Fine Gael are the sort of non-comprehending footstools – apologies, foot-soldiers – who could only blink blankly at President Michael D. Higgins's warnings that economic recession had undermined our citizens' human rights and facilitated the ceding of authority of elected parliaments to debt collectors and bondholders. What was much more out of character was that Labour, with the sole exception of Joan Burton, appeared to have been fatally infected with the same evil spirit of appeasement.

Mr Higgins was not some fanciful poet who was all alone in his views. Figures as diverse as George Soros, a billionaire speculator, and Ashoka Mody, the former IMF mission chief to Ireland, also warned that austerity doesn't work. Their argument was that, far from being a proven, fail-safe science, austerity was the most destructive socio-economic experiment since Malthusian *laissez faire* economics.

Under the voodoo economics of austerity as practiced by our punishers, every feature of progress from employment security, the chance to own your own house, child benefit, free health care and an egalitarian education system gets crushed by an iron fist that imposes eternal reparations on small states, zero-hour contracts for workers and eternal profits for speculative bondholders.

When faced with an economic doctrine that decides that although those most guilty of creating the great European crash were governments, regulators and banks, the punishment would be imposed upon the citizens, Labour's greatest sin was that it stood idly, and invisibly, by. And then these silent non-protesting members of the not-so-great pan-European Coalition of Appeasement wondered why their support was melting away.

Labour did not learn quickly on either austerity or the breaking-promises front. Instead, in the aftermath of Mr Gilmore's departure at an emotional parliamentary party meeting, Pat Rabbitte claimed 'history will vindicate us, the advertising campaign was right.' Brendan Howlin was living in a similar land of illusion when he noted 'we are not austerity junkies'. Such a mindset went a long way towards explaining how the gap between how the public saw them and how Labour saw themselves was becoming insurmountable.

In a sense, it is possible to argue the public dislike of Gilmore and Labour was unfair. In practical terms, it matters little. As with Biffo's Fianna Fáil before them, the public took two swift decisions about Labour's role in the Coalition. The first, understandably, was that Fine Gael was the real boss. The second, chillingly for Labour, was that when it came to all the nasty medicine Fine Gael was so enthusiastically doling out, Mr Gilmore and Labour would be the poor designated Piggys who would be sacrificed as a necessary punishment for the destruction of our lives.

CHAPTER 6

A CLENCHED FIST HIDING BEHIND A SMILE

Enda's cracks start to show

Even for Taoisigh, 'the Enda the honeymoon' – sorry – has to arrive eventually. In Irish politics, you know you are really in trouble when even your eternally supportive junior coalition partners begin to kick up. By late 2013, the Coalition honeymoon was over to such an extent even Eamon 'Invisible Man' Gilmore began to make his distress known. Or rather 'senior Labour figures close to the leader' began to bleat intensely to happy journalists about the 'crass, cack-handed, macho' attitude taken by their Fine Gael Coalition allies to their Labour partners. When it came to the sudden outburst from Gilmore about Phil Hogan's 'chaotic' handling of his department, the Coalition's collective mood was not improved when Mr Kenny hit back by warning he would be keeping a close eye on Joan Burton's progress in hers. Although, at the time,

Typhoid Mary would have been more popular than Joan amidst the Tánaiste's threatened inner circle, such was Labour's level of anger at their Coalition partners, they now closed ranks to defend 'our Joan' from the attacks of those Fine Gael bullies. The spats continued as Labour's by now extremely busy senior sources warned that the story about Enda taking charge of Joan came directly from the Taoiseach's office, with Kenny's imprimatur. Kenny, we were told by the new defenders of Joan, shouldn't be dragging in others to cover up James Reilly's mishandling of the Department of Health, described by one source as 'a car crash a week'. As Labour insiders publicly, but anonymously, slammed the decision of the Taoiseach's office to rattle Joan's cage for its own self-interest as false, macho and politics of the worst kind, the Coalition looked to be heading for the divorce courts at quite the lick.

Sadly, although Labour was lashing Fine Gael's current divide-and-conquer recipe for Coalition chaos, they were not too united within themselves. Senior figures within the party snarled to the press that it was 'fucking amateur hour' in Labour, frustrated that 'every guard and nurse is spitting fire at us and our man is going on about gay marriage and Savita Halappanavar'. Suddenly, senior figures started to notice the venom of backbench TDs directed at Gilmore's leadership, blaming him for bringing Labour to the same level of support that the Democratic Left finished with. Others castigated Gilmore for hiding away in the Department of Foreign Affairs while the liberal wing took over the party and focused on issues far removed from the practical concerns of a country in which people were in constant fear of losing their homes and their jobs. This party infighting was bad news for more than Labour. The instability that it signalled in posed real threats for Fine Gael too.

If the sands were shifting beneath Enda's theatre of political illusions, our Dear Leader showed scant sign of noticing it. Few could blame Enda for his insouciance, for Fine Gael, at least, was knee-deep in the great age of King Enda in 2013, to such an extent that even the least deferential of his ministers began to call Enda 'the boss-man'. Those who knew Enda well recognised the danger in our Dear Leader being addressed in a manner that brought the age of Haughey and his pretensions to mind, for in 2013, Enda was in a supreme state of confidence – which meant trouble was certainly ahead. A disparate group of Fine Gael rebels expressed concern that the Taoiseach was evolving into some form of 'Great Dictator', but it was too late. The toxic mix of Labour impotence and Fine Gael arrogance that slowly dragged the government below the political waves in 2014 was beginning to be forged.

The Taoiseach's view from the political magic carpet he was on, high above the concerns of mere citizens, might have been good but, in fact, Enda had become dangerously severed from the people who had elected him. Somehow he had been fatally seduced by the attractions of EU-imposed austerity, whereby our Troika partners used us as the canary in the coalmine of re-invented Malthusian economics. The big problem for our Coalition Cartel was that they appeared to be far too much at ease with austerity policies, while the Irish electorate remained implacably opposed to them. To the Irish people, the reality of austerity was that Ireland, like the equally small and disposable Czechoslovakia in 1938, had been betrayed to appease the satanic mills, this time of bankers, bondholders and the ECB rather than monomaniacal dictators. In fairness, the Coalition was caught in the original cleft stick. Just as the Czechs would have been destroyed had they fought in 1938, had we pressed the nuclear button on banking default and provoked the wrath of Angela, our fate might not have been pretty. However, while their policy of appeasement may have been necessary, the Coalition's failure to adequately communicate the rationale for such a stance, or indeed to clearly tell Europe their imposed reparations were an amoral deal that sold Ireland into slavery, debased their political credit. As the dividends secured by the lofty sentiments of Enda's first days were squandered with joyless abandon, sadly, it increasingly appeared to be the case that the pre-election bear market was correct: Enda was empty sentiment and not much else.

Europe's demands and the fragmentation of Labour were not the only points of difficulty for the Coalition. Few recall it now, but in the initial weeks of the Coalition, perhaps for up to a month, it was widely assumed that they would engage in a clear-out of the civil service mandarins who, far more than their political masters, were responsible for plunging the Irish state into the mire in which the Coalition found it. The whispering corridors of Leinster House were abuzz with the chatter of panicking mandarins, who were now walking at unwonted speed and getting the early bus into work to escape the planned St Valentine's Day-style assassinations. Slowly and steadily though, the atmosphere of quiet, distressed panic began to ease. A subtle change in language began to establish itself and the messages issuing forth from Leinster House softened. We were now told that, although the Coalition still had the finest of intentions and the bravest of objectives, the dear old wheels of governance move slowly.

And then reform went into hiding. Nothing definitive was said and the intentions as always remained good but, like one of those London T.S. Eliot fogs, the old familiar Eau de Cowen settled over the Coalition. The impression of a slackening in the Coalition's reform impulse intensified as the Coalition began to quietly facilitate the departure of some of the senior civil service mandarins with ongoing huge pay-offs and fine European jobs. This was a far distance from the punitive measures envisioned by the Irish public.

The opposition continued to demand, with all the rigour and focus of jackdaws cawing in a chimney that's gone on fire, that the Coalition solve the problems the Opposition itself had created and, in fairness, there was no shortage of crises for the Coalition to deal with. We had, for example, a group of city and county councils whose governing processes were as chaotic as a herd of drunken cats. But rather than dealing with its inherited problems or tackling the ever-increasing list of new ones, a Coalition that was quite obviously not looking for trouble lest trouble find it embraced the legacy of the Croke Park Agreement as it surreptitiously kicked the Democratic Revolution beneath the carpet. 'Austerity without reform' and, worse still, 'careful now' became the Coalition's two favoured tactics and any prospective democratic revolutionary watchdogs were informed it would be best if they stayed quietly under the table.

The Coalition's 'austerity without reform' approach was most clearly shown in the great caution and fear with which it initially imposed the €100 household charge as part of its 'reform' of local government. It was bad enough that the Grumpy Old Men would not deal straight with us and say that the long-term plan was to bump this up to €1,000. But what really facilitated the Irish electorate's rise in contempt for conventional politics, a rise welcomed with delighted avarice by Sinn Féin, was that our household charge would not lead to any real reform of our council workers' 34-hour, flexi-time, sick-note for every Monday, 'computer says no' terms and conditions.

In fairness to Enda, any report card on the failure of the Democratic Revolution should recognise the ways in which the Taoiseach was hamstrung. One of the Coalition's main handicaps when it came to the revolution was that Fine Gael has never been entirely at ease with radicalism. An instinctive deference to powerful vested interests is built too deeply into the DNA of the Fine Gael, which is really a social club for dynasts, solicitors, hospital consultants and second-division barristers masquerading as a political party. Innately, they crave the approbation of the powerful to such an extent that even their most independent of members Michael Noonan was at his happiest in government when playing the part of the clever pet who could kiss both of Christine Lagarde's cheeks with equal enthusiasm.

If Mr Ahern's signature of 'ah, the hardy lads, working hard' lacked any degree of ideological nuance, Mr Kenny's variant narrowed the ideological field down ever further. Mr Kenny's ideology consisted of a smile, a wink and a nod in public and a private grim authoritarianism. But being Bertie-Lite was never going to be enough for Enda to retain the people's support as the Democratic Revolution faltered. Furthermore, Enda's Bertie-Lite programming was so successful that it seemed no-one could switch our Dear Leader to a new mode. The Irish people were ready for the new politics of honesty that Enda accidentally indulged in at Davos. However, it proved impossible to convince our neat, energetic boy to abandon his innate unoriginal intellectual laziness and realise that, if he wanted to be an honours student, his cautious old ways would no longer work.

When it came to Enda's relationship with our difficult citizens, the sense that the worm was beginning to turn came as early as mid-2012 on a terribly cross day Enda had in Athlone. In fairness, it was understandable Enda was not in a sunny mood, as he was in the middle of a difficult campaign on behalf of the utterly unloved Fiscal Compact referendum. The unhappy Taoiseach was certainly not feeling the love when father-of-three Peadar Doyle confronted Mr Kenny as he canvassed for a 'Yes' vote at the Golden Island Shopping Centre. When Doyle claimed that, 'back in 1958 I was forced out of this country. You are now forcing my children and my grandchildren out of this country,' the old pre-Taoiseach Enda Kenny who hung around supermarkets and crèches helping Mum with her shopping trolley would surely have had a consoling chat with Mr Doyle. Instead, a narked Taoiseach responded, 'I'm not forcing anybody out. Don't make a charge like that on me. They are leaving unfortunately.'

As citizens wondered if Enda was blaming the emigrants for

embarrassing the Coalition by fleeing a country the politicians themselves had broken up, things deteriorated further. Doyle told Kenny, 'I am one of the people who have not paid the household charge. I am telling you personally, and whether I am breaking the law or whether I am not breaking the law, I don't mind because I paid €60,000 in taxes when I came back here'. Mr Kenny told Doyle, who surrounded by anti-household charge and septic tank campaigners, that 'if you want to go and make a speech, you can go and do it outside'. This didn't sound terribly like the respectful dialogue with Irish citizens that Enda had been talking about in 2011. Sadly, the sense of distance between that Enda and his cranky fellow citizens accelerated even further when Gordon Hudson, the chairman of the Athlone Anti-Household and Septic Tank Campaign, advised Mr Kenny to 'take the bridge, head west and stay there'. Enda snapped back, 'you could do with a day's work, I'd say', and was left somewhat stranded by Hudson's reply that he had been self-employed for 29 years but had to 'pack it in because of ye'.

Mr Kenny's remarks were tasteless, to put it mildly, in a country that seemed to be facing into an age of generational unemployment that was slowly turning us into the Indian reservation of Europe. And in a sense, it was a response Dear Leader Enda never really recovered from, for no amount of smiles in the world can erase the image of a Taoiseach squabbling and snarling at the very citizens he was charged, by his own declaration, with protecting. In one brief exchange, Mr Kenny had become one of 'them' rather than one of us.

It was a process that accelerated during that self-same referendum on the fiscal compact. The referendum was the strangest, the most eerie and the saddest of referenda. Generally, referenda are a privilege afforded only to free societies. Our Fiscal Compact referendum was instead a plebiscite on the acquiescence to the nation's rape in which the only selling point for a 'Yes' vote was that a carefully undefined something far worse would come from a 'No' vote. In a further irony that would cause few to smile, this burnt offering came dressed with the promise of a 'national conversation' about Europe. What followed was the oddest of conversations in which Mr Kenny ran like the clappers from the prospect of any live debate on a vote that theoretically represented a defining moment in the history of the Irish state.

As the pressure on Enda to debate the referendum grew, eventually a fiat came draped in the finest of spin. A tradition had been found whereby Taoisigh did not participate in the hurly-burly of such vulgar events as referenda debates. Although we attempted to reconcile ourselves to this new image of gallivanting Enda as some monarch ruling by divine right and who could not be expected to lower himself to talking to citizens, in truth the presence of our mannequin of a Taoiseach might not have made much difference to the result anyway. But his absence provided us with another giant's stride away from the openness and transparency promised in 2011. Instead, in one of its saddest features, this was the referendum where the Irish political elite ran out of things to say. Five weeks is a long campaign and the Coalition parties had no message beyond expressing the vain hope that appeasing the EU's savage gods would bring us stability rather than the ongoing Great Betrayal of the fine words and fancy sentiments of 2011.

In a country where the heads of its people were being constantly plunged under the water by unemployment, emigration and austerity, this was a referendum that was defined by an existentialist abyss of faith. Unlike the courageous Greeks, Ireland's 'Yes to Peace with Dishonour' was a decision drenched in fear. It was a contest that revealed that the Coalition Cartel had abandoned any concept of a process of national healing and solidarity. Instead, the referendum revealed that we were a state more divided at any time than the civil war. The 'Yes' side, consisting of pensioners, political insiders, the public sector and the 30% of farmers Fine Gael are clinging to for dear life, voted for stability. By contrast, the No side voted for anarchy because it seemed in many people's eyes to be the best available alternative.

As for Mr Kenny, those who had dared to hope that, when he spoke of a 'democratic revolution', the Taoiseach was of a mind to take a run at the endemic flaws in the failed Irish political system now knew what political ashes tasted like. Instead, it was becoming clear Enda aspired to be nothing more than the always affable, pleased-to-have-his-hair-ruffled Tetrarch of the Troika. 'Vote "Yes" for stability' was the call of the Coalition, but no-one, and especially not our Taoiseach, warned us that this might be the stability of living death. Of course, after the stressful referendum campaign, we experienced a swift return back to the smiling, the winking and the nodding. The problem for the Coalition was, though, that real Enda kept on breaking out, more frequently than ever.

Real Enda emerged again when it came to his response to the Magdalene report. It wasn't a pretty sight, for it included none of the colour and the high flown sentiment of Cloyne. Instead, the Taoiseach's reaction to the slow sad tale of the Magdalenes consisted of a metaphorical patting of his pockets to see if any of the elderly ladies the Report referred to had robbed his wallet. In his response, the real *petit bourgeois* Enda, the man whose dream Sunday is of a round of golf with the local Monsignor and a quick wave to the inmates of the local Magdalene home as he sprints past, was unveiled.

The most astonishing feature of the Taoiseach's initial response was the enormous difficulty Mr Kenny had when it came to the apology 'thing'. The type of Taoiseach Enda promised he would be in 2011 would have cried us a river of woe. However, when asked to apologise over the Magdalenes' plight, our Dear Leader fumbled about how 'this is not a matter for idle comment or a matter for flippant politics. It is a matter of intense seriousness for those who were involved and for those of us who have responsibility now'. The Taoiseach was, he said, filled with a 'sense of deep sorrow for all of those women who went through that regime', but he also managed to engage in a philosophical dissertation on how sometimes, in this world, people find it very hard to say, 'I am sorry'. In that regard, Enda was speaking knowledgably, for he was a living case study of this phenomenon to such an extent that he used his apology to lay into Sinn Féin's Mary Lou McDonald and her desire 'to have her political opportunistic jibe'.

It was left to Labour, or more accurately Labour's women, to put manners on an increasingly overbearing Taoiseach. Such was their anger over Kenny and how he had behaved that there had been quite the struggle to prevent a walkout by its TDs and senators from a meeting of their parliamentary party to the Dáil plinth as a gesture of protest. Sharp words were expressed by the Labour leadership – in private, unfortunately – before Joan Burton emerged to tell us she was 'very confident an appropriate apology and a response incorporating a scheme to look after these women will be established'. By way of a parting shot she added, 'a very great wrong was done to these women who are at the centre of this issue and I expect all my colleagues are united in this view'.

Labour's Kathleen Lynch was very influential in reforming Enda's response. She had, according to a senior cabinet source, 'buttonholed Enda in the way she can, and let him know in no uncertain terms that "there will be an apology" and that "it was not a case of if you give an apology but when"'. The source further revealed that Mr Kenny, who privately had been hugely cautious over the financial consequences of an apology, was also told by Ms Lynch that 'you would be better off being seen to apologise of your own volition rather than having it forced out of you'. Though Mr Kenny subsequently treated us to a mini-version of Cloyne, the context set by the original response meant it did not wash for many.

The debacle was all the more curious as surely any political survivor of the Hepatitis C scandal should intrinsically know that the one thing a politician cannot afford is to be seen to have a thin soul. Kenny's response to the Magdalenes unveiled the real Enda that lay beneath the pretty political slip he was wearing. As it became evident that Enda's style of government resembled that of a clenched fist hiding behind the false smile of Bertie-Lite, the increasingly eccentric nature of his performance could only be understood within the context of some great internal struggle. The death of the government's reform agenda, despite all the feverish denials that reform had either been planned or abandoned, carried psychological and political consequences. It created a form of disturbance which generated in a strange new eccentricity in the Taoiseach's persona. This manifested itself in increasingly unexplainable acts such as Enda's claims that any files relating to the bank guarantee in the Taoiseach's Department had been shredded by his predecessors. His claims were ludicrous, if for no other reason than they suggested that poor Biffo might have had some sort of coherent plan, let alone a plot, to deal with the Irish banking crisis. Given his conflicted mental state, the Taoiseach's act of stupidity – and there were plenty more to come – was the entirely logical outburst of a political eunuch. Enda's method for dealing with his internal frustration at the execrable political state in which he was trapped was to engage in acts of vengeance and wild accusations against those he perceived as weaker than he.

Banking and the consequences of the actions of our banks would continue to haunt Enda and the Coalition. If we were to summarise in a sentence the most appropriate bill of indictment for Fianna Fáil's fourteen years in government, it would be that Bertie, with the political collusion of the PDs, created a country that was set up to fail. The Great Irish Disruption was the unexpected but entirely inevitable child of Bertie's rule, of a type of politics that encompassed amoral political thoughtlessness and short-termism, where focus-group-driven politicians were only concerned with what was going to happen next week rather than next year. In February 2011, we then elected a government to fix that and lived happily ever after … or that, at least, was the theory.

So, you might ask, how was our Democratic Revolution going, two and a half years into the Coalition's five-year term?

Nothing epitomised the state of our erstwhile fairy tale more than the Coalition's response to the Anglo Tapes scandal. Taped phone conversations between some of Ireland's leading bankers were leaked, which included damning dialogue about how decisions were made and an attitude of utter, if admittedly justified, contempt about the capacity and ability of those who were supposed to be watching the regulatory watchdogs of the banks. Responding to the fury provoked by the revelations about how the wealthy really conducted their affairs, Enda Kenny was in fine fettle within the Dáil chamber as he promised the 'people's' Dáil would get to the bottom of all this with a 'people's' inquiry by a 'people's' Dáil committee into the, ahem, 'people's' banks.

You might then note in a relieved fashion, 'so far, so good then'.

Well, as it happens, not quite. The problem was that Enda's 'people's' committee, staffed by the 'people's' representatives, in the 'people's' Dáil turned out to have all of the legal strength of a house made out of candy floss with foundations of sand built on a marsh. Once again, Enda's response was a thing of all style and no substance.

It was astonishing enough that the Taoiseach's investigation into the banking crisis was feebler than the tribunal system, which had been retired from the investigative field in some disgrace after the vast failure of the Moriarty and Mahon tribunals. The Taoiseach, however, managed to mine the already shaky foundations of his own inquiry before it even started with a mad piece of rhetoric about Fianna Fáil's 'axis of collusion' with the banks. The inquiry, which was supposedly set up for the people's benefit, was infected by a raucous desire for partisan political advantage before it had even commenced. Were it not for the utter impotence of the inquiry, Enda's eccentric outburst would have undoubtedly led to some form of challenge from Fianna Fáil. But they sensibly did nothing, for why on earth would you go to war with the harmless?

Meanwhile, our Coalition of Grumpy Old Men, cosily ensconced in their Mercedes and even cosier with pour-top mandarins, seemed to have forgotten that a proper banking inquiry should be no petty thing. It should inquire into the downfall of the Irish Republic, and find out how a state formed through 700 years of struggle found itself being garrisoned for its own protection by a foreign Troika a mere sixty years after securing full independence. Instead, in a classic example of *Hamlet's* play within a play, Enda's impotent inquiry encapsulated the failure of his own administration. The voters deserved a comprehensive explanation for how Ireland failed rather than a partisan political witch-hunt. Respect demanded it. Respect was absent. Nothing had changed. And that, alas, was becoming the leitmotif of Mr Kenny's reign.

CHAPTER 7

ENTER THE FRAPPUCCINO KIDS AND THE INDEPENDENTS TOO

The emergence of the political fringe

The growing tension between what the Coalition Cartel had said they would do and what they were actually doing began, inevitably, to have unexpected consequences. One of the most curious of these began to gestate at the very zenith of Enda's positioning in the political power game. It was June 2013 and our Dear Leader had just finished hobnobbing with British Prime Minister David Cameron and the rest of the big dogs at the Fermanagh G8 Summit.

Life was good.

Or was it?

For some at least, the event was redolent of the Haughey era when the then Taoiseach strutted around Paris dressed in the finest Charvet could offer. Sadly, his Potemkin pretensions were all too much for one diplomat, who laughed ruefully and commented, 'would you look at him, the little bollix from Donnycarney'. The Donnycarney Syndrome certainly seemed to surround Enda as he sported and played with the leaders of the free world – and Mr Putin – without once suffering the indignity of being asked to park Mr Putin's car. Like Haughey, our Dear Leader had come a long way since the days Pee Flynn would metaphorically ruffle his hair in the manner of Sarkozy and prophesy that while someday Enda might become a Junior Minister, Mayo would always be Flynn country. Although those days are long over, you can be sure the Fine Gael leader has never forgotten Pee – or Mr Sarkozy for that matter. Like an elephant, Enda never forgets.

As Enda networked with the global elite, the adoring media told us in awe-filled tones that Enda actually looked the part by Lough Erne – and, as an added bonus, there wasn't a canary yellow jacket to be seen. Sadly, however, many within Enda's own party had started to wonder whether Enda really was the man or if he was merely the political equivalent of the fake shop-fronts erected in Fermanagh to take the 'Deserted Village' look off the town.

On the surface, Fine Gael was still master of the splintered national political battlefield they ruled over. However, within Enda's mansion of many factions, the erratic nature of the Taoiseach's judgement had begun to open up a number of old and not-so-old party schisms. Faction fighting may be a nightmare of history Enda hoped his party had escaped from, but by 2013 the tectonic plates within this uniquely quarrelsome party had started to shift. Nothing epitomised the escalating fault lines within Fine Gael more than the alliance of Fine Gael eternal bad lad John Deasy and two of its Frappuccino Kids, Eoghan Murphy and Paul Connaughton. Together, they foiled plans to bring their Dear Leader the head of Fianna Fáil's John McGuinness, who had become far too independent and prickly a boss of the Public Accounts Committee for Enda's liking. Of course, as was increasingly the case under Enda, a direct request was not issued, but it emerged into the Fine Gael ether that clipping the wings of McGuinness would put a smile on the wan face of Enda. Trouble had been expected from Deasy but when the two Frappuccino Kids baulked, the plan to remove McGuinness was abandoned.

The stand taken by Deasy, one of the defeated Fine Gael cavaliers from the 2010 heave who had neither forgiven nor forgotten – nor, more importantly, been forgiven himself by Enda – was not surprising. Of far greater concern to the Tetrarch of Mayo was the increasingly loud patter being made by the tiny political feet of his newbie TDs. The enemies of his past were done, dusted and defeated, but he now had to contend with a group of youthful – as in, younger than fifty years of age – TDs who had been elected on the Fine Gael tide and who were becoming increasingly worried about the speed with which that tide was departing. The Fine Gael 'Young Ones' went by the name of the Five-a-Side Gang or, on account of their mostly twenty-something urban status, the Cappuccino Kids. In an indication of the youthfulness of this group, the latter moniker had to be changed when the middle-aged hack who invented it was gently told, 'the Cappuccino thing is a bit dated – we actually mostly drink Frappuccinos these days'. Whatever about the hack, when it came to the Fine Gael hierarchy, the Frappuccino Kids came from a world the leadership knew absolutely nothing about. Mr Kenny and his political familiar, Government Whip Paul Kehoe, had from the start viewed the desire of Kids such as Eoghan Murphy to experiment with unsafe political practices like ideology with a suspicion last seen in *The Valley of the Squinting Windows*. Given that nothing in the political life experiences of Enda, Sheriff Big Phil Hogan and the rest of the good ole boys from the 'Dukes of Hazzard' wing of

Fine Gael had prepared them for the phenomenon of TDs with ideological approaches to politics, let alone ministers, their unease with the Frappuccino Kids was understandable.

The Dear Leader's concern did have merit. The Frappuccino Kids had, in the initial post-election year of grace, avoided any link up with their natural allies in the defeated cavalier Richard Bruton faction of the party, taking the wise view that another man's wound was none of their business, particularly if the wounded man didn't even know he was limping. But instinctively they were closer to that wing of the party that backed Bruton and change in 2010, as distinct to the rural turnips who drove Enda and the politics of 'jobs for the boys' across the line. For a time, the two had co-existed but the uneasy ceasefire was not going to last forever. The Taoiseach had carefully constructed a 'Chairman of the Boards'-style nodding, winking, cheery Western playboy political front. But those who knew politics and who knew Enda intimately saw behind the front. Alas, the problem for our Haughey-style boss-man was that, while the mutts in Fianna Fáil have always been enamoured with the cult of the strong leader, Fine Gael culture is somewhat more idiosyncratic. A party that has always had too many self-proclaimed independent thinkers is not one that would ever be fully at ease with the politics of *Una Enda Voce, Una Enda Duce.*

It worked for a time, but by 2013 the first ominous signs and shrieking apparitions began to appear. Enda's situation was not helped by the shaky nature of his cabinet scaffold, for his pillars of support, Cute Old Phil, James Reilly and Alan Shatter, had evolved into a political variant of dry rot. It had taken a while but Enda's theatre of illusions was starting to fracture. A Taoiseach whose sole core value seemed to be the Bertie one – 'getting into power and staying there' – was starting to look vulnerable. Enda still retained the support of most of those he had promoted and of those backbench turnips who still hoped he might promote them some day. Beyond that, his support depended ever more on time and prayer that the great 'austerity and appeasement' punt would ease the snarling sense of betrayal that was ghosting its way across the electorate.

The wild card in all of this was the Frappuccino Kids. The Kids, with their subversive taste for thought and ideology, were what chemists call a 'rogue element'. The Frappuccino Kids were not, for example, part of the culture of Leinster House. This 'culture' is a strange thing, set in aspic, that has essentially remained the same since the 1960s. Based on tribalism, the herd ethic, loyalty bejaysus, the dynastic principle and the absence of independent thought, it is as separated from the real world as one of those gentlemen's clubs in Whitehall in which dusty old Lords drink port and rail against the loss of the Empire. It is a dynast's paradise, and one that is essentially male. It is a culture that knows little of family life, or of any element of life that has changed since our entry into the Common Market. Rather like one of those non-modernised industries that were mostly swept away in the 1980s under Margaret Thatcher, it is a sclerotic sepia-laden place in which, like new entrants to the civil service, young TDs must serve a minimal apprenticeship of two decades before anticipating promotion.

So it was that into this strange gentlemen's club the Frappuccino Kids arrived, more by accident than intent. As the old guard and the new were of different ages and different generations, the relationship between Fine Gael's frolicsome new political lambs and its big old dinosaurs, such as Cute Old Phil who didn't like any back cheek from backbenchers, began to grate. Our Environment Minister might have been fairly slow-moving, but whenever Enda's lumbering political lurcher managed to actually catch any small trembling form the results were usually lethal. The Frappuccino Kids, however, simply laughed at Phil, for they were not as gun-shy as those who had been defeated in the heave by Enda. Instead of deferring to the dinosaurs, they began to complain over how Fine Gael ministers looked as distant from the real concerns of the Irish people as former Fianna Fáil ministers like Noel Dempsey used to. Worse still, some of the Frappuccino Kids began to create trouble over such political delicates as public sector and social welfare reform. Where, they wanted to know, had Fine Gael's plans for the Democratic Revolution disappeared? Sadly, plans for the Democratic Revolution had disappeared so thoroughly that Government Whip Paul Kehoe was sent out to do a bit of political pitchcapping at the mere mention of it.

Ultimately, the greatest danger the Frappuccino Kids posed to Enda was that they were representative of a country and a generation who believed the Coalition Cartel had forgotten or misunderstood their concerns. Even in a government with 113 seats, it is still important that the Taoiseach be seen in some way to empathise with the country he leads. But Enda, caught as he was in an Ireland that ominously resembled the 1970s, was not capable. By contrast, the new Fine Gael TDs, led by their Dark Prince Eoghan Murphy, were sympathetic members of that thirty-something generation whose alienation from the detached family-unfriendly Coalition was gathering an ominous momentum. Given that the Irish electorate's disconnect from the Coalition was putting every Fine Gael seat in danger, the Kids certainly had skin in the growing game of whispered discontent with Enda on the Fine Gael benches. Considering the Kids were becoming increasingly vocal in their views that Enda was as much of a real leader as Potemkin-style shop-fronts of Fermanagh, two key questions lingered in the air: would our Frappuccino Kids actually do anything? And if they did, who might they have for friends?

Unease was growing in more locations than the nether regions of the Fine Gael parliamentary party. For a start, the growth of Sinn Féin certainly made everyone uneasy. But nothing created more of a scatter amongst the Coalition Cartel more than the rise of a new force in Irish politics: the Independents, Sinn Féin, you see, was a known entity. The Coalition Cartel's calculated gamble was that at some point Sinn Féin would sell out to the Coalition. Really, the only questions were what their purchase price would be and how embarrassing the political walk of shame would be for the Cartel parties the morning after the deal was made. The prodigious rise of the Independents was a much less stable prospect for the Coalition. And even more worryingly, it was becoming increasingly evident over the course of 2013 that an entire nation was turning its face from politics, not merely the usual, easily-dismissed subgroups. At first, the Coalition dismissed the increase in the number of voters in the 'Don't Know' category as an unfortunate rise in forgetfulness on the part of the Irish people, who would regret their initial rebelliousness and return with appropriately bowed heads when the real game to claim the hearts and minds of the Irish electorate began.

It was too late. You see, just because people define themselves as 'Don't Knows' doesn't mean they are politically ignorant or don't care. Instead, often, the 'Don't Knows' care and know too much. Or to put it another way, the 'Don't Knows' in Ireland in 2013 were citizens who, having coldly analysed what lies below the froth of Irish politics, realised its value was nil. By autumn, as the trickle of 'Don't Knows' turned into a torrent, you would think it would be obvious that democracy in Ireland was in a sickly state. After all, the vast majority of its citizens had withdrawn their confidence from the Coalition, the Taoiseach and the mainstream opposition. But the oligarchy of the Traditional Triumvirate of Fine Gael, Fianna Fáil and Labour sailed serenely on, oblivious to the revolutionary rumblings among the electorate.

It has often been claimed the unchanging nature of Irish politics resembles the weary permanence of the dreary grey steeples of

Fermanagh, but over the course of 2013, support for the tired old Traditional Triumvirate of Fianna Fáil, Fine Gael and Labour slumped below 40%. Such a withdrawal of public support from conventional politics should have provoked some questioning from within the Coalition Cartel. The cornerstone of democracy, namely the legitimacy provided by the consent of the citizens, was crumbling. Naturally, the Coalition immediately dismissed the flurry of opinion polls as a little thing of no consequence – the Irish people were merely in their flowers; nothing to see here, move on please. The problem, alas, was that the Irish people were to remain in their flowers for some time. In fact, further flowers, bunches of them, had begun to arrive. The consequences of the failure of the Coalition to deliver on the rhythm of hope and history they had promised had sprung. As in the Cowen era, a listless and disappointed electorate had silently withdrawn its support. And, unlike Beckett's eternally hopefully tramps, they did not even have the consolation of pretending to expect anything better was about to come along.

It did not help that so many of the Coalition's woes were self-created. When politicians are assaulted by the fates, they have some line of defence. This, instead, was an administration that threw banana skins in front of itself on a weekly basis and then wondered why it kept taking tumbles. The Irish public may not have followed all the minutiae of Justice Minister Alan Shatter's various controversies, from the bugging fiasco at the Garda Síochána Ombudsman Commission to his mishandling of Garda whistle-blowers – and indeed, what sane person would have? – but they clearly saw confusion at the heart of the Coalition. Worse still, they saw a gutless inability to resolve that chaos until the courageous intervention by Minister Leo Varadkar brought things to a head. And that was all they needed to know.

The Coalition's problems were far bigger than the public

relations nightmare Alan Shatter. The belly wound that was
bleeding the Cartel to death was spiritual rather than personnel-
based. In a country desperately in need of openness, the Coalition
was defensive. When a graceful apology was required, it proffered
a closed fist. When dialogue with the Irish people was an absolute
necessity, the Coalition told the people to shut up and mind their
manners. When empathy was required, our Cartel simply snarled at
the Irish people and told them, as Enda had in his Davos speech, that
all the country's problems were really their fault. The Democratic
Revolution was collapsing in upon itself.

Smiles were particularly rare in one quarter – the squeezed 'coping
classes'. Ironically, no other social group had ever been courted so
assiduously in theory and ignored more thoroughly in practice than
Ireland's coping classes. Significantly, their ranks were far more
varied than the old bowler-hatted middle-class professionals and
civil servants. Ireland's pressurised coping classes also included the
working poor, the teeming ranks of front-line public sector workers,
Ireland's infamous breakfast roll man and his country girlfriend
who used to work in retail. Although in 2013, the government was
still making verbal love to this group, their audience was getting
suspicious. The dissonance between the Coalition Cartel's amorous
declarations towards the coping classes and the enthusiasm with
which it inserted its hand into their pockets didn't just weaken the
credibility of the Coalition with the Irish electorate. It also opened
the door for Independents to come pouring through.

When the penny finally dropped for the Coalition about the
real strength of the Independents' rise, quite the flap began about
'anarchy' and the prospect of future 'coalitions of chaos'. As is
generally the case when you insult the choices of voters, this turned
out to be a less than compelling line of attack. And anyway, the
real truth of the matter was that if Irish voters were turning to
Independents, and so indulging in what the Coalition characterised

as a sport of directionless anarchy, it was because of the absence of any compelling alternative being provided by the old political order. The *ancien regime* could squawk all it wanted, but as far as the electorate were concerned, it was the politicians, rather than themselves, who had the problem.

This did not stop the commandants of public opinion from folding their arms like a disapproving Irish mammy and telling us that all Independents are fey, dangerous creatures, able to agree on nothing. They issued grim but well-intentioned warnings about how such Independent egotists would bust up the economy, be at the beck and call of vested interests and be unable to agree on anything. Of course, it would be a great shame if our newly-favoured Independents were to behave in a similar manner to Fianna Fáil, Fine Gael and Labour, but it seemed the Irish electorate were hopeful this would not be the case.

As the Independents' rise accelerated, the Coalition and Fianna Fáil remained immoveable in their view that the public's flirtation with our Independents was a midsummer act of madness. According to our established political powers, the public had in a fit of pique, like the mad dog of Oliver Goldsmith's famous poem, decided to bite the leg of the decent conventional parties who had served us so well. Just as Irish mammies warn that those who make beds have to lie on them too, the old Traditional Triumvirate of Fianna Fáil, Fine Gael and Labour prophesied that the electoral prodigal sons currently flirting with the idea of electing Independents in the next election would soon be begging forgiveness after our brief bout of madness and seeking a return to the simpler political games, such as 'Spot the Difference between Fine Gael and Fianna Fáil'. But were those making this prediction fatally behind the curve? A blanket warning against the dangers of Independents didn't recognise the changing nature of Independent politicians. Just as there are many rooms in a lord's mansion, so too do a great variety of Independents exist too. Our metropolitan elites could warn all they wanted about the terrible damage that would be caused by a Dáil full of Jackie Healy-Rae doppelgangers. But it's worth noting that the election of Mr Healy-Rae did a lot more of practical worth for rural development than any amount of high-profile policy initiatives originated by the Coalition. Furthermore, the profile of the modern Independent is a lot more varied than the *Tales of the Healy-Rae Far Side* the Cartel attempted to frighten us with.

The Irish mammies of the political establishment warned that the electorate's love affair with Independents was an act electoral self-harming masquerading as an embrace of anarchy, but their warning failed to recognise the essential nature of our eternally conservative electorate. If our *petite bourgeoisie* were in the mood to become the sons and daughters of anarchy, surely the Anti-Austerity Alliance and the Socialist Party would be triumphant everywhere. Instead, the Irish electorate were sending a somewhat different more diffuse message. Happier times – when Ireland was chugging along like the Mexico of Europe, and during the subsequent hallucinogenic visions of the mad Tiger years – had disguised key flaws in how Ireland was governed. In the wake of election night 2011 though, it had become bleakly clear the party system had definitively evolved into a finishing school for threat-free dullards and ambitious careerists looking to further themselves rather than reform the state. Whether at local or national level, Irish politics – along with plenty of other arenas in Irish society – was filled with weeds that collectively prided themselves on their capacity to choke out difference and radicalism, in search for the safety of a national politics of collective non-thought. This meant that the ever-gathering strength of the revolt against the Traditional Triumvirate was less surprising than you might think. The 2011 Nyberg Report into the Irish banking system had identified the fatal flaw that infected Irish politics and society: our collective 'herd instinct'. Within our political system, the endemic cronyism, the fear to play the role of a party whistle-blower and speak out against how things were run, to question and to be different, merely mirrored our national tendency not to rock the boat. But now the voters wanted a change.

Instead, the parties of the Coalition clung ever tighter to the old discredited ways, as we were to discover via the departure of Fine Gael's Lucinda Creighton over the issue of abortion. The use of the whip system was a key reason behind the absence of any intellectual rigour and debate in Dáil Eireann, which in turn hollowed out our politicians' capacity to defend Ireland's citizens against the variant of rogue capitalism that infected the highest echelons of the economy from 2006. In choosing to go Independent, the electorate was sending a clear message to the country's traditional political parties, if only the parties could stop talking for long enough to hear it. The voters were warning that the devastation inflicted upon their lives by the boneheads of the big three Irish political parties, and the damage they feared from the next biggest, Sinn Féin, had irreparably damaged their trust in the party system.

They were also telling our political classes Ireland cannot be reformed by mere variations of what has gone before. Paddy had finally, after ninety years of passive acquiescence, come to the view that, if he was to have a better future, reform and self-interest must be compatible. In 2011, he might have been equivocal on the matter. However, the lifeless zombie state brought into being by the Great Betrayal of the Democratic Revolution had led Paddy dangerously close to hatching a conviction. Like any laying hen, Paddy was doing a lot of clucking, but no-one in the Cartel appeared to be listening. As far as Paddy could see, it was time to end the politics of group-think and sheep-bleat, and this increasingly meant Paddy was looking to our growing group of Independents such as Lucinda, Shane Ross, Peter Mathews, Billy Timmins, Róisín Shortall, Stephen Donnelly, Clare Daly and the rest to secure that objective.

Paddy had finally got it. By 2013, he understood that the great lacunae in Irish politics are courage, independence and thought, and that the current crop of Coalition bleaters were incapable of supplying them. Now the question Paddy had to calculate was whether the threat to elect a government of Independents would beat courage into the Coalition Cartel or simply lead to chaos. The danger for the old Triumvirate of Fine Gael, Fianna Fáil and Labour was that the more Paddy looked at the Independents, the less they looked like wild anarchists. Instead, in their own idiosyncratic ways, the Independents looked quite like Paddy. This obviously created a further problem for the Coalition, for when they insulted the mad Independents, Paddy started to feel as though they were insulting him too.

Those who remained uneasy at any curbing of the safe old way of doing things, that incidentally cost us our Independence, should have taken succour from the fate of Oliver Goldsmith's fabled dog. After inflicting a bite on his unsuspecting owner, the village onlookers gathered to examine the wound:

> The wound it seem'd both sore and sad
> To every Christian eye;
> And while they swore the dog was mad,
> They swore the man would die.

Instead, as it turned out:

> Soon a wonder came to light,
> That showed the rogues they lied;
> The man recovered of the bite,
> The dog it was that died.

By mid-2014, the voters certainly seemed inclined to bite the

Coalition's leg. We could only hope that we, unlike Goldsmith's unfortunate dog, would live to tell the tale. As for the Frappuccino Kids, as 2014 neared, Enda still had them on side – for now.

CHAPTER 8

THE REAL TRUTH ABOUT LUCINDA AND HOW IT MAY WELL BE TROUBLE

The old ghosts of Fine Gael's eternal civil war rise again

The Frappuccino Kids were not the only curious political phenomenon to evolve in Enda's increasingly fractious Fine Gael. One of the strangest ones was the departure of Lucinda Creighton and the Reform Alliance Gang. The relevant parties claimed it was about abortion, but the truth of the matter was that the breakdown that bedevilled Enda, Lucinda and the Reform Alliance gang had little to do with abortion. It was instead all about the endemic war within Fine Gael that had been going on for five decades. The divide between the Fianna Fáil Cute Hoors and the Fine Gael Pious Protestors, you see, has always been mirrored by a similar divide in Fine Gael itself. The party has its own Cute Hoors and Pious Protestors, and this split is the reason for the party's continuous civil war, one that swings from desultory to full-blown without warning. This ongoing fissure began with the 1960s war between James Dillon, Fine Gael's fascinating mini-Churchill and conservative refugee from the Irish Parliamentary Party, and the liberal Just Society gang under Declan Costello. The battle continued in the 1980s, with the ultra-conservative dyed-in-the-blue-wool Liam Cosgrave pitting himself against Garret 'the Social Democrat' FitzGerald, who was widely suspected of being Labour's Manchurian candidate in Fine Gael. The venomous nature of their dispute was epitomised by the famous 1972 Ard Fheis at which Cosgrave, fortified by a couple of whiskeys, told the party that it had been infiltrated by liberal mongrel foxes. As the self-same mongrel foxes who, ironically, were sharing the Liam's podium looked on in appalled puzzlement, Cosgrave assured the roaring Blueshirt delegates that he would lead a pack of loyal Fine Gael hounds to dig them out and chop them up. They don't, alas, make party leaders like Liam any more.

Far from being hunted down and chopped up, the mongrel foxes ran amok under Garret, until being brought back under control by his successor John Bruton. It should be noted that Fine Gael's was not a classic left versus right ideological divide. It was, instead, a split between those who dreamed of reforming a state that had, with the exception of a small flutter of change under Lemass, essentially remained trapped in the aspic of the 1922 hand-over, and those who wished to continue the Civil War with Fianna Fáil, with the goal of reversing time until the good old days when Cumann na nGaedheal were in charge and the *Irish Press* had not even been born were restored. The simmering tensions between these two factions escalated again under Enda, reaching a climax at Fine Gael's Battle of the Alamo in 2010 when Enda, Big Phil, Little Al and James 'Doc' Reilly saw off the chevaliers. A brittle truce was brokered out of necessity after the 2010 heave, for, despite the broken state of Fianna Fáil, Fine Gael's Dear Leader realised he could not run the risk of opposing or governing with a house divided. So it was that Leo, Simon and Richard were fully brought in from the cold, while Brian Hayes received a chilly form of forgiveness by being sent into exile with Michael Noonan.

To be fair to our Dear Leader, when it came to Lucinda, Enda did do his best. His best might not have been terribly good, but the intent was there. There has always been a bit of a *Quiet Man* vibe surrounding Enda and his turbulent princess. In fact, in a sense Lucinda was Enda's special project. If he could throw Lucinda over his shoulder and bring her home, as John Wayne did to Maureen O'Hara, it would be the equivalent of breaking a thoroughbred horse. The mark of approval Enda sought from Lucinda was a declaration that Enda was the legitimate king of Fine Gael, without any question mark and regardless of any pretenders surrounding his crown. Sadly, the course of that particular ship of dreams was always set for the rocks. It had been doomed since Lucinda made 'that speech' in 2010 at the MacGill Summer School in the Glenties, warning that the worst thing that could ever happen in Irish politics would be for Fine Gael to turn into Fianna Fáil-Lite. The subsequent fury it attracted from Fine Gael's officer class was understandable: as we now know, that was Enda's plan all along. He added some democratic revolutionary trimmings, but the essence of the 2011 election was essentially a hostile Fine Gael take-over of the Fianna Fáil franchise.

For a time, it was hoped that power would be the salve that could heal all Civil War wounds. But even in the times of political plenty, although they jogged along in public, in private the two Fine Gael factions hissed at each other like domestic cats contesting the footpaths of a gated estate. Abortion might have been the eventual *casus belli* for the re-engagement of official hostilities, but in fact the voluntary departure of Lucinda from the Fine Gael fold was much more than a particularly explosive eruption in that eternal internal Fine Gael civil war. When Lucinda lost the party whip after her speech on the Protection of Human Life Bill, hardy pragmatists within the party expressed the hope that Enda's less than quiet woman might yet be back bowing deferentially before King Enda within six months. But even at without the perspective of hindsight, a certain farewell to arms surrounded Creighton's speech. In truth, even if she wanted to stay, Ms Creighton resembled that cat on a hot tin roof which had lost its balance. While the cat might teeter on the roof for some time, gravity will eventually triumph, no matter how agile the cat. When it came to the Fine Gael hot tin roof, it was a case of the Taoiseach's way or Lucinda's way, and Enda was not in the mood, understandably, to lose his spot on the roof.

The strangest and most telling thing about Lucinda's departure from her childhood party was the sense of easy delight she and the other rebels felt. Normally exile, even if voluntary, from a political party is filled with portents of unease and a sense of loss, as it was with Dessie O'Malley, for example. By contrast, not even the possibility of being the future leader of Fine Gael could deter Lucinda, who was 'totally at ease' with her decision to jettison a safe political future. Shortly after her departure, far from being in a fugue of despair, Lucinda instead was relishing the possibility of realising her ambitions to accelerate her battle against the dysfunctional nature of Irish politics and the Irish government: 'I have strong views on it and if I don't fight to change the system from within, who is going to do it?' Although fellow reformers were not exactly queuing up.

Lucinda's departure was certainly not a quiet one. Once freed from the golden Fine Gael cage, Lucinda noisily and regularly made it clear her new intent was to fix the rot at the heart of a system that forces TDs to leave their morals aside in order to defer to the latest opinion poll or the party hierarchy. In her own view, Lucinda's decision to walk the gangplank had been informed not so much by Fine Gael's stance on abortion as by Enda's decision to rule by group-think, a philosophy she argued was a corrosive affliction in Ireland and one that had thrived in the Haughey and the Celtic Tiger eras. Fine Gael's Joan of Arc also made it clear that her belated recognition that Fine Gael was not the party from which to challenge the herd instinct within Irish society was liberating. The bird in Enda's golden cage had been freed and was now singing like a canary.

In fairness, there wasn't much misery on the benches of either Coalition party at her self-imposed exile. That the old insider culture of arrogance, so prevalent during the Haughey era, had persisted into contemporary politics was illustrated clearly by the spectacle of the sneering Labour TD Alex White smirking incredulously as Lucinda made it clear she was prepared to lose her junior ministry if that was the price for opposing a Bill whose foundations she believed to be made of sand. Within Fine Gael, Phil's good ole boys went cajoling, whispering and threatening around the back corridors of Leinster House while the public spin was that, despite all of the furore and the loss of troops, it had not been such a bad old week for our Dear Leader of a Taoiseach. Anxious supplicants for favour, within both the party and the media, raced to portray Bertie-Lite as a tough leader, a sort of milk-and-water pastel variant of Mr Haughey – though obviously minus the yachts, islands and jewel-encrusted daggers. Once the possibility of a single-party government had disappeared for Fine Gael, God's banker Peter Mathews became an independent-thinking nuisance to them, as did Billy Timmins, and so Fine Gael were, they claimed, delighted with their departures, while the departure of 'that bloody woman' Lucinda, and by her own hand too, would at least provide everyone with some peace.

The Taoiseach meanwhile acted like a latter-day David Lloyd

George, issuing warnings to the last wavering Fine Gael deserters that they were headed for a palace of desolation. Unfortunately for Enda, his warnings went unheeded and those who left choose exile voluntarily, undaunted by Enda's fire-and-brimstone threats of expulsion. And when it came to those who were still loyal to the party, many in Fine Gael were getting very tired of the love of Dear Leader Enda, just like the country itself. The mood was epitomised by one forlorn insider, who having been on the wrong side in 2010, who noted, 'we have endured fifteen years of Enda as leader, all that winking and nodding, and we have another five to go. Even tribunal witnesses do not suffer for that long'. The declaration represented an admission that Enda's chief virtue of resilience had worn down his internal opponents to such an extent the only options left to any reform-minded Fine Gaelers was internal or external exile. The cost for Enda was as yet unclear, for all battles exact some sort of price, even from the victorious. But as good King Enda accepted the bowing and scraping of those who anxiously called him 'boss-man', it looked from his perspective as though victory had been irrevocably secured by the Fine Gael herd over the reformers. Fine Gael had finally been turned into a slightly more respectable variant of Fianna Fáil.

The more thoughtful among us wondered, however, whether Enda's adoption of a presidential style might act as a catalyst for the resurrection of a variant of the PD party that had haunted Fine Gael for so long. Suddenly, a critical mass of credible Independent deputies had emerged. Although they were birds bearing very different ideological feathers, they had the numbers required to form a new party to challenge Fine Gael. It was one thing for Enda to pit himself the Ming Flanagan and Mick Wallace 'Muppet Show', and our Dear Leader quite enjoyed the break from Dáil tedium provided by his spats with the 'hard left' of Richard Boyd Barrett and Clare Daly. However, facing a party made up of the very diverse talents of Colm Keaveney, Lucinda, Róisín Shortall, Shane Ross, Stephen Donnelly, John Halligan, Catherine Murphy, Billy Timmins and, at a pinch, Finian McGrath was a far less attractive prospect for our Dear Leader. Intriguingly, unlike our Grumpy Old Men who were snug as bugs in their well-pensioned rugs, the new Independents were mostly of a similar age to that struggling wing of middle Ireland who had, with their families, been conscripted into bailing out the Irish banks so Michael Noonan could look good in Europe and who were becoming increasingly cranky about their status as ECB and Bundesbank sharecroppers. For Fine Gael, it was easy to stifle single-issue Independents, but should those who had been exorcised from the Fine Gael Mother Church and a selection of other like-minded Independents coalesce into an articulate, politically-minded party, it would be an entirely different prospect.

It was perhaps a measure of the absence of imagination in our public discourse that when talk of a new party emerged, our immediate instinct was to dig up the gristly old relic of the PDs. But, in fact, a far more intriguing template had been set by the equally disparate Clann na Poblachta party of the 1950s, a new party of idealistic radicals who successfully challenged the old political establishment. The similarity in the political systems was eerie: back then too, Ireland was a zombie state ruled by a clique of Grumpy Old Men who had utterly forfeited the confidence of the citizens. The prospect of the rise of a new Clann was not particularly threatening to the Coalition as they enjoyed the afterglow of their record majority. But although he did not know it at the time, when the Taoiseach chastised Lucinda for voting against the party whip, he was engaged in a big gamble. The wind was beginning to turn against the Coalition and even in herd-instinct Ireland, the spectacle of conscience being treated like dirt on a shoe could generate forces that would not be easily controlled.

The prospect of a new PD party or a new Clann certainly spooked those few remaining thoughtful members of Finc Gael. They remembered all too well that in the 1997 and 2007 elections, the nuisance factor of the PDs stymied Fine Gael's chances of securing power. They were also acutely aware that such a new party might outflank Fine Gael on a different front. All of the chatter on Marian Finucane and across RTÉ was about abortion. However, a Coalition elected by voters who demanded that Fianna Fáil and all they stood for – or rather didn't stand for – be treated in a similar fashion to Carthage was, astonishingly, becoming vulnerable on what Bertie used to nervously call the 'ettics' front. Paddy had genuinely in 2011 wanted 'something different'. Instead he found himself, once again, being ruled by a government whose core ethos was one of brutal pragmatism, in which the ECB's might was right, all promises, especially those relating to burning bondholders, were disposable, and poisonous intrigue, bullying and clever smears left scant room for real reform. In the world outside this satrap's court, the only options for Ireland's teeming masses were flight, if you were young enough, or mere subsistence. A nation's trust was dying on the vine for the parties of the Grumpy Old Men's Coalition, and it did not exist for Fianna Fáil, a party on political life-support. Sinn Féin was trying hard, but the insatiable taint of rot they could never fully dispose of acted as an invisible but real choke chain upon their surly ambitions.

Over the next two years, the Coalition's astonishing cack-handedness exponentially increased the possibility of a new party rising like the phoenix from the dust and feathers of Enda's Democratic Revolution. Meanwhile, Lucinda began to haunt the Dear Leader in the most subtle of fashions, particularly when it came to the iconic Seanad referendum defeat. Though in the wake of the Coalition's defeat, it was Fianna Fáil who were smiling for the cameras, the real winners of that referendum were Lucinda and the Reform Alliance. Such a claim might seem strange, given that the

Alliance played the slightest of roles until Lucinda trotted belatedly into the campaign. However, timing in politics is everything and unlike Sinn Féin's Gerry Adams who leapt at what he thought was the winning 'Yes' bandwagon, Creighton paced her intervention perfectly.

The real reason that the Reform Alliance were the big winners was that the one clear message to emerge from the semi-moribund referendum campaign was the desire of Irish voters for a new political party of ideas and reform. Mr Kenny's well-marshalled political storm-troopers might have dominated the media aspect of the Seanad campaign to such an extent that one member of the 'No' campaign noted that, in terms of resources and organisation, 'we were like the Polish cavalry charging the German tanks in 1939'. However, despite the poor quality of the raw material, namely the Seanad itself, the 'No' campaign managed to douse the Coalition's already low libido for constitutional reform. The 'No' campaign also threw up one intriguing development: new groups of figures, who had previously been seen as apolitical, fought harder than any of the conventional parties to save it. Some of the more high-profile 'apolitical' members, such as Senators Feargal Quinn and John Crown, did have some skin in the game. But the 'No' campaign's ideological slant made it clear that neither of those two gentlemen were fighting out of self-interest or to preserve their pay and perks in the Seanad play-school.

However, it was the role played by the previously apolitical Diarmaid Ferriter and Glenna Lynch generation of thirty-something achievers that represented the most significant new development. They and the thousands of people who contacted Lucinda were symptomatic of a growing trend whereby Ireland was being roused out of its endemic apathy by the sheer uselessness of its governing class. And significantly, given the growing imperiousness of the Dear Leader, the key election issue was the electorate's fear that abolishing the Seanad would, instead of urging on the Democratic Revolution on, create an elected dictatorship of Grumpy Old Men. The dusty old Seanad was a poor Don Quixote to be putting into the field against our Dear Leader's growing King Enda Syndrome but, in a stark measurement of what had happened to the Democratic Revolution, it was the only one we had.

Michael McDowell, who, in the wake of his role in sinking the Dáil Inquiries fandango, played no small role in sending a second government referendum to the gallows, had for some time claimed that there was a 'market in the political gap' for a new party. The opportunity and the danger that the Reform Alliance had to examine was whether Mr McDowell was right and, if so, were they the party who could take the great gamble to fill that gap? Up to the Seanad referendum result, they had evaded the definitive decision on becoming a new party, for it would be the final act of Fine Gael regicide. But in the wake of the Seanad result, the first timid whispers of 'we are waiting, watching and biding our time' began to sally forth.

The problem, of course, was that their waiting process left the HSE looking proactive. It was understandable the Reform Alliance saw themselves as too new to run as a party in the local and European elections. Instead, they used both elections as clearing houses to find future candidates amidst the ranks of those who didn't like the way Fine Gael had become the new Fianna Fáil. This, however, was a dangerous strategy. Unlike the Dáil Inquiries referendum, which essentially collapsed in a flurry of voter confusion, the Seanad referendum loss signalled the end of Enda's honeymoon. And, more significantly, its defeat signalled a clear collapse of public confidence in the capacity of the Coalition to deliver on Irish voters' ache for real change. Abolishing the Seanad had been the central spar in the great architectural structure of constitutional reform Enda had built – largely on the hoof – prior to Fine Gael's presidential strategies. The public's collapse of faith in a political party in 2008 had manifested itself in the destruction of Fianna Fáil. Now, through an astonishing mix of gaucherie and arrogance, the Coalition was flirting in the same territories.

The problem for the Reform Alliance was that when Paddy makes his mysterious wants known, he expects any suitors to get on with the job quick as you can. Paddy does not like to wait in an orderly queue, even in the ethics shop. However, as the Coalition Cartel sunk ever more into ethical debt, the Reform Alliance appeared to be enjoying the sunshine of Enda's discomfort so much that they had fallen asleep in the political meadow. There was plenty of rarefied thought about, for sure. However, the leisurely progress of the Reform Alliance saw them being nicknamed the Tea Party – not because of their likeness to the American namesakes but rather because of their liking for long slow pots of tea in the Dáil Bar, consumed in a stately manner while the affairs of the world, and occasionally those of Ireland too, were discussed. Meanwhile, the Irish people waited, patiently at first, and then impatiently. Lucinda made the occasional sortie about how the ever-ageing Fine Gael was turning into Fianna Fáil-Lite and criticised Irish politics in a *Sunday Independent* interview for the 'complete absence of intellectual rigour in party politics as it now operates ... [The Dáil is] a palace of zombies where people who are elected give up their faculties and capacities for independent thought'. Undoubtedly, Lucinda was right in her claims that Civil War politics had ended in 2011, and that while Fine Gael temporarily benefited from the collapse of Fianna Fáil, 'if they or any other party believes they can from now on command a core vote as a matter of right, they are deluded'. To Lucinda's eye, all Irish voters were now, and forever more, up for grabs. But simply saying this was not enough. The voters wanted a new circus to replace the old clowns now. It was all good and pretty for Lucinda to talk about putting her heart and soul into working with anyone who wanted to forge something new and fresh in Irish life, but talk on its own just wasn't cutting the mustard. In particular, her concept of a 'movement of ideas' that would operate outside the traditional party structure was not gaining much traction. In theory, it seemed like a fine and noble thing, but to Paddy it sounded rather like the old rhythm theory of contraception. And Paddy, in politics at least, tends to be an all-duck-or-no-dinner man.

So, after a time, Paddy got distracted. He no longer listened when Lucinda talked about how the Reform Alliance intended 'to follow up on the success of our RDS conference with a series of town hall meetings across the provinces'. The claim that the Reform Alliance was talking to people outside the political process who were offering help was also somewhat undercut by the stark reality that wily political foxes like Shane Ross and less wily cubs like Stephen Donnelly were actually plotting to snub the Reform Alliance group, rather than offering to assist it. And there was still that whole abortion genie which kept on putting its head up and winking and nodding, no matter how often Lucinda crossly said, 'abortion is not the reason I got involved in politics. Our problem there was once you break one promise in politics, you break a lot'.

The whole situation became even more complicated when a couple of the political foxes Lucinda had been courting, after rejecting the Reform Alliance, appeared to realise that there might be some votes in an Independent Alliance of their own. It was a bit of a stretch for the three-decade-long member of the Seanad inner circle Shane Ross to re-invent himself as a revolutionary radical. But, rather like John Dryden's view on the close alliance between genius and madness, the line between contrarianism and revolutionary instincts is a fine one and a stockbroker like Shane could do the maths when it came to 30% support levels for Independents. It was an even bigger stretch to re-invent three-term TD Finian McGrath as a reformist outsider, having previously had a very brief alliance with

Fianna Fáil and Che-Guevara-loving Bertie, before Finian leapt off the Fianna Fáil bandwagon just as the wheels started coming off. As Ross, John Halligan and Finian snuggled up ever closer, perhaps the most curious entrant of all into the Independent ranks was Michael Fitzmaurice, who, a week after replacing Luke 'Ming' Flanagan, was cheered to the roof-tops when he suggested a new Country and Western Alliance was the solution to Ireland's woes.

Suddenly, our political system was like Dublin's famous buses: no new parties had come in ages, and then three came along at once. This made Lucinda and her movement of ideas appear to be as close to the rapidly moving political world outside as the last Emperor of China. The one thing, though, that can said about Lucinda is that she rarely conforms to expectations. And though the mice such as Ross and Fitzmaurice were getting quite rowdy in the political bar, the pad of Lucinda's feet became ever louder as 2015 approached.

CHAPTER 9

SHADES OF GERRY'S PAST SHADOW THE RISE OF SUPERQUINN MUM MARY LOU

The equivocal rise of Sinn Féin

When it came to exacting some form of vengeance for the Great Betrayal, one party in particular was doing a great deal of waving, jumping and leaping. If Paddy really wanted a democratic revolution, then his luck apparently was in, for Sinn Féin declared itself more than willing to fill the gap in our growing democratic deficit. Mind you, looking over at that collective of ambitious Haughey-style political scientologists, poor Paddy would have been more than entitled to note that when it comes to the collapse of democratic legitimacy in Ireland, it never rains but it pours. In an already shifty – apologies, shifting – political landscape, the cautious rise of the Sinn Féin political shape-shifters was unlikely to inspire confidence in the thinking wing of our electorate of nascent revolutionaries.

We were, of course, in a different space to the era when the appearance of Gerry Adams inspired references to Byron's famous lines:

> I met Murder on the way —
> He had a mask like Castlereagh —
> Very smooth he looked, yet grim;

But although they are aspiring political kings, Sinn Féin, a party still in transition, secured quite the mixed result in 2011. Though they acquired enough TDs to finally become a mini-Labour party – as distinct to the original Slieveen O'Caolain one-man-band – they profited thinly enough from Fianna Fáil's imitation of Monty Python's Mr Creosote. Instead, though it seems strange now, it was actually the dying swans of Labour who managed to pick up a tidy tally of Fianna Fáil seats. The electorate, even in a set of circumstances that resemble the Marxist dreams about the collapse of capitalism that Sinn Féin professed to believe, were still circumspect about the Sinn Féin option. Still, the Irish voters finally put Gerry Adams into the Dáil. At the time, this appeared to resemble a triumph, although it soon evolved into more of a mixed blessing.

Intriguingly, it was around December 2013, just as the Coalition Cartel locked itself into its prolonged losing streak, that we first began to wonder whether Gerry Adams might be politically mortal after all. The greatest moment of danger for any leader of a normal 'democratic' party occurs when you are seen to be a source of difficulty for future leaders. That, of course, is not a problem if the party has no future leaders beyond your good self. But by the close of 2013, it was all too elegantly clear that Mary Lou McDonald was, for the South of Ireland, a friskily fragrant alternative to Mr Adams. Inevitably in the age of new politics, the differences came to a head in a TV3 documentary on Sinn Féin and Gerry Adams rather than that dustbowl known as the floor of the Dáil. There, it became evident that the biggest victim of the still unravelled dark narrative of Mr Adams's serially contested dark past was, ironically enough, his most likely putative successor.

It seems, in retrospect, that Mary Lou has been at the centre of the Sinn Féin power game forever. In fact, her rise has been remarkably swift. Ms McDonald has undoubtedly been a high-profile Sinn Féin icon for a very long time, but she has, for most of it, also been a peripheral figure. She was the Sinn Féin equivalent of one of Enda's 'lovely girls' – living proof, if you will, that Sinn Féin were not toxic on the ladies' front. But she was an electoral failure. Yes, Mary Lou became an MEP. But for Sinn Féin, as for all other parties, Europe barely ranks above the Seanad in the power game and is certainly placed below the council. Back in the 2007 general election, her MEP seat was a losing docket in the Dublin Central constituency. It was hard to know whether Bertie took more pleasure from ensuring his pal Cyprian Brady with a mere 939 first-preference votes 'accidentally' won a Dáil seat ahead of his party colleague Mary Fitzpatrick or in his deliberate shafting of Mary Lou, which ensured she would even finish behind Fine Gael's Paschal Donohoe. In business terms, it was probably the latter, for Sinn Féin are like an invasive non-native species such as the zebra mussel that, once introduced to a constituency, take it over and choke the life out of the locals. For Mary Lou, there was even worse to come when her precious MEP seat was lost in the most wounding of fashions in 2009: to the old Socialist 'Boxer' Joe Higgins. The Socialist Party's Trotskyite past, it appeared, had triumphed over the Sinn Féin future and Mary Lou was on the political edge ... well, until 2011, when she finally made it home to Dáil Eireann.

The length of her journey and its many interruptions meant she was no more than first amongst equals with the likes of Pearse Doherty when the small Sinn Féin band of fourteen marched grimly in. Once there, however, McDonald gouged out her position on the floor of the Dáil with a similar determination to that which she displayed climbing the Eiger Face of Dublin Central. The Fine Gael backbench rooks initially tried to drown out McDonald with their usual raucous cawing but, rather like Paddington Bear, the Sinn Féin Deputy Leader has a hard stare that would freeze a Jerry Buttimer at a thousand yards. As Gerry floundered to such an extent he was listened to with the silent inquisitorial disinterest reserved for half-wits, the legend of Mary Lou just grow'd and grow'd like Topsy.

The problem for Mary Lou was that the stronger her public position became, the more her party became a not-so-secret drag on her future. The complexities created by this uneasy alliance were most evidenced by Ursula Halligan's gripping encounter with McDonald as the future leader of Sinn Féin shopped amidst the prawns, rustic breads and other middle-class comestibles within the safe settings of Superquinn. Most of Sinn Féin's core vote would be as dismissive as Roy Keane when it comes to the prawn-sandwich-eating brigade. But by 2012, Sinn Féin, rather like the political equivalent of Aldi or Lidl, was looking to expand into the soft lower-middle-class market. By staging a political interview in the midst of an icon of middle-class Ireland, McDonald's, and Sinn Féin's, positioning and imagery, as is so often the case, were superb. After all, a Superquinn Mum like Mary Lou should surely pose a threat to neither man nor beast, nor struggling middle-class and working-poor Ireland. But on this occasion, ironically, the respectability of the location actually contributed to McDonald's utterly uncomfortable response to Halligan's probing questions about the legitimacy of the IRA's armed struggle. Ms McDonald may normally be utterly unflappable but she instinctively sensed the dissonance between the location and the line of questioning. Superquinn is simply not the location for politicians to say they support the right to meet force with force. This awkward interview seemed to drive home for Ms McDonald the clash between her ambitions and her party's position: defending Provos in balaclavas is the political glass ceiling that, to put it bluntly, will always prevent Mary Lou from securing the votes of Superquinn Mom. But there was worse still to come in Mary Lou's quest to attract the Superquinn Mum as, over the course of 2013, the scabby ghost of Gerry Adams started to regenerate.

Gerry's past, alas, turned out to be a particularly frisky old ghost. First of all, the Jean McConville murder returned from the grave of Mr Adams's past courtesy of an RTÉ documentary. Second, Adams's past reached out its skeletal arm with the jailing of Liam Adams, Adams's brother, on charges of child abuse. Poor Mary Lou got busy with the political pooper-scooper, but in a classic case of the old maxim of explaining and losing, McDonald's critique of Micheál Martin's attempt to use this traumatic case to try and score political points was utterly unconvincing. However, the real nightmare for Sinn Féin and Mary Lou came courtesy of the Mairia Cahill scandal, which provided Sinn Féin with, so to speak, a live body.

In November 2014, Mairia Cahill, a young woman from Belfast, came forward to tell her story – she was raped by a senior IRA member, who was subsequently protected by the IRA Army Council while Cahill was subjected to an IRA interrogation. Although Adams still maintains never having been a member of the IRA, Sinn Féin's close links with the IRA inevitably meant Mr Adams and many of his 'friends' were implicated in this latest display of moral rot. Cahill's refusal to be silenced awoke a plethora of other ghosts from the IRA sex abuse files previously suppressed. Suddenly, Mr Adams appeared on the brink of becoming the latest politician to learn

Tory politician Enoch Powell's warning that 'all political careers, unless they are cut off in midstream at a happy juncture, end in failure' is one of the immutable laws of politics. It was an intriguing juncture: up to 2013, it had been thought that the 'curious' structure of the Sinn Féin hierarchy – yes, we are being kind – and Mr Adams's own status as the first war hero in history to never fire a shot in anger meant the Sinn Féin leader might evade that particular law. However, it was a measure of his political decline that, increasingly, when we gazed at Gerry Adams, we saw the face of Charlie Haughey in his final year in power looking back at us.

The idea that Gerry might avoid the endgame that all democrats must endure was unsurprising, for even by the tangled standards set by Mr Haughey, the Sinn Féin leader is the most astonishing political leader Ireland has experienced. Mr Haughey might have been lusted after like no previous false prophet, but even the fanatic desire he tickled in many Irish people is surpassed by Mr Adams who attracts the thoughtless devotion that is the lodestone of the paramilitary soul. But as scandal after scandal threatened the Sinn Féin leader, the similarities between the duo became less encouraging for Mr Adams. In the case of Haughey, such was the power of his fabulous political persona and the vast enchantment it cast during the four decades in which he defined the colour of Irish politics that the thought of an Irish political scene where the old pike of Kinsealy did not dominate the agenda was unimaginable for many. This exotic political creature survived the Arms Trial and his near-treasonable behaviour in cabinet that had led to the trial, while personal bankruptcy had only been held at bay by his rather unique strategy of telling the banks to go and fuck themselves. Haughey, the great escapologist, skipped away from the phone-tapping, the leadership challenges, the PDs, the improbable lifestyle, the destruction of the economy, the lingering taint of the dark that eternally followed him, the political manslaughter of his most loyal lieutenant Brian

Lenihan and even the abandonment of Fianna Fáil's core value of no coalitions.

Then, apropos of nothing obvious – perhaps simply due to age and the slow process of political attrition – Haughey became a hollow man, in what appeared to be the blink of an eye. He still looked the same, still moved in that sinuous manner and still talked in precisely the same ornate but menacing way, but the breath of the hounds of history had finally, after the longest of chases, begun to warm his neck. The endgame was still fraught, but, like Edgar Allen Poe's famous tell-tale heart, the drumming of his past misdeeds became ever louder until finally the great chameleon was so denuded of authority that a political ghost called Seán Doherty was enough to finish the job.

Mr Adams and his alleged misdeeds had hidden in full view for far longer than Mr Haughey was able to, in spite of his added disadvantage of having far greater sins to hide. His ability to do this came from Gerry's undoubted status as a more elusive, ruthless and cunning leader than even Haughey at his peak. It was a measure of his political abilities that, for four decades, Adams, just like Shakespeare's hunchbacked killing king Richard III, had managed to evade all allegations about his 'naked villainy / With odd old ends stol'n out of holy writ / And seem a saint, when most I play the devil'. Just as Charlie created a Gatsby-style palace of deceit to sustain the illusion he was the modern Irish chieftain, Mr Adams invented a veritable Taj Mahal of illusion to hide the more crimson weave of his associations.

It helped that in a Dáil populated by bank clerks, primary school-teachers and, worst of all, career politicians, Mr Adams is unique, for he is no mere TD or politician. Outside of being a war hero who never – wink and nod – fired a shot, Gerry is also a literary figure, an author, a philosopher, a Buddhist who hugs trees and, perhaps most important of all, a form of international celebrity. He is even a Twitter man now, with a teddy-bear sidekick he frequently references called Ted. As with Haughey, Mr Adams's authority is even enhanced by the manner in which he is surrounded by rumour, by fear and, in some cases, by awe, depending on your perception of these things.

Despite his ever-increasing troubles, Mr Adams has, just as Mr Haughey had, made it clear he intends to go on and on, just like one of those Chinese leaders. And in another intriguing parallel with Haughey, it looked in 2013 and 2014 as though it might be the women who would do for Mr Adams. When it came to Haughey, the moment that signalled the grass had begun to grow too fast under his imperially-slippered feet was the election as President of Labour's Mary Robinson. In the case of Mr Adams, the unquiet ghost of Jean McConville and the very alive presence of Mairia Cahill meant that, after a long hiatus, a young country of Google employees and Superquinn Mums was finally learning the Grimm tales of Mr Adams's history.

Gerry Adams's past might not have been a problem before 2013. Though Sinn Féin Nua was not short of political sharks, there was no equivalent of Albert or a new Mary Robinson waiting hungrily in its wings – yet. But as Mr Adams knows best of all, Sinn Féin is now, above all things, a party of pragmatists. They have had to be in order to get to where they are now from where they once were. And so Mr Adams, who was becoming almost as unpopular amongst the electorate as Mr Gilmore – and that ain't easy! – started to hear that dangerous 'isn't it time you should be going?' question far too often for his own good. He should be sure to note no-one is more pragmatic than a Superquinn Mum – whoever that might be within the Sinn Féin set-up.

That at least was what we thought as we waited for Gerry's inevitable fall, and then waited a little bit more. But by 2015, there was Gerry, still grinning down at us in his patented, yet almost accidentally menacing, fashion. Our political and media classes were astonished by his great escape. But in reality, it was not so surprising after all. In what is an unhappy accident if you're a Sinn Féiner, the fascist theory of the 'big lie' appears very applicable to the Sinn Féin methodology of going about things. The politics of the big lie is grounded, as Adolf Hitler described in *Mein Kampf*, in the fascist belief – not, of course, that Sinn Féin are fascists – that the masses in the 'primitive simplicity of their minds … more readily fall victims to the big lie than the small lie, since they themselves often tell small lies in little matters but would be ashamed to resort to large-scale falsehoods'. The happy simplicity of the masses means that not only are the citizens unable to 'believe that others could have the impudence to distort the truth so infamously', but that even when 'the facts which prove this to be so [are] brought clearly to their minds, they will still doubt and waver and will continue to think that there may be some other explanation'.

When it came to Adams's difficulties, it helped that the politics of the big lie – and in truth plenty of smaller ones too – has plenty of Irish devotees. In Ireland, the apogee of big lie politics was again provided by Haughey, who was so adept in this regard he didn't actually bother too much with the lying bit. It wasn't just Haughey though; a willingness to bury inconvenient truths for the sake of the peaceful life is the endemic flaw in the DNA of the Irish gene pool. Mr Haughey was, in fairness, not even close to the worst of the villains who were able, courtesy of our national defect, to hide in full view. For example, when it came to the systematic abuse of working-class children, we preferred to laugh at the 'All Priests Show' rather than inquire into what was, far from lurking below, on open display for anyone who wished to challenge the naked emperors of our note-taking episcopacy. With regard to Mr Adams, when it came to the sexual abuse of Áine Adams, the role played by Mr Adams within the IRA, the crepuscular murder of Jean McConville and the bullying experienced by Mairia Cahill after she was raped, we were told that what our eyes appeared to see were mere spectral fairy tales dreamt up by enemies of peace. And, in a measure of the real state of the Irish electorate's desire for democratic revolution and reform, Paddy was more than prepared to go along with this, for the sake of the easy life.

In the case of Gerry, the biggest lie of all we chose to embrace was that history doesn't matter. The talk was of different times and how the past cannot be an accurate guide to current form. There was even a bit of brutal pragmatism about how the dead are dead and the raped are raped and how all the complaining in the world could not change that now. There is, of course, merit in consigning pasts that are sad to history, and they could certainly do with doing that a bit more up North. But it is a feature of any healthy society that before dark days are forgotten, there must be atonement. This means that, while their decision to sue for peace means we must tolerate Sinn Féin's status as a conventional political party, our response should be one of peace with repentance rather than forgetfulness.

Ultimately, the forces – or rather the great vacuum created by the collapse of the Democratic Revolution – driving the rise of Sinn Féin were stronger than the ever-thinning cobwebs of history. Such was the wave of anger that assailed the country, we were apparently prepared to tolerate any level of moral anomie to secure vengeance on the parties who had betrayed us. Interestingly, however, while Sinn Féin talked soulfully about their own plans for a democratic revolution, any clear plan for implementation was conspicuous in absence. While Paddy might be reassured that within Sinn Féin, there was no unease about the lack of a plan, he would do well to wonder about putting his faith in a party that had no intention of being in government after the next election.

For anyone familiar with the essential core of Sinn Féin, this will not be a surprise. Anyone who spends a prolonged period of conversation with the movement will discover one particularly curious thing fairly speedily. If asked about the ideological views they embrace, you will discover they can name none. While there is clearly an obsession with constituencies, opinion polls and political placement, nothing but vacancy exists when it comes to any vision for a Sinn Féin Ireland. This rather large lacuna means that Paddy is going to have some troubles with Sinn Féin if he's still on the hunt for reform. In that regard, the biggest difficulty with Sinn Féin is not their less than glorious past or the rapidly diminishing, though still loudly vocalised, fears that they might still retain some militaristic instincts. It is that they are political scientologists, devoted solely to the project of seizing power. The Sinn Féin Scientologists are a political army and, like any other army, it is all about process and targets. But what they plan to do after securing power – outside of unifying the island of Ireland, if they are actually still serious about that – is unclear to anyone, even themselves. They are instead exemplary good soldiers who simply march without ever questioning or doubting the *bona fides* of their journey. The party occasionally attempts to disguise its scientologist tendencies with the occasional dabble in socialism, but really Sinn Féin is merely the scientologist variant of Fianna Fáil, with the time-bomb of a few child-abusing paramilitaries attached to the bandwagon's chassis.

Those who are veering towards Sinn Féin would do well to realise Sinn Féin are not even a new version of Fianna Fáil. They are, in fact, far more similar to the Haughey variant, before the need to appear to be reformed watered down the Fianna Fáil brew. The similarities between Sinn Féin and Haughey-era Fianna Fáil are not just those between Gerry and Haughey, for Sinn Féin are also informed by the politics of Fianna Fáil under Haughey. The chief ethic of Haughey's Fianna Fáil's was the will to power, just like modern Sinn Féin. And, despite Sinn Féin's current embrace of political poverty, they will enjoy power in precisely the same manner as Haughey's Fianna Fáil when they get it.

Sinn Féin would discover the hard way that the Irish voter can themselves be as devious as the politicians who invent big lies. The 2014 local and European elections were supposed to be the best of times for Sinn Féin, in which Sinn Féin would finally, under the inspired leadership of Gerry Adams, overtake Fianna Fáil. Instead, the anticipated Sinn Féin surge turned into a very bad case of Gilmore Gale Syndrome. Sinn Féin did triumph at in the European elections, but that was a shadow contest indicative only of far distant future potential. Even Labour, on their day, has been successful in European adventures. The substance of the election was provided by the council elections, in which Sinn Féin trailed in a distant fourth behind the dusty old Fianna Fáil relics, a despised Fine Gael and our mad, disorganised Independents. Sinn Féin, however, were not too distressed by the results. They knew that, were Sinn Féin to expand too swiftly, they would be like the python that tries to swallow too large a carcass and ends up suffocating itself by the weight of its prey. Surpassing Labour, as they did, was a better target to use to build the party up.

While Sinn Féin's West Belfast *Politburo* may dream of Taoiseach Gerry, even this relative success could not disguise growing concerns that Gerry would yet fatally compromise the Sinn Féin project. Although post-election polls began once again to smile on Sinn Féin's prospects, the counted votes indicated that Gerry may still be too big of a political fly for the Irish electorate to swallow. Substantial numbers of Irish voters do seem to be ignoring the many fleas hopping on Sinn Féin's fur. But if they are merely flirting with Sinn Féin in order to get the attention of our neglectful establishment spouses, Sinn Féin's fortunes could change swiftly.

It is in many ways ironic that Gerry, the most cunning and resilient of them all, could yet be the excuse that our even more cunning voters could use to disentangle themselves from their Sinn Féin dalliance. It is even more delightful that Houdini Gerry has found himself tangled up in a Gordian knot of his own making, from which there appears to be no easy escape. No matter how much our peace-making, globe-trotting international ambassador, celebrity poetry-writing tree-hugger struggles, the gravediggers of his contested past continue to drag Adams back to face the ghost of Jean McConville. But as the more mischievous among Irish voters were quick to note, the politician who continued to suffer most grievously from the Mairia Cahill affair and Gerry's other historic woes was Mary Lou. However, our Superquinn Mum had not hung around the hunkers of Bertie Ahern for so long without acquiring a fine nose for the art of survival. Patience, cunning and copious declarations of self-pity did marvels in greasing Mary Lou out from beneath that particular moral bear-trap.

Ironically, a very different moment may prove to be far more indicative of the putative weaknesses of Mary Lou and Sinn Féin. During one of the many sharp exchanges in the PAC, Fine Gael TD John Deasy was interrupted by the Sinn Féin aspirant leader after he called Shane Ross a bullshitter. Without missing a beat, Deasy turned around to Mary Lou and starkly observed 'and you are a bullshitter too'. Intriguingly, a rather startled Mary Lou did not respond to the claim. It was not normal for Ms McDonald to be so quiet when she was under attack. On this occasion, it was as though Deasy had scratched a hidden fear. Could it be the case that the rise of Sinn Féin was echoing that of Mr Gilmore's Labour in 2010? It certainly appeared on close scrutiny to be as insubstantial as the infamous 'Gilmore for Taoiseach' posters of the 2011 election. It could only leave you to wonder whether history was getting ready to repeat itself, tragic the first time and comic the second, with Mary Lou replacing Eamon Gilmore as the sweetest user of a tongue in Irish politics.

Given a scenario such as this, maybe it is just as well our Sinn Féin Scientologists are in no hurry for power. Incremental growth that allows them to tiptoe away from the rank smell of Gerry and towards the sweeter but increasingly sickly scent of Mary Lou will do for Sinn Féin. But what of Paddy? By the end of 2014, it looked like Paddy was, once again, falling for a big lie. Mind you, if Paddy was not to be deceived by such delights, it would help a great deal if he opened his eyes or, more importantly still, his nose.

Ultimately, an old witness statement about Fianna Fáil's Liam Lawlor perhaps provides us with the most apposite description for Sinn Féin's attempt to create an Irish Syriza Spring. During his tribunal evidence, Mr Lawlor recalled making a trip to the Czech Republic after the fall of the communist regime to see if there might be any dealing for property knocking around, leading one witness to note, 'You'd have to feel sorry for the Czechs. First the Germans, then the Russians and then at the first sign of prosperity, Lawlor comes bustling in the door'.

CHAPTER 10

THE STRANGE DEATH OF BOHEMIAN IRELAND

Whatever happened to Irish independent thinking?

In looking at why and how it all went so wrong so quickly for the Grumpy Old Men, it should be noted one of the less chronicled consequences of the way the Coalition Cartel captained the Irish ship into the ground was the slow death of Bohemian Ireland. This was the natural child of Enda Kenny's special love affair with respectability. Mr Kenny may have raced into office promising a democratic revolution, but amidst all the fainting and comparisons to Edmund Burke, one of the less noticed features of Mr Kenny's cunning plan was his enthusiasm for Ireland to become some European variant of Singapore. This Singapore ethic was summed up by the constant Coalition mantra of 'more for less'; it sounded quite nice, until we realised that the 'more' was work and the 'less' was pay. This was, to put it mildly, far less radical than the implications of phrases like 'democratic revolution'. It was an ambition that was the antithesis of Bohemianism, not that Enda, of course, would be put out by that. Primary school-teachers, alas, are not natural Bohemians and our Coalition of Grumpy Old Men was dominated by former members of the profession.

That, it should be said, is not always a bad thing. It would be unfair to think that, because he is of the school-teacher vintage, Enda is naturally grim. Like Jack Lynch in his prime, to whom Enda is often unnervingly similar, he is all for manly fun, for cautious madness such as shooting rats in the schoolyard and the odd few pints – though always in moderation, of course. He is a man most at ease with the scattered-shorts-and-wintergreen smell of a GAA dressing-room in which showers are an unnecessary luxury. But the nature of our Taoiseach school-teacher means that madness should be confined to the GAA pitch and the public house on a Saturday. Beyond that, the school-teacher is only happy with order and a world with a place for everything and everything in its place. Bohemianism, by contrast, smacks of something Charlie Haughey might have engaged in and well, frankly, Enda is a bit frightened of all that stuff.

His school-teacher characteristics mean that Enda was the perfect man for the difficult task of putting post-bailout manners on the unruly Irish. He would, he assured us, take no pleasure in such executive actions. But if the exigencies of an effective new world order required the excision of our Bohemian traits, Enda would lose little sleep over that. His status as a scion of the world of report cards, neat school copybooks and full and up-to-date attendance registers meant he was perfectly designed for the task of keeping Angela's austerity register. There was scant chance of our new headmaster acquiring any rebellious tendencies either, for although he was have been the boss of Ireland, Enda's defining characteristic is deference to bosses. Enda is never happier than when he is the good child, getting high marks and golden stars from his teacher. As Joe Higgins warned, this meant that the Troika had in Enda a brave Irish volunteer as distinct to a reluctant Greek conscript. Sadly, it was Ireland, however, rather than Enda himself, that he was volunteering to take one for the European team.

So what is Bohemian Ireland? It is that strain of whimsy and independent thinking that makes being Irish different. The Bohemian ethic is characterised by a certain devil-may-care attitude to conformity, by a defiance of authority and by a questioning spirit. It is an Irish trait that has survived every variant of oppression from colonialism to the clericalist shadow-state that a nervous post-independence political order imposed upon Paddy in order to keep him well behaved. Fine Gael's Oliver J. Flanagan, the great *bête noire* of liberal Ireland, provided us with one of the better definitions of Ireland's natural Bohemian ways in his great peroration against Ireland joining the European Union in 1972. Flanagan, who certainly was not a natural libertine, warned Dáil deputies about what friends of his had noticed on recent trip to a town near Amsterdam:

> There was no-one to be seen on the streets at 10.30 p.m., that the people were all in their homes either in bed or watching television. When they went for refreshments there were only two people present at 9.30 p.m. On the other hand, at 5 a.m. they were wakened up by the people going to work and were told in their hotel that it was time to come down to breakfast. By 7 a.m. women were returning home from having completed their shopping.

There was much mockery of Flanagan's speech, in which he asked 'would life be worth living if Ireland adopted these standards? There is a typical Irish way of life. I hope it never changes. We may be described as easy-going but a little satisfies us. If we continentalise ourselves, the good old restful Irish way of life may be disturbed and I would not like to see that happening'. Inevitably, Garret FitzGerald attacked Flanagan's speech on the grounds of his objection to the time-keeping of the Dutch; as an objection to EU membership, 'that the people in Europe get up earlier than we do and we would not be up to dealing with them because of the early hour at which they rose' seemed ridiculous. But as it happens, Mr Flanagan had his finger on a particular Irish trait: one of the features of the Irish Bohemian spirit is that no job is particularly important. This attitude means that in times of recession, Paddy's natural position on what is essentially a minor issue is to take to the public house and wait the thing out.

One of the more curious features of our Bohemian mindset is that it has historically thrived during times of oppression. Perhaps, given the amount of practice Paddy has had at being oppressed by domestic and external forces, that should be less surprising. While in theory we were ruled from afar by the English or at home by beetle-black clerics swishing their malevolent soutanes, as long as we could retreat into a safe world of alcohol and non-conformity, then we could at least pretend to be free. This was a stance that provoked our English neighbours into a unique confusion of incomprehension, patronising fondness and occasionally violent outbursts of irritation. One of the more common misapprehensions about Ireland is that it is a cultural off-shoot of Britain. But while we may use the same language and share many of the same interests, the Irish mindset is fundamentally different. Britain is a hierarchical, ordered society. By contrast, we take a much more easy-going, chaotic, Mediterranean approach.

This brings its own flaws, such as our endemic weakness for the company of political and economic tricksters. However, it also facilitates our imaginative spirit of non-conformity, which is strong enough to defy even the repressive instincts of our home-grown pietistic political and clerical class. This non-conformism is not confined to our artistic rebels like James Joyce, Patrick Kavanagh and John B. Keane. In politics, it has provided us with the gaudy macaws of the Lenihan dynasty, the febrile wit of Fine Gael's Yorick, John Kelly, and the speckled legacy of Charlie Haughey. In business too, non-conformist successes such as Tony Ryan and Michael O'Leary are creatures of that same Bohemian spirit. Indeed, for many multi-national businesses, the Bohemian Irish spirit is uniquely attractive, offering them an interesting country to live in and a work-force that can think for itself, rather than a clotted collective of grind-educated graduates.

Though our Bohemian spirit has survived for many centuries, in the first decades of the 21st century, when the Puritans came for the Bohemians, Paddy was in a uniquely weakened position. The slow death of Fianna Fáil, in particular, meant we were utterly defenceless when the Troika, Enda Kenny and a Spanish Inquisition of Grumpy Old Men decided it was time to erase all our Bohemian bad-mindedness and put some manners on us. This was done primarily through the economic concept of 'more for less' – otherwise known as competitiveness. Initially, brow-beaten and demoralised by the great recession, Paddy greeted Mr More For Less with the same puzzled innocence of those Indians who met Columbus. Paddy, alas, was soon to suffer a similar fate. 'More for less', whose chief advocate was Fine Gael's Richard Bruton, became quite the fashion in the nation's counting houses where workers were asked to embrace the virtues of zero-hour contracts as their masters banked the enhanced profits. As the Bohemians disappeared before the march of Mr Kenny's school-teacher values, the Puritans were triumphant everywhere. Such was the extent of the dominance of our Puritans in politics that they managed to safely stow the last of the Bohemian politicians, Michael D., in the presidential mansion, where he is constitutionally obligated to be a conformist.

The Puritan impulse was particularly strong in Leinster House, where non-conformity had been excised by the posse of new Fine Gael TDs who looked, talked and thought in precisely the same moderately conservative fashion we associate with such comedies as 'The Brady Bunch'. George H.W. Bush once famously noted that he wanted to make American families a lot more like 'The Waltons' and a lot less like 'The Simpsons'. He would certainly have been at home in Enda's Fine Gael and Irish politics generally, for within Leinster House the old retinue of rogues, who, for all their flaws, at least knew something of the world outside, had been replaced by a new collective of political zealots who enthusiastically embraced a politics in which all independent thought and difference is to be murdered by the triumph of the focus group and the market researcher.

Sadly, the Puritan attack on independent thinking was a mansion of many unpleasant rules and was not confined to creating a thought-free world in the Dáil. The fiscal cuts imposed by our anti-Bohemian Coalition were bad enough. Worse still were the campaigns the Coalition launched on a weekly basis for health, fitness, computer literacy, efficiency and anything else that would serve the interests of our new culture of 'more for less'. Under the Coalition Cartel, Ireland witnessed a vast increase in the number of the state-sponsored advocates, raging against a terrifyingly untrammelled range of things from cake-eating to those suspicious creatures who prefer cars to bicycles. It should be noted, however, that the virus had begun in the Bertie era, in which the Taoiseach's response to any social dilemma was to arrange a highly-paid advocate to investigate. In fairness to Bertie, he didn't take the advocates very seriously or he wouldn't have set them up. Initially, we too winked at such strange creatures as ethics tsars. But it turned out they took themselves very seriously. And as all of the rest of us were losing our jobs, the advocates kept theirs. Doctors, nurses, teachers and carers were shed like dead leaves from a dying tree, but the vile race of advocates thrived like cockroaches after a nuclear explosion.

The survival of the advocates might have been accidental. But it was suspicious how well it also served the interests of the Coalition Cartel. Some innocents thought the various campaigns that the Coalition's advocates engaged in were forms of the great Democratic Revolution. However, the great list of advocates and their ability to generate a media furore were in fact a useful instrument of social control. Previously, the difficult task of putting manners on Paddy had been outsourced to the church. Although they had been pretty efficient, some difficulties with child abuse had ended their power. Happily, our advocates sped in to fill that breach. Their new task was critical to the needs of the implementers of austerity. The more sins – from dog-fouling to smoking, from drinking to sleeping, failing to cycle, having bad thoughts or walking with your left foot first – that were invented, the more the morale of the previously free and independent Irish citizenry plunged.

The Grumpy Old Men certainly found that such a less-than-brave new world suited their temperaments, for our humble citizenry were so well corralled by the culture of 'more for less' combined with the reign of the advocates that there was no vim or vigour in them to protest against the indignities being heaped upon them. Indeed, it worked so well that even Europe was astonished over the equanimity with which the 'wild Irish' accepted the diktats of austerity. As Shatter hectored us and Phil Hogan introduced us to the joy of the Fine Gael 'put up or shut up' school of governance, perhaps we should not have been as surprised, and disappointed, as we were by the rout of the Irish spirit of Bohemianism. One of the reasons why Bohemians stood out so much in Ireland is that the Irish herd instinct has always been a fruitful lodestone for ensuring conformity. In spite of our public persona of madness, which is mostly for the benefit of the tourists, the essence of Paddy is, in reality, that small peasant farmer who would prefer to die a virgin than lose an acre. The Bohemians might have had a bit of a run of popularity during the age of a Celtic Tiger they not-so-secretly detested, but nations respond to collective shocks in differing ways. In our case, after the wild Bohemian excesses of the Tiger era, our unconditional surrender to a drab Prussian ethic was a form of ideological comfort eating, where we returned to what Paddy hoped might be a place of safety.

It did not help that to a certain extent the ground had been cut out from our real Bohemians by the bankers, builders and celebrity lawyers who so enthusiastically adopted the Bohemian mantle during the Tiger years. Though they were certainly devil-may-care, wild, uncontrolled creatures, their assumed Bohemian status was a fake as the mansions they built. The true Bohemian is not concerned by status or income. These fellows though, even as they played the rake, looked out at the world with piggy little covetous eyes. Their annexation of the Bohemian label meant that Paddy, a creature of extremes as we know, lobbed the Bohemian spirit in with the rest of the Celtic Tiger detritus as he descended into a vast pit of lobotomised conformity.

The chief symptom of this Celtic Tiger dumping was that, instead of anger, a terrible blandness fell over public discourse. Of course, we did take the axe to our Fianna Fáil scapegoats. But once that was done, we reverted to a politics reminiscent of the Haughey era: the only acceptable discourse was protestations of loyalty to 'the boss', whoever that might be. So when Enda banished all of that Democratic Revolution stuff in favour of the numb conformity of Singapore, Paddy simply rolled over. It appeared the easiest thing to do at the time and no-one else was showing with anything better, after all.

In fairness, the demise of the Bohemian was not restricted our poor Republic, for Bohemians across the West were under pressure. The universal forces behind the death of the Bohemian ethic were best articulated by comedian Russell Brand, who warned in the *New Statesman* that we now live in a profit-driven world where even as 'individual interests are being met, we as a whole are being annihilated'. As Brand added that 'we have become prisoners of comfort in the absence of meaning', it appeared for a shining Shakespearean moment that the only person talking sense in this entire morass was the clown. Although he himself is a curious character, in his manifesto Brand appeared to be talking directly to an Irish electorate, many of whom didn't even have the comfort of comfort.

Sadly, as the country's citizens were being devastated, financially and psychologically, Paddy remained in quiet man mode. But Brand's observation that he could not vote for a system populated by 'frauds and liars' whose primary task was to perpetuate a system that is 'nothing more than a bureaucratic means for furthering the augmentation and advantages of economic elites' was increasingly relevant to the reality of life under Enda's so-called Democratic Revolution. And not everyone had bowed their neck to the new Puritanism. Enda and Michael Noonan might have been busy tickling the chins of Ireland's insiders while most of Labour stood idly by, but the death of the Democratic Revolution had left more outsiders than insiders in Ireland. As the culture of fear that had settled over the state after the bailout began to dissipate and Irish eyes began to turn very cold over what was being done to us, many started surreptitiously to agree with Brand.

In his insightful article, Brand cited a speech by Oliver Cromwell on the dissolution of the 1653 rump parliament that attacked the members of the British parliament as 'virtueless horses', noting that you would be hard-pressed to find someone who would be offended by a similar attack on today's government. Certainly when it came to the comfortable Coalition rumps loitering in Dáil Eireann to no apparent purpose, Paddy was swiftly entering 'Go, in the name of God, go' mode.

Brand's warning that apathy and rage were the only two possible reactions for voters to the mechanised indifference and inefficiency of politicians, the alleged servants of voters, began to feature mightily in Irish opinion polls. The similarities between Brand's approach and Paddy's did not end there either. Brand's belief that the solution to the current political and economic crisis requires 'a change that is beyond the narrow, prescriptive parameters of the current debate, outside the fortress of our current system' was becoming ever more relevant to Ireland's political and moral blockage. The problem, though, was that while we all dreamt about replacing 'old, dead ideas' and the 'luxury of tradition', it was pretty damn hard to engage in this process in a land where the Embalmed Radicals, Fianna Fáil, were the main opposition party. As a result, many Irish people simply turned their face from politics, while many of those who were of a mood for rage began to gather under the smiling teeth of Sinn Féin. Others, however, began to wonder if there was a better way to advocate for the needs of the people – outside the decaying political fortresses. And so strange phrases like 'movement of ideas' began to enter Irish political discourse, causing the jaws of pragmatists such as Cute Old Phil and Enda's familiar Paul Kehoe to drop.

One of the reasons that Paddy began to sniff around such queer fruit as ideas was the desolating impact of the principles of 'more for less' on the quality of life of our citizens. In a more civilised time, Greek philosopher Aristotle wisely noted that 'we work to have leisure, on which happiness depends'. By contrast, the heroic Irish evolved into an economy, as distinct to a society, in which leisure had become into the modern equivalent of 'impure thoughts'. We were not quite in Nazi Hermann Göring's 'Guns will make us powerful.

Butter will only make us fat' territory, but we were not too far removed either. The reality of life in post-Bohemian Ireland swiftly evolved into one in which carving out a career and maintaining a personal private life became incompatible goals under the constraints of neo-capitalism. Of course, as our Grumpy Old Men celebrated the ethic of 'more for less', they were oblivious to this. In fairness, how could they understand a strange new world where working mothers talk about sleep like a hungry man talks about food? These decades-long habitués of that strange land where the cheque comes in like clockwork on the hour every month could know nothing of the time-starved country their policies had generated, where mothers and fathers have no time to themselves and being overwhelmingly busy has become a benchmark for success. The cloistered nuns of Leinster House, living safe and separate from the real world, could know little too of the consequent death of intimacy where people are too busy for friends or dating or even sex. Initially, we were so terrified of seeming to be foraging for food in dustbins that we accepted all of these lifestyle changes. However, Paddy is not designed for long-term virtue. And five years into the war that had started in 2008, our voters were starting to look for a scapegoat for the death-march world of work they had found themselves in. It was an indication of how far away from reality our Grumpy Old Men had moved that they continued to be such enthusiasts for a 'more for less' world whose central principles were a denial of humanity that affected how we treated everyone, from our children to our ageing parents.

Significantly, by 2014 support for this austerity-driven 'more for less' ethic began to fade across Europe. Though poor Greece was re-colonised by the Germans, the French tossed out the fiscal compact with a uniquely Gallic disdain. On the level of the ordinary citizen, one of the more intriguing examples of the changing attitude to work was the move in France to ban work-related emails after 6 p.m.

This was entirely different to the world Enda was telling Paddy to celebrate. Significantly, the French 'obligation to disconnect' legislation was inspired by a similar movement in Germany, whose government, curiously, was not enthused by the prospect of applying the fiscal rod of iron it imposes so grimly on others to its own workers. Sense as well as sensibility applied to this type of thinking, for a glance at average working hours across Europe reveals more time spent at work does not lead to more productivity. The Greeks, for instance, clock an average of more than 2,000 work hours a year, the second highest in the OECD, but their productivity pales in comparison to the Germans, who spend a much more sensible 1,400 hours working every year, but with productivity about 70% higher than the Greeks.

So why, given the damage done to the lives of Irish citizens and the clear movement away from such thinking across Europe, is Enda such an enthusiast for the ethic of Singapore? It is not because he is a cruel man or a lover of human unhappiness, for he could not be a successful Irish politician if he was. The reason is simple. A leader such as Charlie Haughey would dismiss the concept handed down by Europe of Ireland as a new Singapore in a single disdainful sentence. Enda, though, courtesy of his Good Child Syndrome, is driven by a need to be noticed and praised by Angela and the other panjandrums of the *La Belle Dame Sans Merci* of austerity. Ironically, there was also a touch of Enda the school-teacher, taking pleasure in punishing the citizens for their mistakes. Ending the uncontrolled behaviour of the bad Irish was a key feature of the voodoo economics of European-driven Malthusian austerity. And bad Paddy had, after all, betrayed the Fine Gael-led sainted Rainbow in 1997. Now, having made our bed and romped in it with Fianna Fáil, Fine Gael were going to make us pay the price.

Inevitably, as Ireland's poor Bohemians were purged relentlessly, Enda's embrace of the ethic of Singapore heightened his separation from the voters. A psychologically damaged nation in need of nurturing found itself being permanently criticised by a cabal of prating Puritans who now dominated and cheapened public discourse in Irish life to such an extent a row about the quality of toilet paper used by a Junior Minister could capture media attention for several months. Nothing epitomised this new cheapness more than the furore over Fianna Fáil TD Niall Collins, who was almost destroyed by the censorious press when he wrote a letter seeking clemency for a drug dealer whose four children faced being taken into care if he was jailed. Mr Collins said he wrote the letter out of compassion and the political and media system turned on him. Mr Collins apologised for his act of compassion and promised not to do it again. Some might think we surely are a sad and cheap little country when politicians cannot engage in acts of kindness lest the censor's office of ethics cuts off their head. That, alas, is what happens when you erase the Bohemian spirit from a country.

But our new Puritan rulers overlooked one small point. When you attempt to completely exorcise a country of its Bohemian spirit, you create an unhappy country. And the bad news for Dear Leader Enda is that unhappy countries tend to dislike their governments intensely.

CHAPTER 11

THE TROIKA ZOO-KEEPERS AND THE IRISH COLONIAL GENE

The Coalition Cartel bungles the Troika exit

2014 was probably the strangest year Irish politics had experienced since Haughey's GUBU year in 1982. For those fortunate enough to be too young to remember, 'GUBU' is an acronym of a Haughey statement on the discovery of a double-murderer hiding out in the Attorney General's flat: Grotesque, Unbelievable, Bizarre and Unprecedented. In fact, such was the madness of the Haughey era, that day was pretty normal. The grotesquery that littered the political landscape of 2014 was somewhat more prosaic, but it was reminiscent of the GUBU era's sense of sinister weirdness crossed with high farce.

The descent into GUBU-esque madness in 2014 was all the stranger given that 2014 should have been dominated by our great escape from Troika bondage. It is rare for Irish politicians, particularly of the Grumpy variant, to adopt the Christmas spirit. But by 2014 the Grumpy Old Men were looking forwards to the Troika exit in the manner of a child looking up the chimney anticipating the arrival of Santa Claus. The political sky was still cloudy, but chinks of light were beginning to peek through for our Grumpy Old Men. The dream that the Troika's exit would finally allow Ireland to live like a normal country had been the sole grappling hook that sustained its citizens in our fall off the cliff. Now that sacramental point was approaching and the Coalition Cartel were the boys ready to take the credit.

The longing across the country and the Cartel was entirely understandable. Everyone still obsesses about the bailout, but it's possible to argue that politics and life as normal had actually disappeared some two years earlier than 2008, when the slow-motion tribunal-led destruction of Bertie Ahern began. That soap-opera fatally diverted the attention of our Taoiseach, his government and even the citizens from the fiscal tsunami roaring its way towards us. We would all too swiftly find out that although Bertie's fall initially seemed reminiscent of an Irish re-telling of *Macbeth*, it was in fact a light comedy of manners when compared to the Jacobean darkness of the court of Cowen. That period from 2008 certainly marked the end of even the illusion of 'normal' politics as Ireland experienced the deepest banking crisis in Europe, the destruction of our domestic economy, a mortgage arrears crisis, the return of wide-scale generational unemployment and the surrender of our hard-fought Independence like a state defeated in war. Having basked, somewhat immodestly, during the Celtic Tiger years in our status as the designated European role model, Paddy woke up one morning to the somewhat shocking revelation that he was living in a rogue state, still unsure exactly what he personally had done wrong. He then received the even worse news that our new foreign masters were intent on putting manners on Paddy as part of the process of sorting Ireland out.

For our Coalition, whose political ambitions shrivelled from the moment they took office, a return to the normality of the good old days of prior to 2008 became the apex of its political objective. This position was understandable. Oppositions generally tend to exaggerate the economic woes of the country in the hope that the situation will only be half as bad as their dire prophecies when they enter government buildings. On this occasion, much to their shock, our new Coalition found the situation was actually twice as bad as their exaggerated predictions. Then, after a half-decade of bailout-induced travail and terror, what looked like a return of 'politics as normal' appeared to come out of nowhere. The first signs occurred when, just prior to the exit from the bailout, Micheál Martin began a daily fatwa on Enda Kenny over the somewhat prosaic matter of medical cards. As Enda limbo-danced his way around the issue, suddenly we were assailed by the strangest feeling of *déjà vu*, for it was as almost like we were back in 2003 or 2004. Though it was nice to think we might finally move on from the era in which the middle classes genuinely wondered would they have to start foraging for food in dustbins, there was one unnerving element to it all. Once again, the relevance of Orwell's *Animal Farm* to Irish politics was clear. In the medical cards debate, Micheál Martin was playing the role of 2003-era Enda Kenny and Enda was doing a more than passable imitation of Bertie Ahern.

Still, few complained when we returned to the land of normal to such an extent that great, carefully crafted, unread national economic plans telling us what the state will be like in 2020 returned to fashion. Some nabobs of negativity pointed out that the similarities to the world of 2003 and 2004 were less positive, as an unloved government, in negative equity with its citizens when it came to the promises and delivery ledger, toyed with an opposition that, like the opposition in Bertie's heyday, lacked an ounce of political credibility. But as we slept gently through the publication of the Coalition's *Song for Ireland*, or whatever their new economic plan was called, the majority of us were grateful for the return to the old politics of schools and hospitals and a break from the last six years during which Ireland resembled Pompeii on a bad day.

Of course, the question nobody asked was whether politics as normal, or, to put it more accurately, politics as normal *a la mode Irlandais*, was as good a thing as we thought it would be. In theory, a still supplicant Paddy associated politics as normal with the civilised way that Nordic countries conduct their affairs. These are curious places where budgets balance, roads and public transport are efficient and even the health service works. Sadly, there was one fatal flaw in Paddy's cuckolded thought process. Politics as normal in Ireland is not efficient and civilised. It is, instead, characterised by witlessness and fecklessness, accompanied by the occasional apologetic clean-up. Politics here has always been a tale of insider-trading for beef barons, public sector trade unions and billionaires, of booms and busts, of disjointed rather than joined-up government, of terrorism and clericalist excesses, of soap-operatic political rises and falls and consequent tribunals. It is governance *a la* Italy and Greece, rather than Berlin or Rotterdam.

Sadly, the attempt by the Coalition to carve out a new political era starting in 2014 – that would be exactly like the old one, with the small exception of Fine Gael rather than Fianna Fáil being in charge – was murdered by the fates before it ever got off the ground. It all started when the exploits of Bertie's litter in the Central Remedial Clinic came to light. The evidence the PAC uncovered, that charitable donations to the organisation for sick children had

evolved into what Fine Gael TD Kieran O'Donnell called 'a slush
fund' for Bertie's cronies, was stunning. It left a citizenry, shocked
to their boots by the debacle, asking whether, after all of the strife
and national trauma since 2008, anything had changed or, worse
still, been learnt. True, it was theoretically a legacy issue. But the
legacy had stayed pretty lively during the Coalition era until the PAC
had started lifting stones. Indeed, its ongoing vibrancy was captured
by a comment by a CRC witness, which suggested few lessons have
been absorbed by the slow-learners of our non-political governing
classes, when they noted that their organisation was 'swinging
around into compliance'.

It should be noted that the witness's sentiment was not infused
with any sense of fear, drama or great haste. Instead, compliance
with the law was still being presented as a matter of choice rather
than necessity. In fairness to the CRC, although the allegations and
concerns surrounding it were spicy, even by Irish standards, it was
only one of hundreds of very odd-looking earwigs crawling out
from beneath the freshly over-turned stones. As Rehab scuttled out,
it and the CRC were merely emblematic of the far more widespread
malaise of self-entitlement that had ravaged the public and private
spheres of Irish life until a Republic, whose capacity to stand
independently was hollowed out by venality, had to seek the aid of
a Troika protectorate.

There was no shortage of fury about the CRC and Rehab. But
there was something key missing from the fury – what were the
democratic revolutionaries doing about this? And the answer was
'nothing'. In the most poignant example of political scapegoating
since the Kaiser sacked Bismarck, the Coalition did force Frank
Flannery to walk the plank. Brendan Howlin busily put through
an innocuous bill on lobbyists that was gently drowned by our
mandarins. But essentially, once the furore ended, political life
continued as before.

But this time, people were becoming, after their brief bout of acquiescence, increasingly stirred up. The economist J.K. Galbraith once fulminated against the evils of private wealth and public squalor. By 2014 we had somehow arrived at an Ireland in which, despite all our sacrifices of the previous years, the two had combined in some unholy union. Private wealth was accompanied by moral corruption, while public squalor was, for some at least, funded by vast tranches of taxpayer-funded wealth. In terms of public cynicism and private self-doubt, the country was at the edge of a critical tipping point.

Logic mingled with a large draft of optimism fights against the claim that we are naturally immoral; to say the Irish character is innately bad is to take as foolish a view of ourselves as the 19th-century *Mr Punch* advocates of the doctrines of phrenology. The interest, for example, of foreign multi-national businesses to hire and invest in Irish workers indicates the Irish character is not utterly dysfunctional. But when Paddy is left in charge of himself, something always goes wrong and it appears to always go wrong at the top. Obviously, the problems at the top are facilitated by the voters, given our ongoing taste for engaging in acts of electoral collusion with this culture. But it is not entirely our fault, for when it comes to seeing alternatives to our familiars and rogues, the Irish citizens are like the half-blind inhabitants of Plato's cave: they can't see beyond the flickering shadows on the wall to the sun waiting outside.

It does not help that whenever we do try to govern ourselves better, the hissing serpent of the Irish colonial gene eternally returns to bite us in the heel. This complaint is dismissed by some on the grounds that the British have, in fairness, been gone for almost a century. But, as the controversy over the 1916 anniversary shows, when it comes to state-building, a century is the equivalent of one swim by a goldfish around its bowl. And we should remember that one of the features of all cases of abuse is that, even when the victim recovers on the surface, scars will eternally lurk below. This is as true for states as for humans. One of the long-term effects of all forms of colonial rule is a fundamental unruly disrespect for a state, which rarely, given its status as a plaything for insiders, deserves respect anyway. In Ireland's case, this disrespect is burned into the national DNA and, while the virus can sometimes be suppressed, it is always ready to rise again. This disrespect is, alas, not a victimless frolic – as we found to our cost. Instead, like gambling or cocaine, although you may escape for a while, in the long run some variant of bankruptcy will arrive in a state where there is neither regulation nor compliance.

This essential truth meant the Democratic Revolution was more than a mere moral frolic. Paddy, if he was to be sure he would never end up clinging on to a spar during a typhoon, as had happened in 2008, needed to fundamentally reform how Ireland did things. The fiascos in the CRC and Rehab that were unveiled at the start of 2014, and the apparent inability of our politicians to fire a more venomous form of grapeshot at them than mere rhetoric, suggested we were as far away as ever from dealing with the consequences of our post-colonial gene deficits. This set the mood of the New Year's political discourse in stone, which meant the VE-style celebrations planned for the end of the bailout had to be put on hold. Our Coalition Cartel were undoubtedly less than impressed by the irony that it was the successors rather than the progenitors of the crisis who were reaping the blighted harvest of the moral squander-mania of the Haughey and Ahern eras. Indeed they were quite vocal on the matter of this unfairness, but the tone for 2014 was set and the vigorously protesting sheep of the Coalition were condemned to a spring, summer, autumn and winter of discontent.

Of course, instead of engaging in acts of self-pity or trying their own blander hand at some Haughey-style messing, the Coalition should have used this as a catalyst for rediscovering the reforming impulse they had mislaid. Instead, politics as normal *a la mode Irlandais* made a triumphant return. If the Coalition was not insulting Garda whistle-blowers, then they were indulging in a slew of all-too-typical Coalition-made disasters. The Bourbon delights of Irish Water, where a bonus culture emerged before the company was even formed, suggested Irish politicians had been getting back to their old tricks while the Troika occupation was ongoing. Once the Troika were gone, the boys – or, more accurately, the consultants – certainly raced back into town. While it was not the only example, Irish Water was the most colourful case study of the return of the unique Bertie Ahern variant of economics, in which the worst features of state socialism and unrestricted capitalism combine to create a series of economic gargoyles that need not fear anything, since the taxpayer stands by to sort out the latest bill. More than a slight air of the politics of the electronic voting machines era also surrounded the set-up of Irish Water, in which ministers were happy to note they were far too busy to engage in such menial tasks as actually managing their departments. That, they claimed, was a job for mere civil servants.

The unexpected sequence of events in 2014 ratcheted the already elevated self-pity levels of the Coalition to new levels. Our unloved Coalition Cartel had, like Yeats's parsimonious shopkeeper in 'September 1913', prayed and slaved and bowed. Romantic and Bohemian Ireland had indeed withered away while our Grumpy Old shopkeepers had added the half-billion to billion in cuts and prayer to shivering prayer to the distant gods of austerity. Our fiscal shopkeepers had circumspectly evaded the delirium of the brave Greeks. They had instead, like Vichy France's Marshal Petain, appeased and acquiesced to the ECB, the banks and the bondholders until, having shivered under the somewhat sanguine oppression of the Troika for three years, the moment of deliverance arrived. Then, instead of seeing the departure celebrated in a similar manner to when the British left Beggars Buoh in 1922, the Grumpy Old Men found themselves experiencing the political equivalent of being pelted with fruit and vegetables.

As Enda's dream of becoming a new Michael Collins failed to thrive, disappointment on the reform front was written in the stars. Our national vice of irresponsibility, willed to us by our former colonial overlords, means that attempts by Irish politicians at being fiscally disciplined or trying to reform the way Ireland is governed for the better are a bit like an Irishman going off the drink for Lent. For a time, the task is embarked upon with great enthusiasm. There is excited talk about how much newer and fresher he feels. He is more efficient at work, goes for a jog every morning and now appreciates his wife and teenage children better. The mantra now is quality time *en famille* rather than bar-stool time. And, for a while at least, it works. Then suddenly the colonial gene bites and the Irishman wakes up from his swoon-like state of efficiency. What follows generally resembles the scene in 'Father Ted' in which Jack, after an extended period of sobriety, wakes up fully, wails 'Priests! Don't tell me I'm still on that feckin' island!' and immediately seeks the succour that only copious amounts of whiskey can grant. The problem with our Grumpy Old Men was that they didn't even go off the jar before they collectively fell off the reform wagon.

It did not help the reform front that, after the Troika fled, the Grumpy Old Men swiftly turned into a human version of the chimpanzees' tea parties that used to take place in the zoo prior to the arrival of animal rights activists. You might think this was not a bad thing, for in the old days everyone used to love the chimpanzee's tea party – or rather they loved the moment when, after the zoo-keepers left, the chimpanzees got to be in charge of the event. You see, while the keepers were in the cage, some degree of decorum had to be maintained by the chimps. And often for a brief time, even after the zoo-keepers left, the chimps would continue to behave in a mannerly fashion. But ultimately, as the excited watching children knew, nature will out, one of the chimps would throw a Victoria sponge at another chimp and before you knew it, the crockery would be scattered and cucumber sandwiches would fly through the air as the children cheered delightedly.

It should be noted that amidst the flying saucers, cakes, the animated gibbering and sneaky bitings, some good chimps – the Richard Brutons and Brendan Howlins of the ape world – would bravely attempt to continue to behave like civilised humans. But ultimately there was no point in their attempts, for the good monkeys sipping their tea in a refined manner from the fine china would be ignored or, worse still, the pack, irritated by their difference, would turn upon them. Those of us watching the great zoo of Irish politics know that only a few chromosomes separate the simian from the human. For three years under the terrible yoke of the Troika zoo-keepers, the Irish political monkeys, helped by the total banishment of those misbehaving Fianna Fáil apes, had been moderately good. Fiscal discipline of a sort was upheld and great plans for reform were designed and progressed. Like the trains on Percy French's West Clare railway, few reached their destination on time or in an entirely unscathed condition, but our approving European zoo-keepers applauded the newly disciplined nature of the Irish and there was always tomorrow to iron out the many surviving difficulties.

Then as the Coalition monkeys' good behaviour stretched into a third year, something fundamental changed in the Troika zoo-keepers' attitude. Suddenly the optimism which had inspired the Troika's positive sentiments about Ireland's good behaviour and prospects for recovery began to decline. They still urged reform upon Ireland but a sort of elegiac tone began to enter the discourse. It was as though – shock, horror – the Troika no longer believed their exhortations and instead were merely urging the Coalition to behave themselves in order to convince the outside world that this time Ireland really had changed. Astonishingly, given the prostrate position we had been in when the Troika arrived, Paddy had actually won. As with their invader predecessors, the Troika feared they were in real danger of becoming more Irish than the state they had come to reform.

In fairness, for a brief period of time after the Troika raced out the door shouting 'don't call us, just don't', the simulacrum of a state intent on modest reform was maintained. However, like the chimpanzees and their tea party, the disappearance of the zoo-keepers meant we were sure and certain to go off the rails. The good political monkeys, particularly in Labour, tried to maintain a smidgen of order. But amidst the screeching of Shatter, the plotting of Cute Old Phil, the fooling around of Enda and the sight of that old political silverback James Reilly thumping his chest over universal health insurance, those who wished to maintain some sanity in Irish discourse increasingly resembled the H.Dip teacher who has to contend with roaring, shouts and flying rubbers being thrown at the blackboard.

Over the course of 2014, as the first dangerous symptoms of pre-election tension began to manifest themselves, the merry political riot became ever more confused. Originally some semblance of order had been maintained in the chimpanzees' cage, with the cake-throwing only between government and opposition benches. However, by the middle of the year, the Fine Gael and Labour tribes had begun to turn upon each other, as Fine Gael tried to maintain its position as Fianna Fáil-Lite and Labour strove to avoid becoming the new Green Party. Worse still, the tribes, particularly the Fine Gael one, started to turn on each other, which inevitably confused matters even further.

Outside of the media, the happiest onlookers were the Troika who, having arrived roaring like lions, left in the manner of lambs.

The contentedness with which they left did beg some intriguing questions. In retrospect, people began to note that, although we had talked a great deal about what we thought of the Troika, we had never asked the Troika what they thought of Paddy. The Troika, and the politicians who dealt with them, certainly hadn't offered any views beyond the usual verbal coleslaw about the heroically stoical Irish. But the great speed with which they left, anxiously saying 'don't call us', suggests their view of us was not at all so complimentary.

It should be noted in passing that they have of course banned chimpanzees' tea parties in the zoo on the basis that, whatever about fighting, cake is harmful to monkeys. It's just a pity that it is apparently impossible to do the same when it comes to Irish politics. It looks as if the chimpanzees' tea party will continue to be the prevailing method of politics in Ireland, and we won't have the Troika zoo-keepers to regulate the next batch when the current group of chimps scamper off to their retirement pens.

Home rule for our monkeys did not advance the prospects of the Democratic Revolution. Instead, such was the level of chaos that followed once we got a run at governing ourselves again that it is hard to know just how many times the Democratic Revolution died. Some will highlight Pat Rabbitte's 'promises' moment, when he admitted on national television that election promises are made to be broken. To be fair to Pat, he didn't actually saying what everyone immediately blamed him for – not that this mattered too much. But he got too close to the nub of things for comfort.

Instead, it is more likely that future historians will, if history is not by then illegal, note the Democratic Revolution's death date as when Micheál Martin, late in 2014, asked why retired public sector mandarins, already bejewelled with generous state pensions, were being re-hired by Irish Water. Mr Kenny appeared almost genuinely indignant as he scolded Martin for his temerity in not realising that 'for many years a system has applied there – are we to change it now?' At the risk of being accused of sounding smart, we do dimly remember a time where the entire purpose of Mr Kenny was to do just that.

When it comes to reform, the Coalition parties will inevitably try to resurrect their dusty old bag of froth and feathers in time for the next election. However, Paddy should not believe anything beyond the stark reality that the Democratic Revolution is as bereft of life as Monty Python's parrot. Once, the Coalition might have been brave Don Quixotes mounted on donkeys. But by the end of 2014, it was clear that release from Troika penal servitude had allowed our former secret society of developers, mandarins and insiders, whose dominant ethos consists of silence, cunning and non-disclosure, to creep right back into the heart of government buildings. And while the trade union anti-social partners were not quite back in the parlour of government buildings, you could be assured that if a party is just about to start, those fellows won't be shy about inviting themselves in, even if they haven't got a bottle to bring to it.

In a sense, we should not be too hard on Paddy or the Coalition Cartel. When it came to their imitation of the chimpanzees' tea party, the seeds of their defeat were sown by the Irish colonial gene. It would have been better, of course, if we had actually tried to break out of our old way of doing things. That, however, would have required the political sophistication of leader such as Obama and our poor political monkeys were simply not in that league.

CHAPTER 12

GRUMPY OLD MEN ON THE ROPES

The Shatter Shark Theory greases the political slide

y the midpoint of 2014, the Grumpy Old Men had more things than the Democratic Revolution to worry about – or rather the absence of the aforementioned revolution had given them plenty of things to worry about. The Irish electorate were in Eamon Dunphy 'betrayed, traduced and betrayed utterly' mode. And when we reach that special sacramental place of self-pity, casualties are inevitable. The strange thing was that the Grumpy Old Men began to drop off in the manner of an Agatha Christie novel even before the electorate had entered Dunphy mode. The template for these departures was set by Mr Shatter. Given the mess that preceded it, we thought this would be a thing of blood and death where the skies would darken with cawing rooks and our man would strap himself to a rock like Cú Chulainn. Instead, the terrible Mr Shatter was bundled out of office rather in the manner that a good bouncer clears a sleeping drunk out of a pub, so efficiently he is outside the door knocking to be let back in by the time he wakes up. Ever since Mr Shatter lost his cabinet seat, he has been trying to find his way back in to the Dáil and suffering the same fate as one of Haughey's senators, who got so confused during a berating that he could not distinguish the door from the wood panelling in Haughey's office. Eventually, the infuriated Haughey told the fool to 'leap out through the fucking window', which, in a way, was what happened to Mr Shatter – though in a much more polite fashion, of course.

Shatter's prolonged fall introduced us to many political concepts, but the most important one for the future health of the Grumpy Old Men was the Shark Theory of politics. One of the more unwise habits of politicians is their tendency, when in trouble, to throw a human sacrifice to the sharks in the media and the opposition in the hope that this might distract them. The problem with this theory is that far from clearing the sharks away, it often causes even more of them gather in the expectation that this is a handy spot for grub. This was certainly the case with Mr Shatter as the sharks were fed first with the portly morsel of Oliver Connolly (if you can't remember, don't worry: not important), then a Garda Commissioner (quite important) and finally, as ever more sharks gathered around the Coalition boat, Minister Shatter himself. And though Mr Shatter, unsurprisingly, didn't taste so good, this didn't deter the sharks from hanging around, hoping that after a grilling by Justice Fennelly at the Commission of Inquiry, the far more attractive morsel of Enda himself might be next.

In truth, Mr Shatter, for all of his subsequent bleating, colluded in his own fall. It was bad enough that, at a time when the government needed to be making friends, it had a Minister for Justice who was capable of starting a riot at a Buddhist convention. But from the moment the extraordinary GSOC and whistle-blower crises broke, the minister resembled the sort of fellow who tries to kill a snake with one blow to the head and misses. The inevitable denouement to such an act is more flailing blows at the hissing creature, yelps pain when the snake manages to sink its fangs into any poor beleaguered soul hanging around and other unhappy results.

The tale of Shatter's fall was interesting beyond his own undulating agony, for it was also a morality play in which the future fate of our Grumpy Old Men was written in large capital letters, had they but the political eyesight to see it. The story of Shatter was, after all, a turbulent drama that began with the small fault-line of a couple of minor whistle-blowers kicking up. A generous inclusive response would have killed this particular problem stone-dead. Instead, in contravention of every principle the Taoiseach had sworn to uphold when he was in the mood to celebrate brighter colours, those who had dared to speak out were trashed publicly and privately. As what should have been a short story evolved into the political equivalent of *War and Peace,* incorporating contempt for the ordinary citizen and the defence of insider elites, it did not help that Alan was the sort of political hysteric who was utterly shorn of the capacity for empathy.

It helped even less that Mr Shatter was merely a more florid variation of the Grumpy Old Men of the Coalition. Mr Shatter might, supported by the apparent belief of his political cheerleaders that he was a cross between Christ, Socrates and Voltaire, have been somewhat more egotistical than his colleagues. However, he was only the noisiest orchid amongst a bunch of political flowers who had no small regard for their abilities, even if proof of their greatness was rather hard to find. It also helped Mr Shatter that he was special to Enda. In the mindset of Mr Kenny, having clever people hanging around him proves, contrary to all other assertions, that the Taoiseach is not a dunce. It would have been great if Mr Shatter were in fact the intellectual Enda believed him to be, for such creatures are a sufficiently rare breed in Irish cabinets to merit some form of special defence. However, the evidence that Mr Shatter was some sort of peculiar genius was, on closer inspection, remarkably thin. The unloved minister was certainly very clever when set against the context of the slack-jawed turnip wing of Fine Gael's backbench deputies or in his legal career soothing the feelings of trophy wives and securing vast settlements when South Co. Dublin husbands were caught with their trousers skimming their ankles. But could it be the case that, as they so often do, our Fine Gael yokels were confusing the capacity to insult people with intelligence? If the art of politics is about being offensive and creating an enemy a day, Mr Shatter was a political genius. However, the really successful politician needs to do more, to be able to strategise, to bring the people and their own Departments with them and to win the support of the public for their reform agenda.

One example of the political ham-fistedness of Enda's *petite-general* was his sinking of the central plank of the government's key, though now discarded, strategy for Oireachtas reform, namely the Dáil Inquiries referendum. And though Mr Shatter did manage to get the referendum on judicial pay through, it accelerated a collapse in relations between the judges and the executive that was only rescued by the intervention of sensible people like Chief Justice Susan Denham. A closer measure of his capacity was his ill-fated Insolvency Bill, which turned into the political equivalent of Zanzibar's declaration of war on the British Empire, which lasted for some forty minutes before a shell blew up the Zanzibar navy – a single sailing yacht.

As a cavalcade of troubles piled on Mr Shatter's head, there was another reason for Mr Kenny's reluctance to dispose of such a lightning rod for trouble. His problem was a simple one. When it came to Alan Shatter, the Taoiseach and the Coalition were like those who bought Anglo Irish shares in 2007. Mr Kenny, Mr Gilmore and the rest of the cabinet had invested so much of their political credit in Mr Shatter that, even as his political share value was going through the floor, cutting their losses immediately appeared too high a price. Sadly, like the poor old Anglo punters, in the end they had to cut Alan free and lose the political pot anyway; in all these affairs, no matter what you do, at some point the bell in the political stock-market rings and the chits are called in.

The fall of the house of Shatter wasn't entirely Alan Shatter's fault, but enough of it was to make his position untenable. By the close of the affair, the cruel truth was that, for all the talk of the scales of justice, everyone had suffered too much and nobody cared enough to grant our fallen hero justice. And though Alan went easily enough in the end, the lesson that everyone, including the cleverest man in the world, is disposable should have sent more than a few shivers across the spines of our Grumpy Old Men. They were also running low on credit, for although Mr Shatter did not bring any others overboard with him, his misadventures destabilised the foundations of the Coalition and the Grumpy Old Men's political longevity in the profoundest of fashions.

Mr Kenny's tribal 'might is right' approach to the sordid affair certainly did his party of democratic revolutionaries little good. The Taoiseach may have equivocated all he wanted, but when it came to the Shatter trouble, Paddy was not at all impressed. It certainly didn't look like the bright new politics shining with the innocence of a child's eyes promised by the Democratic Revolution. Worse still, that very small part of the Irish tribe known as the Fine Gael core voter – the Spartans of Fine Gael, if you like – who actually don't want the party to resemble Fianna Fáil-Lite, were appalled by the spectacle of Garda Commissioners resigning in mysterious circumstances after night-time meetings. That was the sort of thing they associated with Fianna Fáil. This meant that although the Fine Gael Spartans did not vote for any other parties in the local and European elections in 2014, they did walk away from the party in a sufficient numbers to seriously wound it. Labour's refusal to utter a censorious comment, even after Fine Gael's Leo Varadkar did the spadework for them, meant they suffered plenty of collateral damage too. Inevitably, Labour defended its timorous stance on the basis of that any intervention was precluded by their colonial powers-style carve-up whereby Enda deals with erring Fine Gael ministers and Eamon confines his zone of influence to erring Labour ministers. But tart comparisons were quickly made over the ease with which Mr Gilmore surrendered the head of his difficult political child, Róisín, and Labour's willingness to take a back seat on the Shatter affair and so give up any high moral ground they might have held.

In fairness, Labour's strategy is certainly one that facilitates the quiet life, and the last thing the Grumpy Old Men needed was a series of Dick Spring-style controversies over the antics of the exponentially increasing stumble-bum Fine Gael wing of the cabinet. But we had travelled a long way from 'Gilmore for Taoiseach' country when a Labour leader could stand witlessly by while ducks and drakes were made of whistle-blowers and the Justice department to facilitate a Fine Gael Taoiseach's political pet. Significantly, as Alan was finally plucked from ministerial office in a similar manner to the cruel magpie picking the chick out of its nest, the sting of the Coalition's defeat was heightened by the name and nature of the victors. The Independent trio of Clare Daly, Mick Wallace and Luke 'Ming' Flanagan were the big winners for it was this maligned group who brought the whistle-blowers to light. It represented a stark exegesis on the vast carelessness of our collective governing class that three disparaged TDs, in some cases with good reason, were needed to lift the carpet covering how we are policed and, in spite of highly questionable assaults on their character, reveal the maggots crawling below. It was certainly something Paddy took note of and stored until he got his chance at the ballot box.

Ming was to have his own form of revenge when he declared his candidacy for Europe in 2014. The Fine Gael rooks, of course, cawed more loudly than usual at the very notion of Ming the MEP. The problem, though, was that the electorate began to think very carefully over what should be the defining issue of the 2014 election. The bad news for Enda was that they had decided this should consist of electing the candidate who would give Dear Leader Enda the biggest boot in the bollix with their election. Chasteningly for Enda, this was a fellow with long hair – and sometimes, worse still, a pony tail – who, in Dame Enda's view, had never worked a day in his life, who came into the Dáil chamber without a suit and instead wore an Oscar the Grouch T-shirt and who smoked drugs. 'That's the man for us,' said an electorate who were in the mood to give their Taoiseach, who now greeted them by running away, a going-over with a chainsaw rather than a mere slap on the wrist. Really, you could only compliment them on their prescience.

The departure of Shatter, that wasp wrapped in a snarl, brought other, more complex matters to mind. Light-touch regulation, in the public mind, was a concept exclusively connected with our banks. In fact, whether it is the church and child abuse, political ethics, building controls, the environment, the medical profession or the Gardaí, light-touch regulation has been an endemic feature of Irish governance. Sadly, the consequences of the Irish love affair with this unfortunate concept proves the truth of Dwight D. Eisenhower's warning that institutions that are not regularly examined deteriorate swiftly. The Gardaí have, in fairness, been regularly examined by a plethora of inquiries, which have on far too many occasions painted a portrait of a force that has degenerated, in certain areas, into a form of unarmed militia dominated by a culture of 'blue silence' and 'negligent oversight'. The problem is that these examinations, with the brief exception of those during the reign of Michael McDowell, have too rarely been followed by action – well, for those examined at least. At least the often too easily disparaged Mr McDowell tried. By contrast, our democratic revolutionaries' attempt at remedying light-touch regulation consisted of Mr Shatter's fatal embrace with Garda Commissioner Callinan.

It was a strange and poignant sort of affair really. Four decades ago, when he first entered the Dáil, Mr Shatter might have been a radical Young Turk. But by the time he came to power, our pension-approaching Justice Minister was fatally detached from the much-changed country that had elected him. He looked and sounded fit more for some 19th-century parliament than the present-day Irish one. The sinister news for the rest of our Grumpy Old Men was that he was hardly alone in that regard. This meant that even as the sharks spat the last gristly bits of Mr Shatter out and turned their noses hopefully up towards the trembling remnants of the Good Ship Coalition, the troubles of the Grumpy Old Men were far from being over.

Were the Grumpy Old Men wiser, or had they had at least recognised the Shark Theory of politics, they might have mended their ways fairly swiftly. Needless to say, of course, they did neither. And as 2013 progressed, we barely had time to bid farewell to each tumbling Coalition domino, for just as one Grumpy Old Man fell overboard, the next one seemed ready to topple. When it came to the stark decline of the Grumpy Old Men, one of its curiosities was how swiftly Pat Rabbitte became the next problem child. One of the strange things in Irish politics is that just as a politician reaches their Holy Grail, suddenly things begin to go wrong. In a real sense, Rabbitte embodied the Labour dilemma. It is not that he had performed badly in government. Instead, Pat's big problem was that his presence didn't appear to have made that much of a difference.

Put simply, Pat looked too comfortable being there – or, to put it another way, he looked as if he had been there for twenty years. That should not have been as much of a surprise as it appeared to be. Part of the quiet brilliance of our political system, as devised by our mandarins and as Sinn Féin Nua may yet find, is that it excises all radicalism from those who reach its summit. Some, of course, are never very radical to begin with, but Labour's revolutionary student leader turned Democratic Left founder always had a radical streak. Then slowly the system began to suck Pat in, to such an extent he became leader of the Labour Party. In a strange way, being leader of Labour almost appeared to disappoint him. Were he still in charge of a small radical party such as the Democratic Left or, better still, Sinn Féin the Workers Party, his radical and often venomous streak might have been given free rein. But when you are leading Labour, you have to draw your teeth and drain your spirit by being pleasant to putative Coalition partners such as Enda Kenny.

The most dangerous thing that happened to Pat was that he started to become a national institution. Nothing epitomised this more than the caricature of Pat in Doheny and Nesbitts. The location was significant, for no-one who is a threat to the establishment sips there. It is where insiders go to imbibe. Worse still, Pat became a wag and there is no safer creature in Dáil politics than a wit. Slowly, the system took over as Pat sipped pints with Michael Noonan and made nice with Cute Old Phil Hogan in the Dáil chambers. All this meant for Pat was that when times of political trouble arrived and the pantomime needed someone to boo, the establishment had done so good a job of appropriating him that he was the public's favourite target.

Some of the Grumpy Old Men fell as gently as Newton's apple. Ruairi Quinn was one of these. The Minister for Education would have liked two more years. But after five decades in power, even Ruairi had to confess he had a long innings. Even with the best will in the world, a man whose political formation began with the student revolutions against Second World War French leader Charles de Gaulle in 1968 was not exactly representative of modern Ireland.

Others such as James Reilly survived in body but not in spirit. Reilly had always been a curious sort of political macaw, mixing guileless radicalism with a strong man ethic of 'my way or the high way'. Ironically, his very political eccentricity was why he was a source of hope, for normal politicians had not managed to deal too well with the grand vizier's court of the HSE. Ultimately, the curia of the HSE proved too strong for James. The minister could fume and pontificate all he wanted, for the mandarins simply listened and smiled and waited until his brave ideas left the minister's office, before guiding each one down a variety of obscure corridors to strangle them.

In the end, it was not so much the ongoing implosion of the HSE that did for James. Instead, the time-bomb, loudly ticking like the crocodile's clock in *Peter Pan*, was the issue of universal health insurance. It represented a classic case study of the difference between what politicians say and what people hear. During the election, Irish voters thought UHI meant that they could stop paying health insurance and get their operations for free. Sadly, the plan as rolled out actually consisted of compulsory, and more expensive, health insurance for everyone with no additional benefits at all. Indeed, it meant that middle-class Paddy would now have to wait in the queue behind unemployed Paddy, unemployed Patricia and their ten feral unemployable children who, of course, weren't paying anything at all to get in first.

The culture of 'more for less' had reached its great apotheosis.

If the accident-prone Reilly had retained a millimetre of political credibility, he might still have been able to sell this firewater. But Reilly had ruined his last china shop. Even Labour would not swallow the political flies that Reilly was trotting out over UHI. In a display of his commitment to the children of Ireland, Enda shoved Reilly into the Department for Children, which immediately relegated its status to somewhere below Arts and Culture.

In the end, Gilmore would go too. The most curious feature of his departure was that it so closely followed the pattern set by Mr

Shatter. The prophecies about how the end of Mr Gilmore would be managed were dark. There was hopeful talk of blood and fire and old Sinn Féin the Workers Party men gathering like Spartans in Thermopylae to bleed the soft Labour boys dry. As Labour blood started to seep into the carpet even before the votes were tallied in the 2014 elections, political junkies were transfixed by the hope of that a good cleansing bloodletting would happen as a result. Instead, in public at least, Gilmore's departure was so civilised that there wasn't a coup, let alone a *coup d'état*. The original plan of Labour's ageing Student Princes might have been to tear down the walls of the city, or rather the party, to prevent 'that woman' from occupying the boss's chair. The problem, alas, with the designated champion of the *ancien regime*, Alex White, was that his support did not appear travel beyond the gates of Leinster House. Some, indeed, suggested it struggled to even reach that far. Mr Gilmore fell away from power in a manner similar to meat falling off the bone, and Alex White was defeated by Joan. In the end, it wasn't even that the Tánaiste attracted hatred or anger. It was, instead, just the chilling disinterest those who are young reserve for the opinions of those elderly ones who know nothing of their world but still insist in intruding on it. On his departure, Mr Gilmore simply said, 'the renewal of the party needs a new voice at the microphone'. Strange to say and poignant as the sentiment was, it was one of his finest moments in government. The Invisible Man had realised what he was.

In retrospect, now that they are gone and we have new ministers to hate, the fate of our Grumpy Old Men induces sensations of pity and not a little guilt. Exiled unfairly before their time in 1997, they were past their prime when suddenly they were sucked into office by the great Fianna Fáil vacuum, which meant they almost had no alternative but to leap. In fairness, although their chain-mail was rusty and their swords wooden, they were willing, even though the invitation was to lead the country further into austerity hell. Fianna

Fáil, by contrast, simply rested and tended to their self-inflicted wounds, groaning at the indignity of it all, while a non-sympathetic Sinn Féin simply licked their feral lips. But before pity gets too fierce a grip on us, it should be noted that no-one forced our Grumpy Old Men to volunteer for service. And though reduced, the terms and conditions of office were quite good. And they did manage to achieve some things while in office. Utter despair was replaced by the possibility of a future. Some form of fiscal soft landing, if only for a minority, was secured. Ireland became respectable again in the eyes of the world. We were not Greece. People did not starve in the streets. A form of social cohesion was maintained. Ultimately though, our Grumpy Old Men left too many possible trophies behind for praise. In a country that had been levelled by the utter ineptitude of our insider classes, they had the chance to remake the state in the shape of whatever vision they could conjure up. But, alas, they were Grumpy Old Men and so they had no vision beyond a little tidying up, a return to respectability and the restoration of the failed elite that had brought us to this pass to power. That, added to their grim disposition, which was utterly unsuited to the needs of the people, sealed their unfair fate.

Amidst the carnage, there was one curious survivor who reigned triumphant amidst the sorrowing masses of Grumpy Old Men. From the moment he tried to get Irish farmers to embrace environmental sustainability, Cute Old Phil had experienced much travail and been responsible for quite a few of the Coalition's disasters. Yet despite all of his woes, somehow our man secured all that he had dreamed of, courtesy of the EU Commissioner job. Afterwards, Phil was as close as a man can get to a perpetual state of bewilderment, barely believing he had secured that which he had utterly coveted. Somehow, Phil had broken the great iron rule that says all political careers ends in failure. Instead, he had created a new one: Phil's 'heads you lose, tails you lose again' conundrum. Enda had been stuck between the devil and the deep blue sea when trying to decide if he would get into more trouble for keeping or exiling the Coalition's political albatross. In the end, he decided in favour of the absence that should make the heart grow fonder. It was hardly a decision made with the sort of iconoclastic rigour we hoped for from our long-departed Democratic Revolution. And Phil's reward was hardly the type of ending to a morality tale in keeping with the high chivalric ideals we started off with.

Little of this, it has to be said, mattered to Phil. But as he visibly shivered in anticipation over the vast fruitful plains that lay ahead, one thing struck us. The visible delight of Phil over his escape suggested that real horrors awaited those left behind. One of those left behind looked particularly unnerved. Amidst all of the chaos and uncertainty, one other Grumpy Old Man had survived. But as he stood alone in cabinet amidst the ruins of his retinue, Dear Leader Enda looked terribly isolated.

CHAPTER 13

THE VOTERS HAVE A DEMOCRATIC REVOLUTION OF THEIR OWN

After pride, finally, a great fall comes

I n *The Fall and Rise of Reginald Perrin*, a classic 1970s sitcom, one of the stock jokes is that whenever Perrin's mother-in-law is mentioned, an image of a galloping hippopotamus flashes through Perrin's mind. If Irish politicians are wise, a galloping hippo should cross their minds when thinking of Ireland's working poor. But, as we know, they are not wise. Instead, they approach the squeezed middle in the enchanted gauche manner of the victims of a particularly elaborate Venus flytrap. For the Irish politician, particularly if they are in opposition, the squeezed middle is a beautiful waving flower bearing gaudy colours. If their eyes are not dazzled by the clashing colours, then their nostrils are entranced by the unique scents that emanate from this political blossom. This is particularly the case when the squeezed middle is in heat and looking for a political mate, for this is a combination that often drives politicians mad. Entranced and hypnotised, even when they see the fates of others, they cannot control themselves. Instead, fatally and unavoidably, they are drawn in – until, with a snap, the flytrap's jaws close on their squirming forms.

Death by the squeezed middle flytrap can, of course, take some time. Bertie Ahern grappled with the flytrap for a decade and a half before pleasure was replaced by pain. Sadly, the Grumpy Old Men enjoyed a far shorter lease of fascinated pleasure. The problem with the Coalition's courting of the middle classes was that, in the wake of their successful first kiss, the Coalition became sleepy and arrogant. Our poor political lovers failed to successfully consummate, let alone satisfy, their middle-class temptress, which meant that by 2014 the squeezed middle was squeezing Dear Leader Enda and his Invisible Man Tánaiste between their electoral teeth in a less than loving fashion.

The Coalition, once they realised they were in the grip of death rather than the embrace of love – and that took some time – did try the usual tactic of sweet promises in an attempt to loosen that grip. Suddenly, after a two-year lacuna, Mr Gilmore and Mr Kenny began to ask after Superquinn Mum again and to offer to hold her vastly reduced shopping bag. In the chilly atmosphere of 2014, this resembled Con Houlihan's famed description of Dublin goalkeeper Paddy Cullen's reaction when he was caught off his line by Kerry's Mikey Sheehy. Houlihan's comparison of Cullen's panicky dash back to his line with a woman who has smelt a cake burning racing back to the kitchen perfectly captured the ungainly, panicky state of the Coalition. Sadly for the poor Coalition, their cake was not so much mildly singed as baked black, and there was little evidence that the old trick of scrapping the burnt top to find something edibile below would work.

The problem for the Coalition Cartel was that it was caught in an economic and ideological cleft stick. The Coalition knew that their political health was tied up in the knot of putting more disposable income into the pockets of the citizen. Sadly, the diktats of the policy of dumb austerity they were bound to implement meant all the Coalition's actions contradicted their sweet words, so that the Cartel came to resemble that crying Nile crocodile whose deceitful tears could never be trusted. As the Coalition became embroiled in ever more squabbles with the class whose support it needed to survive, the appalling strategic dilemma they found themselves in appeared to blind them to the horrors of their position – or rather they tried to talk away the obvious with fanciful explanations along the lines of Bob Hope's famous appeal to his wife not to 'trust your lying eyes, honey' when she caught him in bed with a starlet. Thus the Coalition cheerily presented property tax as a treat that would rebalance local government and water tax as a benevolent conservation measure that would improve the lives of children, seals and baby rabbits. Paddy merely saw the wolf of yet another tax increase.

Of course, there is a downside for the squeezed-middle Venus flytrap too. They may entrap our politicians, but once caught, even if the flytrap does not like the taste of them, Irish politicians are extraordinarily difficult to spit out. In fact, you can really only do it once every five years, which means that if you don't get to like the taste of them early, you have to do a lot of spitting. Although the Coalition continued to hang in listlessly, by April 2014 the Irish voter finally definitively started the spitting-out process. Given the Irish electorate's natural inclination towards the dusty old nurse of mediocrity, out of the fear that something new would lead to trouble, the Coalition was not initially too nervous. After all, despite the foul mood Paddy was in during 2011, he ultimately decided to elect a Taoiseach who drew his inspiration from the grey ascetic form of

Liam Cosgrave. However, by the time the usually harmless local and European elections came around, the traditionally cautious Irish electorate, who, like Irish mammies, are usually prepared to forgive anything, turned feral themselves.

Of course, when faced with this possibility, our political class played their traditional role, averting their eyes from the tutu-clad elephant tap-dancing across the room. On one level, you could hardly blame them. During the Troubles in the North and the rise of the Provisional IRA, which polarised political opinion on both sides of the island, one of the greatest questions that politicians in the Republic were faced with was whether the centre would hold. By 2014, the new issue amongst the citizens of Ireland was whether its survival was of any intrinsic worth. In 2011, Ireland had genuinely wanted their Democratic Revolution. Instead, they were given the burnt offering of a minimalistic restoration. Initially, this was enough for a people whose confidence had been shattered. But as a feeble recovery began to take hold, the political tectonic plates started to move and the Coalition's feet were missing the beat.

The Coalition saw the decision of our alienated electorate to favour a future government of Sinn Féin and Independents as a form of political madness, which, like lesbianism in Victorian England, was promptly quarantined from discussion lest the notion spread. Unfortunately for the Coalition, the electorate swiftly developed a bit of a Sinn Féin–Independent habit. This scale of this shift was not entirely surprising, for the prodigal sons of Fine Gael and Labour had thoroughly squandered their political capital on pointless fripperies like retaining Shatter for long after he became a political liability. At first, the Coalition Cartel – its Fine Gael wing, at least – remained bullish about the future. But as it became increasingly clear the only vigour surrounding the Little Nells of Labour was the consumptive nature of their political coughing, Fine Gael's polite society started to consider how they could coalesce with Fianna Fáil, and so ensure everything would continue as normal.

There was one little problem with this cunning plan. Such was the sourness of the voters' mood towards traditional politics, a Civil War-ending reunion of Fianna Fáil and Fine Gael would not have enough public support to be elected. Even a government of our Traditional Triumvirate, Fianna Fáil, Fine Gael and Labour, was, by 2014, struggling to muster sufficient support in the polls to secure a majority. We were definitely in 'there's a problem here, Enda' country. Of course, the establishment Triumvirate could still hope that the Sinn Féin–Independent rise would follow the thorny path of the Gilmore Gale, which ran out of puff at the very gates of government. Our establishment noted that such a disparate grouping could never form a stable government, for unlike the current loving Fine Gael–Labour union, a Sinn Féin–Independent alliance would contain too many disparate working parties for the thing to succeed. This, however, underestimated Sinn Féin, who are ultimately a party as free of ideology as Labour and so able to go down a bit of the road with anyone.

Given the spooks and shades that Mr Adams is surrounded by, even Sinn Féin privately concedes Taoiseach Gerry is not the prettiest or most sustainable of sights. However, were Gerry to follow Fine Gael's precedent of 1951, when the Fine Gael leader General Richard Mulcahy declined the Taoiseach's office in favour of party colleague John Costello because of some Civil War 'bother', we would be very close to being in business. That is not to say Gerry couldn't be in the cabinet, but something like Foreign Affairs – where he would be kept out of the country a lot! – or Arts, Culture and the Diaspora – where he could be kept out even more! – might allow Mr Adams to do the same job as Enda minus the title. Indeed, Mr Adams might not even object to not getting the Taoiseach's gig so long as he retained the real power of being Sinn Féin President. Governing and hard choices are not, we suspect, Mr Adams's thing.

The disappearance of Mr Adams would have the added benefit of freeing the Taoiseach's office for his designated media successor, Mary Lou McDonald. A woman Taoiseach would be a new departure in a political system that struggles to hire them as Junior Ministers, but, like Mary Harney (alas, in more ways than one), our supremely opportunistic Superquinn Mum was increasingly one of the few politicians the Irish public had confidence in. The Coalition sirens could sing all they liked about 'danger here', and they did. But the more Paddy looked at the Sinn Féin–Independent alternative, the less terrifying it appeared to be. Sinn Féin's Simon Coveney, otherwise known as Pearse Doherty, would not frighten too many bondholders were he to become Minister for Finance. But while Sinn Féin might, beyond Simon, Mary Lou and Peadar Tóibín, be a bit short on the sweetness, intellect and light front, there is no shortage of Independent TDs who have the capacity to be impressive ministers.

It is difficult to see how any cabinet with an innovative thinker like Stephen Donnelly in Education or the plain-speaking, honest-dealing John Halligan in Social Welfare or Noël Browne's second coming, Róisín Shortall, in Health could be seen as a threat to society as we now know it. And while it might be a bit poacher-turned-gamekeeper, the performance of Shane Ross on the PAC suggests that if he didn't start a national strike, Mr Ross could be a perfect fit in Brendan Howlin's Public Sector Reform gig. For the Irish public, who exist in a very different world to the rarefied *Tom Brown's Schooldays* atmosphere of Leinster House, the rough truth of things was that the more they looked at such a Sinn Féin–Independent cabinet, the more appealing it appeared to be. It certainly looked a lot better than the somewhat queasy leftovers, many closely nudging their sell-by date, that the Coalition was proffering.

Some sniffed the zephyr of unease earlier than others. As the Coalition approached high summer in 2014, Pat Rabbitte warned in an interview with the *Sunday Independent* that they would not fulfil their ambition to remain in office until 2016 if the current drift did not end. 'Drift', unnervingly, was a central theme of Rabbitte's message that 'the single-minded focus of the first three years has to be restored'. Mr Rabbitte did not mince his words when noting that, if the 'drift' of the last three months were allowed continue and if the Coalition divided into factions, 'it is pretty obvious, really, that we won't see 2016'. The political classes reacted with real alarm to the prospect of the Coalition train not making the 2016 terminus. For the rest of us, it was even more alarming to hear a cabinet minister warn that 'the government has to put a coherent plan together', considering the more innocent of us believe they're working to a plan all the time. The admission that there actually wasn't one had more than a trace of 'beware the ides of Biffo' surrounding it.

There was much sense too in Rabbitte's warning that 'the Universal Social Charge is punitive. It is not acceptable in any democracy, where you are dependent on the allegiance of the people, that that citizens become liable to the top rate of tax at the industrial wage'. The public, he said, 'understand that the government has difficult decisions, but it's gone as far as it can in terms of cuts and taxes for them'. What people were saying on water charges, he added, 'is that this had fucking better be the last piece of the austerity jigsaw'. In fact, like Dagwood Bumstead and his perennial difficulties with catching the bus, Mr Rabbitte's prescience resembled the tipster who comes up with the result of the race after it has been won. The people had already decided water was a step too fucking far and the only people this was news to were the Coalition.

Given the overall context, it is extraordinary that, both before and after, so many believed the 2014 elections were a tedious affair. This, after all, was a contest where a minimum of three party leaders stood to lose their crowns – well, until Mr Adams, with one swift leap over the desecrated body of Jean McConville, escaped scot-free from that particular chaos. But there was nothing tedious about the voters' Democratic Revolution that occurred. The voters' smart-bomb targeting of the Labour Party represented a stark declaration that Labour as it was constituted after 2011 was a failure. Nothing epitomised the voters' mood towards Labour more than the results in Dublin. Here, Labour had poured in a fortune in the unconvincing hope that saving Emer Costello's MEP seat might pull Mr Gilmore away from a set of sharks that were wagging their tails with excitement. In fact, the European results were an astonishing commentary on the state of the Coalition. Only the small matter of a couple of thousand votes, which saw Fine Gael's Bonnie Prince Brian Hayes squeak in on the last count, prevented Dublin electing a Sinn Féin, an Independent and a Green MEP.

Happily there was no need to for the hungry sharks to fret, for the fine dining was about to start. Their covetous desire to feed on the succulent rump of Cute Old Phil was to be denied. However, when the results came in, Mr Gilmore finally knew how Michael Noonan had felt in after Fine Gael's disastrous election showing in 2002. The Grim Reaper wasn't so much waiting as tapping his foot impatiently. In fairness to Mrs Doubtfire of Dún Laoghaire, given his status as the Invisible Tánaiste, Mr Gilmore's actual departure was actually somewhat ennobling to the profession of politics. Time was also called on the next of Labour's high-profile Grumpy Old Men, Pat Rabbitte. But as the sharks burped contentedly, the question galloping ever faster through the frantic minds of poor Labour was whether three rather than one heads might be enough.

The results, which also saw Luke 'Ming' Flanagan being borne off in triumph to Europe, were greeted with some horror by those commandants of public opinion who make Sam the Eagle in *The Muppets* look like a bundle of fun. The Coalition and their media counterparts took on the role of Irish mammy to our bold electorate, warning that while Paddy the voter might be enjoying himself now, he would yet end up returning to the aristocratic Simon Coveney a week before the general election, tipping his cap and muttering apologies for his disobedience. But how grounded in reality was their warning? Increasingly, the wise old men of the media appeared to be as behind the pace of the evolution of Irish voters as the political parties. They, like the Coalition, were unable to process the more diffuse message the electorate were sending about the great failure of the Irish state. The collapse of the Democratic Revolution and, in particular, Labour's failure to drive the Revolution through the resistance of the Cuprinol 'does what it says on the tin' conservatives of Fine Gael, added to Fianna Fáil's failure to regain voter trust, had created a highway, rather than a gap, in the political market. By choosing to fill this highway with Independents, the electorate were sending the Coalition a clear message, if they would but stop the talking and listen. That the message was so clear was surprising, for normally the Irish electorate sends its messages the same way that ancient Greek gods sent cryptic omens to their worshippers. Due to their cryptic nature, they could easily be misread. But the ides of 2014 were impossible to misunderstand: the Coalition had been found guilty by the coping classes of betraying the Democratic Revolution. The jaws of the Venus flytrap were starting to clamp down hard.

It soon became clear the Coalition's response to the annihilation of public faith in their administration, in so far as there was a response, was to stick it out to the bitter end in the hope that luck or simple exhaustion might take the edge of the public's detestation. It will be interesting to see how Labour's plan to retrieve the support of the voters by doing nothing at all will work. The suspicion is that it won't go at all well. In fairness, the Coalition were short of any better alternative, given they were responsible for the greatest collapse of a mandate Irish politics had seen since – wait – oh yes, Biffo's rout.

Amidst the post-2014 count desolation, one small ray of sunlight brightened up the court of King Enda. If some politicians are blessed by their enemies, Mr Kenny was surely blessed by his Coalition partners. We were so used to describing Labour's meltdown that it was easy to ignore Fine Gael's little imbroglios, although that became somewhat more difficult after the council election results. Initially, as the vultures trotted over to Mr Gilmore to say hello, the fur and feathers flying around the Labour Party did a fine job in disguising the woeful nature of the Fine Gael performance. But nothing could disguise the reality that the wolf had gone from nipping at the edge of the Fine Gael flock right into the centre where the fattest, sleepiest sheep hang out.

The loss of 105 council seats brought the Fine Gael total down to 235, meaning Kenny had fared almost as badly as Brian Cowen in the 2009 council elections. Cowen's humbling total of 218 seats marked the beginning of Fianna Fáil's electoral end. Now, tired of the long wait since 2011, the Irish electorate had decided to start the Democratic Revolution themselves and this time, the Coalition was not invited.

Of course, council elections are obviously not as dramatic as general elections when it comes to the loss of heads. Council elections mostly consist of battles between the poor old party churls. General election battles, by contrast, witness the deaths of knights and, if you are lucky, a few kings and queens. However, after Fine Gael's first ever electoral reversal under Mr Kenny – if you discount the Presidency, and everyone does – it didn't take long for nervous TDs to start doing the general election maths. When the prospective Labour deluge was factored in to the declining Fine Gael vote, a minimum of fifty Coalition TDs and ministers were facing the political axe in the next general election. Already, the new intake of first-time Fine Gael TDs, the Frappuccino Kids, were starting to get distinctly nervous, for after the departure of all the

Fine Gael councillors, they were next in line to be mowed down. But some ministerial knights were getting fretful too. They might reside far above the poor council churls, but knights still need a few peasants to get them up on to their political steed. Suddenly, a chill surrounded the Dear Leader. Increasingly it was being noted of Enda that twelve years was an awful long time to lead a party; inevitably, the energy levels were not the same. After the blood was swiftly washed off the Labour floors and walls and the mop was bleakly squeezed out, the key question was: had our Grumpy Old Men actually learnt anything?

The subsequent Dáil debate would, we were told, tell us much.

It did.

They hadn't.

The Taoiseach crankily read out the list of the dearly departed ministers and then, in a despairing attempt to improve the mood of the country, returned to the ghost of old triumphs. The millenarian language of 2011 was a thing of the past; instead, Enda declared that 'crucially, our reputation as a safe bet for inward investment has been restored'. If Paddy was over the moon with the sentiment, he was hiding it well. 'Delighted, I am sure', was Paddy's sarcastic response to Enda's observation that 'Last December, thanks to the hard work and considerable sacrifice of the people, sacrifice that at times they must have thought would never end, we exited the EU–IMF bailout'. Oddly enough, Paddy did not show much joy either over Enda's revelation that 'our clean exit of the bailout, without requiring a precautionary credit line or a second bailout, as predicted by many, has improved Ireland's standing and has allowed us to raise new funds so that we can safeguard the public services that our people depend upon in their lives on a day-to-day basis'. The mandarins might have been delighted, but it certainly had not made a whit of difference to the man standing on the 46A bus or the poor country girls commuting on overcrowded trains from Portarlington, who wondered, as they clung on to their underpaid jobs that would never pay off their overextended mortgages, if they would ever be able to buy anything nice for themselves again.

As Enda trundled on about 'returning our country to full employment so that we can best reach our goal of making Ireland the best small country in the world in which to do business', it was drab a vision as you might suffer at a chamber of commerce dinner. There was just one moment of unease, when Mr Kenny noted 'there is still so much to do and all of it is so urgent'. For a moment, it was as though the Taoiseach, like so many of his predecessors, was pleading with a hooded figure bearing a scythe to hold off because he was nearly there. Sadly, the man with the scythe, having heard it all before, rarely entertains such pleas. As for Dear Leader Enda, his conclusion that 'belief, fragile as it is, exists deep in our people' was about as convincing as a water diviner without a stick.

Micheál Martin, by contrast, was confident and assertive as he noted the Coalition had loaded ten new tax increases in 2012, twenty in 2013 and a further ten in 2014. The Fianna Fáil leader also had a cut at Joan Burton observing that 'the Tánaiste may well have stored her "Gilmore for Taoiseach" posters in the garden shed, but she has no such alibi for the large and still growing list of broken promises and unfair decisions for which she and her colleagues have been responsible'. Neither was Gerry Adams slow in unveiling the nakedness of the Coalition Emperor. Mr Adams is not normally a great fan of history but he was more than pleased to return to Enda's 2011 speech on the nomination of his government. Adams dryly noted that 'three years is a long time in politics. In that time all his fine words have faded'. Adams's comments on how Enda had failed to fulfil his covenant to close the gap between politics and the people, between government and the governed were so apt that for once, even the Fine Gael cawing rooks were silent. As Adams noted 'this reshuffle is a mediocre piece of political drama that will have no positive outcome', it was the often mocked and disparaged Mattie McGrath who best summarised the great fall of the Coalition Humpty Dumptys: when it came to the real qualities of Enda and the Coalition, Paddy, Mattie said, had 'found out'.

CHAPTER 14

FIANNA FÁIL BECOMES THE PARTY YOU CANNOT KILL

Could Micheál Martin be our next Taoiseach, after all?

Amidst all of the political chaos, one small, harmless and utterly unnoticed group crept into view. The growth of the phenomenon of Fianna Fáil nostalgia was pretty unexpected. But after two years on the dry, experiencing the delights of the drab puritanical respectability of the Coalition, Paddy was ready for road again. In fact, he was desperate for it. For a while, Paddy kept his desire secret, like the 18th-century papists who visited mass rocks. Paddy knew his nostalgia was wrong. But he could not help chuckling over such events as the debauched grandeur of the fall of Biffo. Was it really the case that Fianna Fáil used to go to think-in events and appal barmen with the spectacle of the Taoiseach hitting the bar to hold court before his supplicants, all desperate to ingratiate themselves?

Some were nostalgic from the very start of the new regime of the Pious Protestors. Innocent idealism is a rare commodity in Leinster House and that it was found in the persona of a journalist was all the more unusual. This, however, was the spectacle we faced when a younger member of the breed exclaimed, in the first month of the reign of our new Coalition, that it was surely great that after the chaos of Biffo, we would now have a 'hardworking and idealistic government that would reform the dysfunctional nature of the Irish state'. Sadly, as is so often the case with hope in Leinster House, optimism was decisively spayed by harsher realities as a somewhat crotchety hack snarled, 'great is it? Do you not understand what has happened here? We have replaced a perfectly good government of lunatics with a reforming administration driven by a work ethic. Where will we ever get the likes of what we had before? A Taoiseach being compared to a drunken barman by an American comedian, a cabinet that hates each other and their Taoiseach, leaking like Irish Water pipes against each other, a collective of Green nutjobs that are more concerned about puppy farms than promissory notes, Mary Harney playing the Queen of Hearts in *Alice in Wonderland*, Mary Coughlan, the Marie Antoinette of Donegal, more fear, loathing and spectres erupting from the floor-boards than an Edgar Allen Poe short story, Conor Lenihan? Jesus, we never had it so good.'

The veteran hack paused for breath before issuing a final despairing snap of 'having a reforming new government may well be good for the country but this is a damn bad day for journalism'. Whatever about the moral anomie that lay behind the outburst, its basic premise was at the time correct. Few enough, and with good reason, will be nostalgic about the policies of Mr Cowen but in terms of dramatic farce, not even the writers of *The Hangover* could have invented a better alternative. It was, of course, somewhat depressing to be living in a country that was falling off a cliff but, in the media at least, this was accompanied by some exhilaration crossed with panic, for, if nothing else, you were never short of work. Sadly, if working in Leinster House under Biffo was like a permanent episode of *One Flew Over the Cuckoo's Nest*, the return from exile of the Grumpy Old Men was more like going on to the set of 'Downton Abbey'.

A vast chill settled over the journalists of Leinster House as we returned to the land of servants and masters that is so characteristic of life under the occasional reign of the Pious Protestors. For those who had been in the trenches during Biffo's many battles, it was like returning from the First World War with a VC only to find yourself being ushered back into your old humble spot by the Gate Lodge. But we are merely humble hacks and we know our place. And should we forget it, there is always a vast queue of politicians, political advisors, fellow colleagues (particularly of the RTÉ variety), judges (particularly of the Supreme Court PD stripe), celebrities, barristers, entrepreneurs, civil service mandarins, billionaires, captains of industry and toadstools – apologies, footstools – of those captains of industry, all of whom are vastly higher earners than journalists and all of whom are always anxious to remind us that we are overpaid, under-clever and, worst of all, still here.

Journalists are well used to receiving such a message. The problem for our Coalition was that the self-same queue were equally keen to inform the working poor of their many flaws. The queue's disposition was informed by their belief that they were engaged in the political equivalent of God's work. However, while God's work generally starts off on a well-meaning note, at some stage the incapacity of those inferior ones who do not understand or, worse still, sufficiently respect the importance of their tasks leads to the evolution of unhappiness.

Many believe that the great decline of Fianna Fáil occurred well before poor Biffo was dragged reluctantly into the ring to take on a little fellow called 'world economic recession'. We instead trace it to that moment where too long in government converted some Fianna Fáil Cute Hoors into Pious Protestors. When it comes to the fall of the Fianna Fáil Humpty Dumpty, the ethicists of the state generally blame excesses such as the Galway races. We contend rather that such events were a positive, for they allowed Fianna Fáil to get sufficiently close to Paddy to still catch the essential smell of him. What really destroyed the party was the triumph of the puritanical Dermot Ahern–Noel Dempsey wing of the party. Suddenly, Fianna Fáil started to believe they were superior to Paddy. As part of this process, Fianna Fáil began to believe they didn't have to listen to poor Paddy either. Instead, great experts, all of whom were wrong, were hired to advise Fianna Fáil on the economy and light-touch regulation and we all, alas, know where that ended.

The Coalition might have well thought that after 2011 they had finally excised Fianna Fáil from their dominant position in Irish life. And Fianna Fáil themselves did little to persuade us that the opposite was the case. But such was Fianna Fáil's role in all aspects of our culture, they have, rather like the younger brother of Ireland's errant colonial gene, entered our DNA in a manner that means no matter how hard Enda and his Coalition compatriots try, they cannot exorcise the Fianna Fáil stain. They did try to give us regular history lessons about Fianna Fáil's villainy but Paddy is like any other bad child. When he doesn't want to learn from history, then he won't.

What was particularly strange about the Fianna Fáil recovery was that it came despite, rather than because of, the party. When the Coalition began definitively to fail, a strange flaw began to emerge amongst the ranks of Fianna Fáil. Instead of going for this opening with the snarling opportunism of their predecessors, Fianna Fáil began to experience a dangerous moment of hesitation. In the past, as the fall of the Rainbow Coalition in 1997 clearly displayed, old-style Fianna Fáil, a coalition of the damned and the ruthless, were maestros in the art of closing out the political deal if one was available. With the current crew, however, the sense began to grow that they were still suffering from the political yips in the wake of their spectacular electoral defeat. It was almost as though Fianna Fáil had learnt to love the hair-shirt, the nettle soup and the whips and chains – of the penitent political Matt Talbot rather than the pleasurable variety – too much. The problem for Fianna Fáil was that although the politics of the eternal apology is all well and good, it is a politics of absence, for an apology without subsequent actions does not solve or remedy anything. After the 2011 election, Fianna Fáil got stuck in the apology groove. It was as if a party obsessed by history was unable to see that a bigger threat was posed by its failure to grasp its future due its fear of its past rather than its past in itself.

This meant that the poor Fianna Fáil mendicants continued to be a party without a narrative – or rather the only story they had consisted of apologies. But an apology is not a narrative. It is at best a gesture of supplication. The long-term consequence of Fianna Fáil's decision to flee from their past in the manner of disgraced Israelites caught worshipping the golden calf meant that by 2014 they were still as peripheral as when they entered the Dáil in 2011. It seemed they were incapable of either noticing or taking advantage of the growing view of the coping classes that the Coalition, for some mysterious reason, was against the people of Ireland.

This was all the more surprising given that it was those who would traditionally be considered Fianna Fáil's own people that were suffering. This struggling coping class, who find themselves left without any disposable income the day after they receive their pay check, became the Irish Moby Dick, the elusive whale all the parties wanted to catch. In 2013 and 2014, they were partying with Sinn Féin and the Independents. But in the long run, such ahistorical creatures as country girls and part-time employed breakfast roll men are always available for a bit of fun with old-school Fianna Fáil. In 2011, former Fianna Fáil voters had constituted the bulk of the borrowed votes Fine Gael and Labour had secured. To put it at its mildest, these voters had not enjoyed their fling and were more than available for a return to the Fianna Fáil fold. The problem, however, was that they had to be asked first. And as Fianna Fáil continued to resemble the girl folded into the wallpaper during the slow set, the voters got bored fairly fast.

Perhaps it didn't help give Fianna Fáil confidence with the asking that the electorate were not above playing ducks and drakes with the poor Embalmed Radicals. Nothing epitomised this more than the campaign of Seán Gallagher for the Presidency. Though Mr Gallagher ran as an Independent, he was seen as the political equivalent of a prospector's licence for a rejuvenated Fianna Fáil. For a time, as Gallagher soared, it appeared that the Irish electorate was prepared to erase from their memory the extraordinary spectacle of a Fianna Fáil cabinet that had resembled a collective of absinthe-sipping French existentialists who, for their own psychological safety, had decided to become as detached from the real world as Robinson Crusoe. But it turned out the deceitful voters had only been playing at forgiveness, for at the decisive point the electorate swished their collective tail in the disdainful manner of a salmon that, having spotted a flaw in the carefully presented bait, turns away.

The inability of Fianna Fáil to recover a bit of its devil-may-care spirit was typified by the suspicion that grew within its ranks for what we shall term 'dislikeable mavericks'. Fianna Fáil was not unique in this, for one of the features of our estranged Democratic Revolution was a dislike of mavericks. This should be surprising given that democratic revolutions are normally characterised by freedom of thought and the surf and play of new ideas. But as we know too well, what we got instead of change was the great age of orthodoxy. In fairness, distaste for such orchids as freethinkers is natural for governments, as they are expected to prioritise the Prussian virtues of unthinking similarity. But if we have no space in opposition for such characteristics, then the age of bleating sheep has surely arrived.

Fianna Fáil's fear of mavericks is clearly visible in their special relationship with their own John McGuinness. It often appears as though the plump, unfeathered hens of his own party are more afraid of John McGuinness than the Coalition. To outsiders, it might appear that in a Dáil full of Boss Hogg types, McGuinness is the much-needed Clint Eastwood 'Man with No Name'-style outsider riding into town to clean up the mess. But although he has the respect and trust of Irish citizens, in the closed world of Leinster House the view is colder. In there, even his own party bleats about how difficult and dour he is. He is certainly slightly crankier than the Fianna Fáil lads who saunter around Leinster House with the easy insouciance of pedigree dogs that have found an unpoliced back entrance to the butchers. However, unlike the rest of his party, he managed to devise a plan of attack upon the Coalition. This was facilitated by the fact that, in spite of his reputation for being a cold contrarian, McGuinness is a closet idealist whose political analysis is both moral and sophisticated. McGuinness is best known as the great inquisitor of the PAC. But the millenarian turn of his political philosophy became increasingly evident as Fianna Fáil's uneasy Dark Prince began to speak of the evil that follows when a country is governed by those who believe it's all about the economy. Under their sway, Irish democracy, he warned, had been turned into 'a veil, behind which autocrats can act with impunity'. In claiming the public now knew what the inner workings of our 'democracy' looked like, that our supposedly democratic Republic was, in fact, an incompetent and self-satisfied autocracy run by a relatively small number of insiders who are long past their sell-by date, McGuinness was speaking a language that was unknown to Leinster House – well, except perhaps for the Socialist Party TDs. There was also some of the radicalism of Fianna Fáil in its early years in McGuinness' warning that 'individuals, families and communities are the bedrock of this Republic. Now, they are bystanders, ballast on the bottom of the ship of state'. The crux of the matter, he warned, was 'where stands the citizen in his own country? A long, long way from power and influence, I believe. That now lies in the hands of weak politicians and an unelected few, mainly group-thinkers, who reinforce each other's attitudes and actions and do not want change or transparency and accountability.'

McGuinness's articulation of the Great Betrayal of the people was a long way away from the milk-and-water bleats of Fianna Fáil leader Micheál Martin and he went even further still with his warning that 'democracy is the name, but autocracy is the game'. In his analysis, the ballot box was a placebo; the Dáil an ineffective talking shop; the upper levels of the public service a place where privilege and position came before responsibility; and politics itself 'an empty, noisy vessel'. Perhaps his most damning judgement of all was that the Coalition had failed because 'the first duty of government is to keep its people safe, not to keep them in the dark'. It was language that belonged more to the American evangelical school of politics than the muttering into their own sleeves school of politics the Fianna Fáil pedigree mongrels were more used to indulging in. Strangely, despite the American cadences, it carried the ring of authenticity. Significantly, McGuinness's declaration of support for those whistle-blowers that are loved far more in theory than in practice by our elite was particularly emotive. The treatment of concerned citizens who lay their livelihood, their happiness and that of their families on the line in doing the State some service had become for McGuinness 'a measure of how this State now operates, and how it casually disregards the standards it so forcefully demands of its citizens'. His warning that few of the practices that occurred during our various whistle-blower controversies contradicted his view that 'the State is without compassion and is self-serving, inefficient and, at its highest levels, often arrogant, dismissive and overpaid' was very timely.

The bad news for Fianna Fáil was that McGuinness's caution that the state's 'ruthless methods of dealing with opposition and new ideas are the hallmarks of a failing culture well on its way to implosion' was as relevant to Fianna Fáil as the Coalition. Similarly, his criticism of 'this tottering, failing culture ... [of] institutionalised politicians ... [who] behave like nodding dogs in the back window of a car – amiable, decorative, slightly amusing, and useless' was a bit too close to home for Fianna Fáil's comfort. McGuinness, it has to be said, was not alone. Another John the Baptist, Éamon 'Dev Óg' Ó Cuív, also warned that the Fianna Fáil crisis would not be solved by giving up the drink, smiling nicely and acting like a busy fool running up and down the country. He, like John McGuinness, realised issues such as the destruction of this state by a cabal of EU autocrats and bankers and the nature of what a Republic should be are not solved by focus groups. Sadly, though, the henpecked Fianna Fáil hierarchy still preferred group-think to me-think. As for the plump unfeathered hens amidst the Fianna Fáil TDs and senators, who generally strolled around Leinster House acting the goat, they just stared quizzically at Fianna Fáil's new prophets.

As the establishment hit back with a Grand Inquisition over the quality of toilet paper Mr McGuinness had used in his office, there was even talk that McGuinness might have a tilt at the Fianna Fáil crown. The talk came coincidentally at a difficult time for party leader Micheál. In the strange new world Fianna Fáil found themselves in in 2014, Bertie Ahern's one-size-fits-all unisex catchphrase, 'ah, the hardy lads, working hard', had been replaced by a new variant. Increasingly, each crisis in Fianna Fáil, whether it was of the existential variant or the absence of tea-bags, attracted the new stock response: 'well, in fairness, Micheál is working very hard'. In truth, poor Micheál would want to be working very hard, for plenty in Fianna Fáil weren't – but that was a different problem. The question that Fianna Fáil were finding increasingly difficult to answer was whether hardworking Micheál was a busy fool rather than a man making real changes. There was no lack of will or of effort, from Micheál at least, but, like a car stuck in wet mud, all Fianna Fáil's revving was getting them nowhere. 2014 should, under the old rules, have been the best of times for Fianna Fáil, given the collapse in support for the Coalition. Instead, Fianna Fáil imitated the witches in *Macbeth* with their cackling warnings of 'Double, double toil and trouble; / Fire burn and cauldron bubble' to mind. Whatever about bubble, there was no shortage of toil and trouble ahead for Fianna Fáil if they were to get back into power, which was not good news for the lads who were thoroughly enjoying the golf and the gold-plated membership of Copper Face Jacks that come with opposition life.

The problem for Fianna Fáil was that every reason given as to why Mr McGuinness should not lead clubbable, harmless Fianna Fáil was precisely why a citizenry winnowed into apathy by the state of Fianna Fáil under nice Micheál would find him attractive. Eventually, the sense that Fianna Fáil needed a Savonarola rather than a fusspot meant McGuinness began to attract some interest within the party. Fianna Fáil, if it was to be reformed and saved, needed a leader who could instil fear in his troops, and that was never going to be Micheál. Micheál's dominant trait, in so far as dominance applies to Micheál, is fussiness. He is, in short, a man for Ps and Qs rather than the political Putin Fianna Fáil needs. The main charge Fianna Fáil's pedigree dogs could rustle up against McGuinness was that he would go mad if in power. But perhaps we need a bit of madness in how we are all too politely governed. And, in a display worthy of party leadership, McGuinness had corralled and controlled a very diverse political stampede of egos within the PAC, a committee that requires far more sensitive political hands than most ministries.

For a brief moment of time, the Fianna Fáil leadership seemed up for grabs. In a chilly analysis of Micheál's position, one frontbencher warned 'it all hangs on the Dublin [European] election; it would become very difficult if Fianna Fáil came in behind Eamon Ryan or Nessa Childers'. Another source talked about how, on his trips, McGuinness has 'been getting a rapturous response, standing ovations. People are tired of Micheál's milk-and-water Fianna Fáil sounding like Fine Gael'. As it turned out, although Fianna Fáil trailed in a long, long way behind Nessa and Eamon in Dublin, the Fianna Fáil leader was to survive. On the day of the election count in 2014, McGuinness struck too soon. In the early morning, it looked as if Fianna Fáil faced an existential crisis. Then, the capture of a couple of percent that were as cheaply won as anything Fine Gael and Labour secured in 2011 meant that by evening, the mood had changed. Existential radicalism, not that it was ever really in, was out and fussy conservatism was in. The Fianna Fáil likely lads looking over Micheál's shoulders into the future decided it might be better for them if Micheál's blancmange style of leadership were to continue to, if not exactly thrive, certainly survive.

Fianna Fáil were not alone in their suspicions of dislikeable mavericks. Other parties were simply more efficient in eliminating them. Fine Gael and Labour, for example, sorted out their mavericks by exiling them. Intriguingly, the one party that does not appear to have any mavericks at all is Sinn Féin. Funny that.

Nothing could erase the unease surrounding Micheál's fusspot-style regime. Tragically, Fianna Fáil had lost its wild streak at the very moment when Ireland was preparing to revolt against Enda Kenny's alien graft of Ireland as the new Singapore. As an intriguing – or dangerous, depending on your point of view – sense of uncertainty entered the Irish political landscape, the time had come for the old devil-may-care Fianna Fáil, who had no time for rules or the prognostications of pundits, to enter the race. A vast sense of rebelliousness had entered the psyche of the working poor who were more than inclined to defy the Coalition's edicts of 'don't vote for Sinn Féin or Fianna Fáil, for they will ruin our perfect world'. All Fianna Fáil had to do was tell Ireland that history was bunk and they were finished with the apologising thing. Instead, their cautious response to the opportunities they were presented with killed the possibility of any counter-attack stone-dead.

Nothing epitomised the party's continued domination by the figures of its past more than its Ard Fheis of 2014. The party might have been engaged in its usual lacklustre agenda, endorsing niceness, the evils of irresponsible drinking, mandatory cycle helmets, gender recognition processes, the decriminalisation of marijuana (hurrah!), but only for medicinal purposes (boo!) and a client-centric social welfare system, whatever that might be. History, however, kept intruding, for in a conference centre with a plaque honouring Bertie, our main interest was focused on whether the Bull O'Donoghue might gallop in the door and shake the hand of a quivering Micheál. The past reared its head again during local election nominations, the most interesting feature of which was the attempt to dislodge Mary Hanafin from the council ticket. It failed and Mary got elected.

We should remember, for it is easy to forget, that Fianna Fáil did actually win the local elections, in spite of the fact their manifesto consisted of nothing more than the Coalition consistently shooting themselves in the foot. This facilitated the unique situation where Fianna Fáil became the first party to win an election while simultaneously backing away from an electorate who had no-one else to vote for. The reality of their situation was more acutely captured by the European elections. In Dublin, a land of former Fianna Fáil giants, the party ran a county councillor who ended up being transfer fodder for the real parties. They fared no better in Mid-West where they ran a dinosaur and a senator and although the semi-independent Republic of Brian Crowley won a seat, he soon departed from the Fianna Fáil fold and went fully Independent.

It didn't take long for Fianna Fáil to realise their local election victory was a handful of dust. But the shortness of time that they took to secure that epiphany was long enough to ensure they were now stuck with Micheál and his pedigree dogs, come hell or high water. Of course, while their situation at the end of 2014 was weak, it was still fluid. The sad thing was they didn't seem to have the intelligence to recognise their ongoing weakness or the courage to take advantage of the fluidity. It is admittedly difficult to be optimistic when you are constantly told the one iron law in Irish politics is that there is no way a *bête noire* like you can secure power in the next election. Instead, the best Fianna Fáil are told to aspire to is a chaste, barren life of political respectability, in the hope that at some stage it might dare to reach the heights of being Fine Gael-Lite in a decade or so. Were the ghosts of Fianna Fáil past, power-players like Lemass and Haughey, to pay a visit to the modern incarnation of their party, they would recoil in horror at the prevailing belief that Enda Kenny has set the template for how Fianna Fáil leaders should behave. Should they deign to speak to Micheál, they would tell Micheál that, given Fianna Fáil's turbulent past, no party is better qualified to realise all laws, even of the iron variety, are made to be bent. But by 2014, their lost capacity for rule-breaking had left a Fianna Fáil party that didn't appear to really know why it even existed. As for Paddy, suddenly he too was faced with quite the agonising dilemma. Could it really be the case that the only way he could punish those guilty of the Great Betrayal of the Democratic Revolution was to vote back into power those whose own betrayal had necessitated the need for that revolution in the first place? It was a riddle that would even cause a sphinx like Haughey to grin.

CHAPTER 15

PADDY LIFTS HIS HEAD – NOW WE ARE REALLY IN TROUBLE

The Coalition Cartel faces into the abyss

Looking at why it all went so wrong so quickly for the Coalition with the virtue of hindsight, it is now evident the exit of the Troika was more of a tinker's curse than a church blessing. During the Great Disruption, Paddy was like the man with the boil on his neck in Flann O'Brien's short story, whose head was bent so low his snots were bouncing off the pavement. Then one day, sometime around the middle of 2014, Paddy realised the sky wasn't going to fall in and lifted up his head for the first time in about five years. Unfortunately for our Coalition, Paddy didn't much like what he saw. Instead, not to put too fine a line on it, his response consisted of a belligerent wail of 'what the fuck are you doing to me?!'

From that moment, Paddy was as intractable as the famous mule that would neither drive nor lead. When it came to the subsequent summer, autumn, winter and spring of discontent, we should not be too hard on Paddy, for as a voter, Paddy is not, despite his terrible reputation, too difficult. Fianna Fáil's former Minister for Finance turned European Commissioner Charlie McCreevy once famously said that all Paddy wants is a few pints, the GAA and a bit of 'how's your father' on a Saturday night. Of course, poor Charlie was dismembered by our elite for his cheek in speaking the truth. But in essence, all that Paddy really wants is for our politicians to leave him alone to at least enjoy those few treats – and if that is an ask too much, that they don't irritate or make life too hard for him.

Obviously, the Coalition failed badly on all those fronts. Mind you, it was not entirely their fault, for even they had the nous to realise austerity was unpopular. The problem, though, with austerity is that it is often a little like marriage, whereby the getting out of it is not as easy as the getting in. They certainly thought they were getting out of it after Michael Noonan's budget in October 2014. To understand the delight of the Coalition Cartel as they cooed and fawned over their fiscal baby, it is worth returning to Noonan's budget of 2011. Seeing as this was the first budget to be delivered by a Fine Gael minister in a quarter of a century, it could have been assumed that, after such a lacuna, the boutiques of rural Ireland would have been cleared of stock as the celebratory tribe prepared for their moment of triumph. Instead, on that eerie day, the Dáil with its deserted car parks and empty bar bore a closer resemblance to the *Mary Celeste*. As isolated TDs flitted through mothballed corridors, it was clear the state's bankruptcy was an orphan. Of course, when a state has been gagged and tied to the train tracks by its lenders of last resort, there is generally little to celebrate and a great deal to be evaded.

And despite all his wit and natural intelligence, it swiftly became clear Michael Noonan was a man spending as long as he could saying nothing so it would not become apparent just how little he had to say.

By the time his cautious collation, with its heavy emphasis on what the world thought of us, had concluded, Noonan resembled the sort of farmer who spends more time looking at his neighbour's estate than his own weed-strewn fields. Given the financial condition of the country he was budgeting for, Noonan's 'careful now, down with that sort of thing' script and conservatism were understandable. But none of his clever fiscal shimmies could disguise the fact that this was still a scarecrow of a budget. Brian Lenihan's budgets were disastrous, but they were also, by the standards of the time, a little brave. By contrast, despite Noonan's attempt to drape some sort of strategy across its skeletal form, this was an anti-budget, which, as it turned with every breeze and bowed to every zephyr, brought us precisely back to where we had started. After a decade of dumb spending – that was, in fairness to Fianna Fáil, agreed with at the time by all parties – the best response to our current crisis that the finest minds in the civil service could come up with was a decade, if not more, of dumb austerity.

Nothing epitomised the fiscal madness of it all more than the scenario in which yet another steep cut in capital spending was balanced out with extra expenditure to pay off axed public sector workers. Functioning states in times of depression use government spending to revive the economy. Under Ireland's dumb austerity regime, capital spending, which would create real jobs for troubled mortgage holders and the 90,000 unemployed construction workers nationwide, was being slashed to pay lump-sum retirement payments to already overpaid teachers – and all without a squeak of protest from our democratic revolutionaries. It was difficult to see how turning Ireland into a variant of one of those Florida retirement towns where all economic activity is centred on fulfilling the needs of retired civil servants would restore Ireland's lost entrepreneurial spirit. But as we languished in a world of misery where Europe and the banks were, with the acquiescence of puppet governments, a parasite on the Irish people, this was only one of a thousand cruel and foolish policies that were destroying the nation's morale.

Noonan's 2014 budget was supposed to be a far more radical affair. Yet during and after its delivery, the sole response, once again, was silence. Such was the grip the tendrils of austerity still retained on hope that even the cawing rooks of the Fine Gael backbenches could scarcely raise a cheer, let alone a standing ovation. The silence lasted for a day. And then a great brouhaha broke out. It wasn't about the budget though. That, like some netherworld changeling that squeals at the sight of light, lasted a day and died. The voters simply looked at it and asked one devastating question: was it for this small piece of candyfloss that we had experienced seven years of austerity? Instead, the great national howl of rage was over water charges. Pat Rabbitte's prophecy earlier in the year had been right. The limits of toleration for austerity had been reached.

As frightened eyes looked out from government buildings, Ireland experienced its first spontaneous revolution of the proletariat since the PAYE marches of the 1970s. Given Colbert's famous definition of the art of taxation as extracting the maximum of feathers with the minimum of fuss, it was no wonder the Coalition, and in particular its Finance Minister, felt doleful. Our poor Finance Minister had been trying to stick a few feathers back into the naked Irish goose and all he had received was pecks. But even without the spectre of water charges hissing and shrieking away in the background, the severity of the public mood was understandable. One astute commentator came closest to explaining the public mood by noting that the budget was the equivalent of the Gardaí returning 10% of your property after a burglary. You're not going to refuse the 10%, but understandably your attention will still mostly be focused on the missing stuff.

There was also an element of delayed reaction surrounding the voters' response. Paddy's psyche had been repeatedly violated by seven years of austerity and eight austerity budgets, if we count in the year where Brian Lenihan had three goes with the hatchet. The Coalition's modest offering, though beautiful in the Cartel's eyes, was not going to do much to revive the trust of Irish citizens. Their sense of moral outrage was, as they gathered a smidgen of courage, intensified by the realisation that the two separate governments, Fianna Fáil–Green incompetents and Fine Gael–Labour eunuchs, had cosseted and protected the banks and the developers, kept the top level of the public sector intact from cuts and then wanted Paddy to dance for a 1% cut in the top rate of tax, which, thanks to our lovely new ethic of 'more for less', wouldn't apply to Paddy's wages anyway. That, of course, was why the cut was included: 1% off the top rate of tax fulfilled the Coalition's intention to bring in tax cuts but as it was applied to a small group, it was the cheapest tax cut that could be made.

As he came to terms with the latest great escape of the good old elite that had ruined the state, Paddy was as mad as Michael Douglas in *Falling Down* and he was not taking it any more. Now, as he scanned anxiously for signs of weakness in the Coalition that would allow him to give it a good kicking, a perfect little diamond was presented to him. Better still, it was Dr Frankenstein Coalition's own creature. It had been thought the HSE was a once-off that could never be repeated again. But like one of those Russian Matryoshka nesting dolls, where each doll is the perfect smaller replica of its predecessor, Irish Water had done just that. Right down to its back of an envelope-style conception and 'who needs notes' gestation, our reforming Coalition had created something of its own whose relationship with the HSE resembled that of Narcissus and the pond. Each, from overstaffing to incompetence to public distrust to secrecy, was the perfect mirror of the other.

By this point, when confronted with the Irish Water delight, Paddy no longer had his head down. Paddy, instead, was braying loudly on the streets. This small final toxic wafer of austerity finally caused Paddy to explode. Ironically, the man who saw trouble coming most clearly of all was the Invisible Man. From the start of the year, Eamon Gilmore warned that water charges would be the thing that would eventually kill the Coalition. It certainly was the story that wouldn't go away, starting with the moment in January when Irish Water's chief executive, John Tierney, formerly of Dublin City Council and Poolbeg incinerator white elephant fame, told Sean O'Rourke of RTÉ that his organisation had spent €50 million on consultants. The Troika were barely out the door and already old politics was showing its slip.

That was bad enough, but the knickers swiftly went out the window next when Cute Old Phil Hogan was let out of the kennels. Phil headed, as usual, into his favoured style of bluff and bluster, telling us not to sweat the small stuff like €50 million. Phil was a blue-skies thinker who couldn't be obsessing about minutiae like that. Our man, of course, also had his middle eye on Europe so his concentration levels when it came to mere domestic affairs were slipping. As Phil huffed and puffed like one of those broken down steam trains needing rescue in the Thomas the Tank Engine series, the Coalition started to worry what other legacy issues Phil had left waiting.

For a time, the damage was confined to a mere internal Coalition squabble between Fine Gael, who wanted to kill the issue by announcing a €240 average charge, and Labour, who wanted to say nothing definitive at all in the hope that the water equivalent of the tooth fairy might just take the terrible thing away. Despite all the talk about Coalition and cabinet splits, the spats around the biscuits of the cabinet table were minor enough affairs. But the problem the Coalition faced was that the voters and, in particular, the working poor were mightily suspicious of this 'average' figure. Their experience of 'average' figures when it came to tax and this Coalition was that they tended to get the very high end of that wedge. And after a decade of austerity, the working poor simply did not have the money to pay.

Water continued to be the running wound that neutralised the Coalition to such an extent that even they eventually realised it could be the loose stirrup that would cost them the election. The problem was that by the time they got around to water tax credits – which only confused Paddy, who was, in any case, willing to be confused, so he could become angry about being confused – it was too late. By this stage, bad Paddy had gotten loose. For seven years, he had been battered, bruised, told he was one of the PIIGS by the Germans, lost his job, his house, endured thirty different tax increases and now a Janus-faced Coalition was telling him that the first sign of things getting better was the arrival of a new tax to pay.

Paddy decided he was fed up of tipping his cap and saying 'sorry, sir'. Paddy Jekyll went on a sabbatical and Paddy Hyde was let out on the loose. Rather like the French army in 1917, Paddy was in a state of mutiny. He was fed up of the trenches of austerity, of living in a death-in-life zombie state where you couldn't afford to have children, let alone a job or a house or any of the other things Charlie McCreevy correctly divined as being amongst the chief desires of Paddy. In even worse news for the Coalition, by the close of 2014, Paddy was starting to enjoy being furiously irrational. He was finding it liberating.

As the Coalition Cartel nearly fainted at the prospect that popular democracy might infect the country, they took the wisest route possible. Their decision to do so was all the more surprising given that it had the added bonus of actually being the correct one –

well, politically, at least. Initially, the retreat of the Coalition Cartel
on water charges matched the flight of King James after the Battle
of the Boyne and redemption for this confused collation seemed
as distant a prize as ever. Luckily for the Coalition, bomb threats
to Labour's Alan Kelly's office and the Siege of Jobstown combined
to save the day. The Siege of Jobstown, during which Tánaiste Joan
Burton was held hostage in her car by angry protestors, filled middle
Ireland with a vast chill. The alienation of Dublin voters from the
Coalition Cartel had been so great that in the Dublin South West
by-election, Socialist Party candidate Paul Murphy and Sinn Féin's
Cathal King had secured nearly 60% of the first preferences between
them. The Coalition parties had, by contrast, won less than a third of
that. But then the mini-riot at Jobstown diffused the revolutionary
fervour of middle Ireland. It had a far more deleterious effect on
the forces of revolution than a thousand baton charges could have.
Middle Ireland looked at the cursing, the spitting and the swearing
at women and children and its revolutionary resolve melted away.

The efficacy of the melting process was undoubtedly facilitated
by the rare spectacle of a decisive Coalition U-turn. Minister for
the Environment Alan Kelly wisely eschewed the normal Coalition
policy of pretending a U-turn wasn't occurring at all and that voters
were just showing their ignorance by claiming their eyes were seeing
what they were seeing. On this occasion, the Coalition had to make
it clear that they were in a state of total, abject and immediate
flight from the people's righteous anger. There was a run on bells,
whistles and white flags as all the nice stuff about conservation,
personal responsibility and infrastructure was thrown out the
window. Instead, the only topic on the table was how to bring the
fixed charge down as low as possible while staying within the EU
rules about keeping the semi-state company off the balance sheet.
Though Paddy was still in foul humour, he knew it was going to be
hard to die in a trench for a water charge of €60 for a single person

and €160 for a family. Pragmatic Paddy, after a brief Syriza moment in the sun, was back in town and after the Jobstown riot, Pragmatic Paddy was here to stay. As for that scratching at the political window – well, that was the sound of old-school Bertie politics slipping the latch over, as the concept that politicians should serve the interests of the people rather than their parties sank even lower in the political pecking order.

For a time the U-turn did not work, shackled as it was by the baggage of Crony-gate. Crony-gate was an astounding squabble occasioned by the attempt of Enda's Fine Gael associates to appoint a poorly qualified Fine Gael Seanad candidate to a national cultural institution. The attempt devolved into farce when Fine Gael ended up ordering its own TDs and senators not to vote for the Fine Gael candidate. Such was the state of darkness in which the Coalition entered 2015 that people now began to wonder if Enda would see out the Coalition's full term. The Taoiseach had already lost his backbenchers, but now questions were being asked as to whether he could even hold his cabinet. The question was indicative of the serious nature of his position, for the greatest patronage any Taoiseach has is ministerial office. The problem Prime Ministers worldwide face with this, however, is that patronage is like cocaine. The anticipation and the hit are things of joy. But the high dissipates terribly fast. And a Prime Minister who has distributed all of his offices is like a cocaine dealer without any product. He is of no use to any one any more and is far more likely to be shot than kept. Of course, residual ties of loyalty – or, more likely, fears of ministerial rivals – mean that, for the most part, ministers remain loyal to Prime Ministers. Prime Ministers can, after all, remove ministers at the stroke of a pen, although the damage that this can do to both means it is rarely attempted. But what happens when a minister's position deteriorates to such an extent that their primary ambition of retaining their Dáil seat, the very locus and meaning of their existence, is under threat?

One curious feature of our Dear Leader's cabinet was that, by the end of 2014, so many of its members belonged to the wing of the party that had voted against him in the 2010 heave. They were all, of course, professing loyalty now, but nothing could disguise the brutal fact that five out of Fine Gael's twelve ministers had opposed Enda in 2010. The most sinister feature of all this uncertainty, from the increasingly addled perspective of the Dear Leader, was the sudden emergence of the Leo question. No-one, it must be stressed, was saying there should be another heave against Enda – 'oh Jaysus, no! Perish the thought!' But ... well, there were tensions. There was no gainsaying that the times were hard. And like the dear recently departed Mr Gilmore, the Taoiseach was experiencing communications problems with the ungrateful people of his party and of Ireland. Not, of course, that anyone was guilty of any tangible thought-crime about Enda's but, really, wouldn't it be great if he took that Presidency of Europe job?

Although we hadn't reached journey's end yet for Enda, it seemed as if the car was starting to travel a lot faster. Our Dear Leader had noticed too. There is a tradition in the GAA that, just before the match starts, opponents give each other a couple of mild digs with the hurl, just to let them know they are up for it. This seemed to be what Enda was doing when he publicly upended Leo at a Fine Gael think-in in the autumn of 2014 with the warning that when it came to health, he wanted to hear what can be done, and when, not how it can't.

In fairness, since becoming the Minister for Health, Leo had consigned so many of James Reilly's proposals to the bin that he was flirting with the danger of resembling the sort of dodgy builder who inflates the price of the prospective job with bleats of 'Jaysus, who built this house? They left a right mess – it'll cost you, I tell you, to clear this up'. But considering the best job Leo had done for the Coalition to date was culling a UHI proposal that even the HSE admitted was unworkable – and they should know – it was a tad unfair for Leo to be throwing down the gauntlet like that. You might have been tempted to say the honeymoon between Enda and Leo was over, except for the minor fact that it had never really begun. Of course, in detailing the catalogue of woes he found in the Department of Health, Leo wasn't in any way casting aspersions on the judgement of the man who handpicked his predecessor. Dear me, you would want to be an awful suspicious old soul to be thinking Leo was engaging in the politics of 'nudge, nudge, a nod's as good as a wink to a blind bat'. Though if you had started to fret about Enda's judgement, you probably wouldn't find a queue of people in Fine Gael to say you were very wrong.

Enda wasn't wrong to be worrying about Leo. Around this time, in a measure of how deep the existential crisis the Coalition Cartel were in was, a lot of people started to find Leo very interesting. It may seem strange, but the most dangerous thing about Leo for Enda was that people found him interesting. That might not appear to be a significant point of differentiation, until you ask just how many politicians do interest the public – in a positive way, we mean. There is Michael D., Joan, Michael Noonan, Mary Lou, maybe Lucinda and then – well, we are in Old Mother Hubbard land after that.

It might seem curious, given how little he has said, that Leo is of such interest to the public. As a minister, he has, for the most part, preferred a chic minimalist style. But in a Dáil where far too many people talk far too much about far too little, the Minister for Health's 'less is more' persona has created a sensuous veil of mystery that intrigues the public. Though no-one could say he has risen without trace, he has governed in a far more subtle way than most thought possible. As Enda's struggles increased, Leo was unseen but, like the Holy Spirit, his presence occupied many Fine Gael minds. In particular, he occupied the minds of those who feared that, far sooner than Fine Gael would want to, they will have to make a decision about the future of their party.

Significantly for those who were having bad thoughts, Leo was the last man standing who possessed the potential to regenerate our Cordelia of a Democratic Revolution. In that regard, Leo's strange strength is that he is defined by that which he is not. He is not a Cute Old Phil man, though ironically he could yet replicate Phil's role in acting a bridge over troubled Coalition waters. It may seem surprising, given his gruff exterior, but Phil was often the Talleyrand that smoothed over Labour and Fine Gael squabbles, generally via a pint in the Dáil bar. And oddly enough, perhaps because he was efficient and didn't get them into too much trouble, Leo swiftly became Labour's favourite Fine Gael minister. Nor is Leo, after all that waste and trauma of the 2010 heave, a Richard Bruton man. He is just about an Enda man, but in a puzzled semi-detached way as though he is not quite sure what Enda is about or quite how he got there. But seeing as Enda himself regularly experiences such moments, that doesn't mean Leo is an anti-Enda man. Unlike the rest of the happy Fine Gael slaves though, Leo doesn't call Enda boss-man. He is still a Lucinda man, but doesn't make a fuss about it – and that's a tale for another day anyway. Ultimately, the most curious thing about Fine Gael's heir apparent Leo is that he is his own man, for were Dear Leader Enda to ask most of his TDs if they would let Enda singe his brand on to their buttocks with a hot iron, the only race would be to see which of them would unbuckle their trousers most speedily. Nothing, it appeared, had changed from the old iron age of Haughey, during which dim-witted senators would leap out of upstairs windows if Charlie asked them to.

As Mr Varadkar glided into the post-Enda leadership game with the easy indolence of a well-fed shark, it became clear how complete the reverse take-over by Fianna Fáil of Fine Gael had progressed during the Democratic Revolution. Earlier that year, the most tribal of Blueshirts, Phil Hogan, just prior to his departure, spoke of how he wanted to be remembered as the Department of Environment's equivalent of legendary Fianna Fáil TD Neil Blaney.

Now Leo too joined the fashion for citing Fianna Fáil heroes. Asked upon his appointment to the Department of Health if he dreamed of being the new Noël Browne, Leo instead expressed a preference for emulating Fianna Fáil's Donogh O'Malley. Chillingly for Enda, Leo's embrace of the Fianna Fáil ethic suggested any move by the minister for the top job would not be infused by the spirit of well-heeled amateurism that had done for Little Richard. If Leo moved, it would be with intent and it would be for keeps.

Leo reminded others more strongly of Seán Lemass. Like Lemass, Leo is a strangely private individual in the public sphere. Though he does not dislike the electorate, which is always a bonus, he doesn't follow the example of so many of his contemporaries who race around their feet like overly energised King Charles spaniels. Instead, he gives them the strange respect of speaking honestly to them. Ultimately, despite his own better instincts, when it comes to Fine Gael's eternal status as a house divided, Leo is, as Lemass was for Fianna Fáil, on the reforming mongrel fox wing of Fine Gael. And by the time 2014 ended, there was apparently no shortage of need for reform when it came to Fine Gael and to a leader who had been coursed to the very point of annihilation. The John McNulty Crony-gate scandal had been particularly wounding, for although the Fine Gael and Fianna Fáil monkeys might come from a similar gene pool, the ever-thinning core of Fine Gael voters differentiates themselves from Fianna Fáil by their opposition to this school of politics. The Fine Gael monkeys, you see, do not just believe they are different to Fianna Fáil counterparts. They also hope and believe they are better than the Fianna Fáil apes. Yet there Fine Gael were, again, down in the tar-pit, playing pork-barrel politics with our sacred cultural institutions. And that was before we got to the new phenomenon of the Fine Gael Angry Birds, pecking away in the background over Enda's 'Father Ted'-style attitude to the ladies.

Amidst all the confusion, the Democratic Revolution had

reached its nadir. Irish citizens had fled from a government that was spiritually oppressive. Such was the destruction of the party's popularity wrought by their participation in the Coalition, Labour's ongoing survival looked increasingly under threat, while Mr Kenny was existing on the verge of political legitimacy. As all parties experienced a fretful Christmas, Ireland was a country in a unique state of equivocation. The implosion of our Coalition and Taoiseach meant all things were possible. Some even dared to suggest, despite all the sickly omens, that a Coalition comeback could not be ruled out.

My, but how we all laughed at the notion.

CHAPTER 16

THE PHONEY WAR BEGINS

Finally, we reach the beginning of the end

Uneasy indeed were the sleepless heads of our various political leaders as they faced into 2015. It used to be the case that when it came to the dreamy musings of our politicians, the dour Irish voter was merely a party pooper. These days, however, the Irish voter appeared to have turned into the party executioner. Having warmed up to their murderous role in 2002 by turning Fine Gael into a zombie party, the electorate in 2007 went the whole hog and executed the PDs. Not even their status as the most clever political unit ever, led by the most modest and clever politician ever, could save Michael McDowell's not-so-yummy mummies and not-so-babyish barristers. Paddy, having replaced the PDs with the Greens, then got out the carving knife and abolished the Greens in 2011. They had a pretty good go at Fianna Fáil as well, although ultimately, like the python who tried to swallow the elephant, they were unable to consume Fianna Fáil completely and had to spit them out. The regurgitated Fianna Fáil, still in a more dead than living state, did not make for a pretty sight.

Spring 2015 marked the end of the beginning of what was going to be, whether we wanted it or not, the longest election campaign ever. The question our Coalition parties worried about was whether Ireland's serial-killing voters had a hat-trick of party political executions planned. A lot of Labour rabbits were certainly looking nervously out of their burrows when it came to that prospect. All was not yet lost for Labour though, for already questions were already being asked as to whether their battle with Sinn Féin would resemble the tale of the hare and the tortoise. After a competitive first lap, the Sinn Féin hare had streaked away for the first four thousand metres of our five thousand metre race, but although the Labour tortoises were still almost fatally detached from the herd, they were holding onto the hope the ending of that particular fable promised.

Outside of the Sinn Féin bolters, Fine Gael was the only party who could say their existence after the next election was probably secure. But in a karmic punishment for the Great Betrayal of the Democratic Revolution, they were being pushed ever more definitively towards having to pursue a post-election choice of coalition partners between the devil of Sinn Féin and the snot-green sea of Fianna Fáil. Intriguingly, despite their status of being, outside of Labour, least safe of all, Fianna Fáil appeared to be imitating the behaviour of the hare by taking a mid-race nap. It was a strange and dangerous strategy. Those in Fianna Fáil who were in Leinster House obviously believed surviving the 2011 election was a form of political garlic that had given them electoral immortality. But as Fianna Fáil's poll ratings slipped ever closer to the 19% mark, the possibility was growing that, far from plucking off the low-hanging fruit of a few cheap seats, Fianna Fáil could actually lose seats.

Nothing epitomised their equivocal state more than their

uncertainty over whether the March 2015 decision of John 'the Bull' O'Donoghue not to run was good or bad news for the party. The cautious nuns in HQ were, of course, offering up serial novenas of thanks over the decision. Fianna Fáil is new and modern now, to such an extent they even have a digital wing where a surfer dude leads out puzzled Fianna Fáil TDs to interact with the internet and the Twitter machine. And the last thing our new modern, hairless, harmless to neither man nor beast Fianna Fáil needed was a florid maestro of mixed metaphors, who resembles a fellow that has broken out from a particularly colourful J.B. Keane play. However, while you can say what you want about the Bull, at least the man who famously warned of Fianna Fáil's then *bête noire* that this country needs Green Party economics like lettuce needs slugs was interesting.

Indeed, when compared to the new, respectable Fianna Fáil, all of the *ancien regime*, be it the Bull or Mary 'quite contrary' Hanafin or even that imp Bertie look fascinating. Their submission to the *festschrift* of respectability had, ironically, created a scenario in which the future of Fianna Fáil bore an increasing resemblance to the old intractable 'Irish Question' that caused such havoc in 19th-century English politics. Fianna Fáil, of course, was not causing any havoc. Indeed, that was the problem. But there were similarities nonetheless, for the famous observation that whenever some benevolent British ruler came close to solving the Irish Question the mischievous Irish secretly changed the question could be extended to cover Fianna Fáil. The party found itself in the ironic situation of trying to ward off the possibility of death by respectability, after spending the preceding four years trying to secure it.

In fairness, when it comes to Fianna Fáil's doleful circumstances, the party was under pressure on any number of battlefields. There was quite obviously the Sinn Féin front where the voters who used to think Labour but vote Fianna Fáil had been stolen by Sinn Féin donning the clothes of Fianna Fáil, in much the same way Bertie the Socialist used to have a nose through the wardrobe of Joe Higgins. Indeed, Sinn Féin have purloined the Fianna Fáil wardrobe so efficiently that they are behaving in precisely the same way Fianna Fáil used to act in opposition under Bertie or Haughey. Many criticise the irresponsible nature of Sinn Féin's non-policies, where everything the government does is a disaster and every Sinn Féin solution is not quite ready to be unveiled just yet. But at least they are opposing. By contrast, though sweet, the refusal of new Fianna Fáil to take on the Coalition with the snarling opportunism of the past has left Fianna Fáil as shorn of a narrative as their struggling Labour dancefloor partners. Stopping Sinn Féin is not a narrative, you see. It is an objective, which is quite the different thing.

Mind you, by March 2015 even the Fianna Fáil Embalmed Radicals were no longer quite so relaxed. But were they too late? For outside of Sinn Féin, Fine Gael was not in the mood to start paying off the interest, let alone the capital, of those votes a winking Cute Old Phil 'borrowed'. The complexity of Fianna Fáil's state was intensified by its complicated tango with Labour, in which Fianna Fáil recovery and Labour's escape from a Green Party-style meltdown are basically incompatible. And that is even before we turn to the havoc that the Country and Western forces of the Michael Fitzmaurice wing of the Shane Ross Independent Alliance may inflict on Micheál's rural rump. Suddenly we began to wonder whether Fianna Fáil rather than Labour would be the ones receiving the obsequies after the votes were tallied.

Then amidst all the jockeying and uncertainty, suddenly something far more extraordinary than all the other extraordinary events of the previous four years began to happen. Suddenly, in politics everything went quiet. There was still noise and thunder, but it was as though we were watching a gunfight where all the lead had been taken out of the bullets. In retrospect, historians will

surely call the first three months of 2015 the Irish phoney war. As
with the original phoney war of 1939, in spring 2015 everyone knew
a great conflict had started. There was just one problem: no-one
could find where, outside of the occasional limp-wristed sortie, the
battle was. Instead, everywhere, even in the normally fertile trenches
of the Health and Justice departments, was eerily calm. As with the
original phoney war, the silence was almost reassuring. But we knew
great and secret preparations were afoot.

So what was the cause of the great silence? A key factor was that
the Coalition had stopped shooting. Given that the opposition had
never started, silence, blessed silence, was inevitable. What was
curious was that the Coalition had gone on ceasefire, even though
they were the ones advancing. Then again, there was a certain logic
to it all, seeing as every incidence of Coalition gunfire in 2014 had
led to either Fine Gael or Labour being shot in the foot. Stopping
that particular self-defeating process meant things were always
likely to start going better for the Coalition.

Suddenly, as the Coalition Cartel began to behave like a normal
government should, phrases like 'Coalition comeback' began to
emerge in a similarly furtive manner to people's admissions in 2011
that they supported Fianna Fáil. It was perhaps a measure of how
terribly the Coalition had performed in 2014 that the timorous
turnaround was easily secured once Enda simply stopped acting
the goat. It also helped that a belatedly humble Fine Gael also
realised they were not masters of the universe. Instead, at Enda's
Ballroom of Romance-style party conference in Castlebar, the party
pledged its troth to Labour in a manner that would have left a gold-
digging blonde who has found a 90-year-old billionaire with a heart
problem in a Florida retirement village embarrassed. Fine Gael had
sifted, weighed and measured, and decided that the best route back
to office consisted of offering the voters the choice between a stable
but loveless Fine Gael–Labour marriage or a Sinn Féin–Fianna Fáil

coalition of chaos. Serendipitously, Labour had arrived at a similar diagnosis.

As for our will o' the wisp Taoiseach, he was just about to acquire a new nickname. Mrs Thatcher once famously warned a Conservative Party conference, 'you turn if you want to. The lady's not for turning'. With Enda, it was more of a case of 'U-turn? I'll U-turn wherever you'll like me to'. Enda's affinity for a U-turn was not exactly new, for the reversals of U-Turn Enda are many and varied. NAMA, for example, went from vilified 'secret society' to a loved and respected feature of the state. If Paddy, as Enda claimed, really likes to hear the story, he need not bother asking Enda or the rest of the most tight-lipped government in the history of the state. As for civic respect … Suddenly, however, Enda started making U-turns in the direction the voters liked, not, of course, that they gave Enda much thanks for it.

The age of U-Turn Enda started with the Seanad when, having originally staked his political credibility on abolishing a house that in Enda's eyes was incapable of being reformed, Mr Kenny informed us all that if he was elected Taoiseach after the next election, he would give 'serious consideration' to appointing 'particular kinds of people' from the Seanad to cabinet. That wasn't the end of the surprises from U-Turn Enda, for the Taoiseach, who has had no shortage of problems with the 'women' thing, now apparently intends to ensure half the cabinet will consist of 'lovely girls'. Dear Leader Enda has remained in U-turn mode over the course of 2015, a change that is apparently the result of mysterious focus group research. Seemingly, Enda has been told by his pointy-headed pollsters that he has to start behaving himself in areas such as cronyism, political reform and the women thing. Clearly, the Democratic Revolution is in a strange old state when the Taoiseach needs a focus group to tell him the citizens want gender equality and political reform. But it had been in a funny old place for four years, so why change now?

The Coalition, meanwhile, started to speak in a unified way on the hour every day about all the wonderful things they were planning to do for Paddy, if he would only give them the chance. Every day there were references to a new golden age of tax cuts, of jobs, of pay increases and jobs commissions. It was the sort of seduction routine that would have impressed any card-sharp. Meanwhile, as part of the Coalition's Operation Transformation, a new modesty entered the discourse of our political Mary Magdalenes. There were no more snarls about the trouble Paddy would get himself into if he went off with that dirty Sinn Féin girl or those loose Independents. But there was much elliptical talk about the virtues of stability and the implied evils of Sinn Féin. By contrast, Fianna Fáil was hardly referred to at all.

However, as the U-turns kept on coming and although Fine Gael and even Labour too began to rise ever so delicately in the polls, some wondered if Enda might be creating the rod for his own already scarred political back. This had nothing to do with any fussing about the Democratic Revolution, for that thing was lying on the flat of its back with its paws up in the air. It was, of course, understandable that after a series of wretched polls, our Dear Leader began rotating so often he is now in danger of being reincarnated as a spin dryer. But U-Turn Enda may yet learn the hard way that those who live by spin tend to die by the electoral sword. It is bad enough that a national leader is evolving into a willing blonde mannequin propped up by pollsters with clipboards. But if all your U-turning is actually proof that you stand for nothing, then you should at least be discreet about it, for if you do all your U-turns in plain view, then no-one will believe you about anything.

Meanwhile, in an indication of the utter volatility of the political landscape, just as a soft breeze began to caress the Coalition's back, the previously rampant Sinn Féin found themselves beating a hasty retreat behind the Maginot line as the carpets of history were rolled back, revealing another heap of writhing maggots. Like all shocks, the turnaround came as quite the surprise. In the wake of the Sinn Féin March Ard Fheis, no-one had been seized by Gerry's faded rhetoric. Instead, their attention had been caught by the youthful desire and hunger of the delegates. Nervous escapees spoke of a desire and a hunger that were redolent of the Fianna Fáil machine in its heyday. Those who spoke of Sinn Féin's fine young cannibals noted that for all the confident talk, especially from Fianna Fáil, Sinn Féin would be outworked on the ground, Sinn Féin looked like it was gearing up for a ground war that grinds out seats.

In another example of how Sinn Féin was starting to look more like Fianna Fáil than Fianna Fáil itself, Sinn Féin appeared to be blessed with abundant supplies of that critical political resource called Teflon. Teflon, particularly when combined with abundant supplies of brass, is the most useful of things in politics, but there is one problem with it. Teflon, it appears, is not a renewable asset. Instead, rather like one of those Eastern fables about genies and lamps, it always runs low eventually – even for a Bertie Ahern.

Up to 2015, the industrial qualities Mr Adams had been supplied with disheartened his enemies. However, as yet another sexual abuse scandal began to rumble within the Sinn Féin innards, it appeared that Mr Adams's Teflon supplies were running dangerously low. The difficulty Sinn Féin was about to face is that the public tend to pick individuals to hold culpable for the failure of institutions. And in this case, the figures who were being most closely linked to Sinn Féin's failing were Gerry Adams and his ever flexible political friend Mary Lou. And more significantly, they were not seen to be providing too many credible answers. Sexual abuse had replaced terrorism as the new case study in Sinn Féin and the politics of the big lie, and Sinn Féin found the going a lot tougher when it came to this new front.

Mind you, Sinn Féin's ongoing legacy problem on the terrorism front was as problematic as ever. This was epitomised by Mr

Adams's woes in America, when asked 'How do you orphan ten children?' in relation to the murder of Jean McConville. Mr Adams coldly replied, 'That's what happens in war. That's not to minimise it. That's what American soldiers do, British soldiers do … That's what happens in every single conflict'. Outside of subsequently noting that his response did not go down too well in America, who impose rather higher standards on their army than Sinn Féin, Mr Adams avoided the real issue: that in any civilised country, Jean McConville's murder would be treated as a war crime akin to the shooting of prisoners of war by the Nazis.

For some, Gerry continued to be a cross between Buddha and Che Guevara, while his solid reserve of Teflon protected Gerry from questions on governance – he's never actually been in charge of anything and particularly not the army council – because, of course, a graven icon like our hero cannot be expected to fuss about such minutiae. But by March 2015, the Irish public's patience was really being tried. Like Haughey, Adams had hung in with an iron will. But all the quirkiness of Gerry's Twitter adventures with Ted could not fully disguise that there was very little of the poetry associated with successful election campaigns to be found in Sinn Féin's brutal pragmatism about how the dead are dead and the raped are raped.

Still, at least when it came to alternatives to the Traditional Triumvirate of Fianna Fáil, Labour and Fine Gael, Paddy had a choice now, with Sinn Féin, a plethora of Independents and Lucinda Creighton's new kids on the block, Renua, touting for Paddy's first preference. But in typical Paddy style, having got the chance, did he actually want it? When it came to the launch of Renua, all the public attention may have been on Terence Flanagan's Father Dougal moment on 'Drivetime', when he stuttered to a halt on the minor issue of what exactly the party stood for. But when it came to Lucinda's new party, the far more sinister background music was the Coalition comeback, as on the very same day as Renua's launch, a Paddy Power–Red C poll confirmed what many of us suspected. There had been a swing back to Fine Gael and Labour, with Fine Gael at 26% and Labour at 9%, meaning they were getting very close to breaking the critical 40% barrier that would give the Coalition 70 seats. It was a long way from the masters of the universe territory of 2011. But Labour's determined break-out from Green meltdown country and Fine Gael's consolidation certainly suggested that a little bit of prosperity has seen Paddy revert to his inner mantra of 'steady as she goes there, lads'.

It was far too early for Renua to despair, for the Coalition's comeback was a very qualified one. A new glass ceiling of citizens who were disgusted with the extent of the Coalition's Great Betrayal had emerged. They could not countenance voting Fine Gael or Labour so soon. Though we had apparently decided to sweep the poor little Democratic Revolution mouse up into the dustpan, this meant the most likely outcome of the next election was still one where Fine Gael and Labour will need to be part of a new home-grown troika. And one possible third leg for that putative political stool had finally kicked into action. But while Renua's launch was well prepared, and even better intentioned, the new party was facing into significant headwinds. Once you strip away all the ideology stuff, ultimately the essential determinant of success for any new party is best summarised by the famous Warren Zevon song where a son, in trouble in Cuba, pleads with his father to 'send lawyers, guns and money'. It is probably excessive to suggest guns are needed – though they haven't done Sinn Féin any harm – but lawyers, money and candidates are pretty firm predictors of political success. And whatever about lawyers, money and candidates were in short supply when it came to Renua.

There was no shortage of idealism and a determination to be radical, but when it comes to Irish politics and success, idealism and radicalism go together like … well, like the PDs – in the long rather than the short run. On the plus side, at the launch, the absences were nearly as interesting as the omissions. The departures of Peter Mathews and Fidelma Healy-Eames certainly erased the Fine Gael rump appearance, and those who joined certainly took the Popish plot look off things. Ryan Tubridy's 'Late Late Show' interview might have obsessed about abortion, but at the launch Renua made it pretty clear that this is a party that is about reform rather than the rosary. In fairness to Tubridy, he did make a valid point when Lucinda used the 'it's our first day' defence once too often about Terence and his awfully big brain-freeze. Tubridy's snarky observation that Renua was 'playing senior hurling now' was wounding, particularly because Renua faced the same problem as any small rural club blighted by emigration: they struggled for numbers. Lucinda is good, but she cannot be the goalkeeper, full-back, centre-back, centre-forward, full-forward and supply the ball. Even Charlie Haughey would have rebelled against that level of control.

Fast Eddie Hobbs did manage to outline a definitive policy position. Sadly, this policy managed to alienate 300,000 public sector workers in two mighty sentences about no new pay increases. As the mandarins in 'Yes Minister' used to say, this was a very brave position indeed. Despite its courage, and outside of the tricky absence of lawyers, guns and cash, the new party will be playing against the wind in one other key area. Renua and its rivals on the Independents front are a living case study of Shakespeare's warning that unless you take that 'tide in the affairs of men / Which, taken at the flood, leads on to fortune', then, alas, 'all the voyage of their life / Is bound in shallows and in miseries'. The bad news for any new party coming in was that the tide that had previously surged for our Independents was on the ebb. There was still a gap in the market, but competition had increased and potential political profit margins were shortening.

In fairness, at least a new party had, albeit somewhat uncertainly, entered the rarely brave old world of Irish politics. We will have to wait to see if it fulfils Machiavelli's view that there 'is nothing more difficult to plan, more doubtful of success, nor more dangerous to manage than the creation of a new system', but there is certainly no shortage of doubters waiting for Renua to fail. Indeed, one of the most intriguing features of the development of Lucinda Creighton's new party is the palpable desire across the establishment for 'that woman' to fail. Of course, Renua is not Lucinda's party. But everyone knows that the life and death of this fluttering political fledgling is lying in Lucinda's cupped hands. The world also knows that, should the new party fail, then Lucinda will find herself in the sort of political desert Charlie Haughey ended up in after the Arms Trial. In Irish politics, it is bad enough if you try to kill the king – but if you then try to kill the very party that spawned you, then forgiveness will never come. The desire for 'that woman' to fail is conspicuous for another simple reason. Lucinda's party, founded as it is upon the concepts of character and independent thinking, represents an existential challenge to the grand old Irish way of doing things.

Of course, the last thing Enda Kenny needed in an election year was for his expelled troublesome priestess to turn into a PD- or worse, far worse still, a Clann na Poblachta-style pebble in his shoe. The bad news for Enda was that Renua bore a far closer resemblance to the Clann than the PDs. After the launch, those who like things done the traditional way chuckled and said, 'forget the policies, who are the candidates?' But if Renua is to be the touchstone that will determine whether, for once, Paddy has been roused out of his endemic apathy by the sheer uselessness of the governing class, this would not be achieved by a few opportunistic discards from the Traditional Triumvirate.

Amidst the hope and the messes, the one thing that cannot be gainsaid is that if that duplicitous fellow Paddy is still genuinely in the market for a democratic revolution, there is a party in the field that can deliver. Difference has suddenly trotted into Irish politics to say hello. It will not be easy. But at least Renua can be cheered by the fact that at least they are not Fianna Fáil, for then they would really be in trouble.

Ultimately, the biggest difficulty Lucinda faced was the existence of Shane Ross in the woodpile as other alternatives began to stir. The alternative Independent Alliance of Shane Ross, Michael Fitzmaurice, Finian McGrath and John Halligan appeared to have had a more fruitful series of conversations with our ambitious Independent councillors than Renua. Shane Ross had been on the trail since Christmas and councillors had been chased in a manner normally only seen in a Seanad campaign. The hope, in particular, was that Michael Fitzmaurice might play a key role. The planned-for split was that Ross, McGrath and Halligan would capture the urban vote and Fitzmaurice's Country and Western Alliance would turn them into a national movement. Unlike Ms Creighton, the new Independent Alliance was still determined it would not operate like a conventional political party. It was an understandable decision, given that the original tight-knit group contained a former Fianna Fáil candidate, a former member of the Workers Party, the Fidel Castro-supporting Finian McGrath and the somewhat differently oriented champion of free enterprise Shane Ross. Ideological coherence would certainly be difficult. However, as the Irish voter noted, he would be at least spoilt for choice on the new party front. Independent TD John Halligan warned, 'we are at a watershed moment. This is building from the people. The voters want an alternative and won't forgive us lightly if we don't provide it'. That remained to be seen.

One thing was for sure. If it was choice Paddy wanted, he wouldn't be getting much of it from the Traditional Triumvirate of Fianna Fáil, Fine Gael and Labour. As the election slowly creaked into gear over the course of 2015, they became locked in a self-regarding, self-obsessed war that was as phoney as the earlier spring campaign. The actual difference between the political alternatives the Triumvirate presented was so minimalistic that the main bleat of Fianna Fáil was that the Coalition Cartel had stolen their clothes and wouldn't give them back. As the jackdaws chattered forwards and back, had anyone who left Ireland in 2011 and resolutely ignored current affairs returned in 2015, they might have thought the Democratic Revolution had never happened at all.

Oh wait …

CHAPTER 17

THE COALITION CARTEL BIDS THE HOUSE ON A SPRING STATEMENT

But have they forgotten this is the most deceitful season of all?

As we entered the run-in to the longest ever election campaign, a curious little vignette summarised the eternal verities of Irish political life. At the humble location of Oxford University, the former IMF mission chief in Ireland, Mr Ajai Chopra caused the slightest of ripples in the Irish political pond via his claim that the ECB had acted in an 'outrageous' manner and went beyond its remit when it pressured Ireland to commit to years of austerity. Mr Chopra, who had been far less garrulous about these matters when he was the IMF chief panjandrum here, said he wasn't surprised people in Ireland were upset about the letters between the former ECB President Jean-Claude Trichet and the late Brian Lenihan in 2010 in which Mr Trichet threatened to cut off funds for the Irish banks if the government did not apply for a bailout. In a contribution that restored happy memories of that time when a certain now Invisible Man had thundered about Labour or Frankfurt's way, Mr Chopra claimed that the possible effects of burning the bondholders that were put forward by Europe were exaggerated. Mr Chopra also accused the ECB of being 'gung-ho' in terms of imposing lots of austerity early, and he said the Irish government was also 'quite aggressive' on the fiscal front.

At a different time, it might have been the catalyst for quite the furore were it not for one slight technicality. Once again, truth and accountability were arriving to the Irish political roadshow that little moment too late. Paddy had moved on from the Troika and all that pain and all the lessons that most assuredly had not been learnt. Even if Chopra's revelations indicated there were new lessons to be learnt, Paddy was not in the mood for turning back, given how bad the first time had been, thank you very much. Once again when it came to an Irish crisis, the salmon of knowledge had escaped in an unscathed condition. Instead Paddy, or, in this case, Michael Noonan, was now busy wagging his finger at Greece, warning that if it didn't behave like Ireland and be a gentle, compliant canary in the coalmine, it would be the worse for Stavros.

In a sense, Paddy was even more right than the Coalition Cartel in his determination to be not at all fussed about the dramatic revelations. Once again, Paddy was getting the plain unvarnished truth when the time was far passed to do anything about it. Rather like our great age of tribunals, the political statute of limitations had long passed and it was too late to impose any punitive sanctions. All that was old history now and though we still had a live banking inquiry – well, fellows like Mr Trichet, the great architect of our woes, weren't for turning up to that dog-and-pony show. Mr Trichet instead said he would talk to a few Irish politicians. The subsequent imagery, where a group of supplicant Irish politicians were hectored, berated and lectured by Mr Trichet, who was sitting at the top table of a posh European event, did not suggest much had changed since 2010.

In truth, Paddy's head had been turned by a very different thing. When it came to the narrative of the Coalition Cartel, the journey had begun with the whimper of Michael Noonan's first budget, where the Coalition set the vibe of 'careful now' in stone. However, by 2015, the Coalition Cartel had been seized by a decidedly different mood as they prepared to enter the great election war roaring like a new political lion, musing excitedly about their 'Spring Statement'. The political sun had finally come out. It was now surely time to bask for a little while and risk the occasional purr. Those who were of a wary disposition did fret over a reprise of the unfortunate 'stars in their eyes' fiasco, where on the first anniversary of coming into government, some Fine Gael genius had come up with the idea that the party's TDs would attend a photo-call carrying cardboard cut-out stars detailing the Coalition's achievements. A humiliated and privately furious Taoiseach was forced to abandon the proposal after Pat Rabbitte stuck a political fork in the concept by calling it silly and misguided. In fairness, the saner wing of his TDs stuck a few more forks in the cooling carcass, as they openly suggested that having a pack of gobshite TDs brandishing placards praising themselves, while people were losing their jobs and homes, would enrage the electorate beyond reason. The collapse of the photo-call was also facilitated by the fact that, even in Fine Gael, there was a scarcity of TDs who would be stupid enough to engage in such a stunt.

The Coalition Cartel was also wise to be wary about its spring frolic for another reason. Politicians have always been fatally attracted to the concept of spring. It offers metaphors of growth and renewal, of new buds and transformation. But spring can be a deceitful little imp too, for its all too transient sun can be replaced out of nowhere by hailstones that dash the dreamy buds of May into the ground. Still, despite the fate of movements as diverse as the Prague and Arab Springs and indeed our own Spring tide, all of which were doused by colder, more fundamental mistrals, our politicians eternally return to the spring concept. And in 2015, the majority of the Coalition were of the view that a Spring Statement, which would act as a sort of mini-budget, was the way to go. The Coalition Magi had been on a harsh road for a long time. It would surely do little harm if, now that the sun was finally on their faces, they got to experience the budget twice, first as a spring surprise and then as an October delight. Certain Coalition ministers now declared that there was a value in regularly having an economic discussion about the trends in the national economy. It was a desire that, oddly enough, had been absent for the first four years of austerity. Touchingly, Brendan Howlin was particularly anxious for such a debate. It would apparently facilitate his duty to engage with public sector unions about how to unwind the emergency financial legislation that underpins pay cuts without putting the country's progress in jeopardy. Of course, the Coalition would have to ensure that the efficiencies that have been brought about as part of the Haddington Road Agreement were maintained. The Coalition was quite anxious to note that any concessions announced in the Spring Statement would be, at worst, a case of Social Partnership-Lite. Mind you, as any good Catholic knows, when it comes to sin or the rhythm method of fiscal contraception, there is no such thing as being half in or half out.

Then, suddenly, the mood of cautious optimism began to change amongst the Cartel. The Coalition's unease was intriguing. In theory, their success in our 'Definitely Maybe' election of 2016 should be simple. All the Cartel has to do was discover what Paddy wants and give it to him in the way the goose gets fed by the gavage. The problem, alas, is that divining what mercurial Paddy wants can be quite the moveable feast – or fourteen-year famine if you get it wrong, as the Rainbow did in 1997. When it came to election 2016 – or 2015, depending on who you speak to – convention said this was not a complex issue. Paddy, we were told, wanted cash and preferably by the wheelbarrow load. Paddy was, by this point, tired beyond belief by the ethic of 'more for less'. He wanted to feel a jingle in his pocket and a bird on his arm. We could hardly blame Paddy either, for nothing epitomised the consequences of the long rage of austerity more than the emergence in 2014 of a strange phenomenon in rural Ireland. Traders at fairs across the country noted the people attending were so cash-poor that they had no money to give their children to spend at the fair. As children and parents wandered aimlessly through fairgrounds with no money to spend on the rides, it was the nadir of austerity, and of life as it should be lived too. The unfocused wandering of parents in a purposeless delight-free circle was, in a sense, a metaphor for an island that had quite forgotten the very concept of delight.

In the early months of 2014, deceitful Paddy had appeared to be quite open in his intentions. It was a case of 'damn ethics, hospital waiting lists and schools – we want the cash'. It goes without saying that for all their 'careful now' talk about modest prosperity, the Coalition Cartel was up for meeting Paddy's unmannerly needs. After all, for most of the Cartel, the greatest nightmare of their political careers occurred in 1997. Before that election, the Rainbow Coalition of Fine Gael, Labour and the Democratic Left had laid out a fine low-fat repast that should have left the voters more than satisfied. Fianna Fáil, however, promised Paddy a fiscal lock-in and the poor Rainbow got locked out for fourteen years. Some difficult creatures, mostly of an *Irish Times* stripe, did ask if the new plans of the Cartel contradicted their regular criticisms in the past of Charlie

McCreevy's economic philosophy of 'when I have it, I'll spend it'. This, however, failed to recognise the key issue was less economic than political. The Coalition Cartel finally had some moolah. The electorate wanted that dosh. The Coalition was going to spend it all right. But it is never, damn it, as simple as that.

One of the most intriguing features of 2015 as it advanced towards Easter was that Paddy was becoming caught betwixt desire and experience. Of course, Paddy, being Paddy, wanted to 'party on'. But the innocence of 1997 was gone. He might have wanted the dosh, but a bruised and, as a result, fiscally conservative Paddy was, when he thought more deeply about things, somewhat gun-shy when it came to allowing politicians let the throttle go on government spending in order to massage their own interests. The Coalition was in danger of being caught in a strange cleft stick: if they did what Fianna Fáil would do – which was what they really wanted to do – and adopted a simple 'spend, spend, spend' approach, they could end up hoisted on the very strange petard, where excessive spending could turn into a vast strategic mistake. Like the diligent primary school-teachers that they mostly are, the Cartel was trying hard to learn from history, but there is a difference between learning and copying. One of the most important things you can learn from the past is that the greatest error in war is to use the tactics that were successful in a previous campaign in your next one, for they may be obsolete when applied to your current woes.

When it came to suspicious Paddy, the question the Coalition had to ask was whether it might be too risky, as can sometimes be the case with famine victims, to overfeed him too swiftly. At a minimum, suspicious Paddy might squint and start accusing you of having indulged in an extra year of famine so you could look all the better when it came to the election year. The Coalition must have been nervous of this, for the closer we got to the Spring Statement, the more uneasy the Coalition Cartel became. The mood deteriorated even further when the Easter teaching conferences arrived. Suddenly, the Spring Statement, which had initially seemed a harmless enough frolic, turned sinister as a line of voters, or rather public sector unions, began to form a disorderly line, waving cheques and IOUs that they apparently wanted the Spring Statement to cash. As the stitches began to melt on the Coalition Emperor's new clothes, Brendan Howlin suddenly began to squawk anxiously about how resources were very finite. Even if the Cartel had the use of the magical bottomless sack of the Bertie era, it would have represented a major job to sort out the unions' endless list of desires. But Brendan was right. We were still living at the edges of the dry age of austerity.

It was unfortunate for the Coalition Cartel that, just as Paddy started getting interested in its Spring Statement, the Cartel started getting so panicky that they cancelled all of the political bunting, the flowers, bottles of champagne, Lord Mayors, bells, whistles and calculators to decide how much we're getting in the tax breaks planned for the perfect Spring Statement lift-off. The initial fine talking about the significance of the Spring Statement was replaced by the Coalition's line that the statement was merely a dressed-up version of a formal document the government is obliged to present under EU rules. Apparently, one of the legacy issues of being one of the PIIGS is that, by the end of each April, every government in breach of EU debt limits is obliged to present a stability programme update – unless they are French, of course. In another example of their endemic attraction to the politics of the three-card trick, it turned out that the Coalition had taken the slight risk of dressing our previously unnoticed meetings with the EU probation officer in a fancier set of clothes and been rumbled.

Sadly, as is often the case with Paddy, the more frantically the Coalition said 'move away there now, nothing to see here', the more Paddy gathered around, craning his neck to see what was going on.

And when he didn't see anything, Paddy started to grumble that the Coalition was obviously hiding what was going on. The Cartel nearly succeeded in deterring the storm with the warning that the Spring Statement would mostly deal with macroeconomic issues. Nothing chills the blood of citizens, or, worse still, citizen journalists, more than the prospect of having to endure a macroeconomic statement. But it was too late. The horse has bolted and the grey goose had disappeared too. Paddy wanted his Spring Statement, and he wanted it to be a good one.

Paddy's desires in that regard exposed the fundamental error in Enda Kenny's claim that Paddy likes to know the story. It was a classic case of 'close, but no cigar'. Paddy does like to know the story, but only when it is a nice one. When it comes to politicians and sad stories or moral tales with virtuous lessons, Paddy gets diverted fairly easily. In the case of the Spring Statement though, Paddy had gotten it into his head that Enda and Joan were going to tell him a nice story. This meant that he had the knives prepared for any failure to live up to a promise that actually hadn't been made. And rather like the sad tale of Mr Cowen's terrified approach to the Taoiseach's office, the growing reluctance of the Cartel to tell him what he wanted to hear began to make Paddy feel awful suspicious. As journalists sharpened their knives with phrases such as 'the Emperor's new clothes' and 'damp squib', the mood was turning against the latest production of our political *Wizards of Odd* before the story had begun.

Though the unease within the Coalition was understandable, the situation was not irretrievable. The Spring Statement did not have to be about the economy. Not everything is about cash in hand, even for Paddy. It could have been about the espousal of new values and a confession of sin. Though politicians hate apologies in the same way that the fox loitering around a henhouse dislikes a barking dog, a belated declaration of penitence for the Great Betrayal of the Democratic Revolution could have been attempted. Outside of the minor issue of finally hearing the truth, the electorate love nothing more than penitent public figure, even if they are politicians. In Ireland, this started with Ben Dunne, who casually confessed to a vast list of sins – after he had been caught – and was blessed, forgiven and freed to sin as much as he liked immediately afterwards.

The truth of the matter was that there was good cause for an apology. For all of the modest prosperity fluttering fitfully around the sails of the previously damned crew of the spectral Coalition ship, the abandoned Democratic Revolution was the phantom of the Irish political opera. The Coalition Cartel could point to modest economic successes. But when it came to fulfilling the promised moral revolution, they had, by any standard, failed, failed utterly. The sacked and pillaged nature of the state they inherited in the 2011 election meant they could have attempted anything, for Fianna Fáil was not the only institution that had been left in ruins. They were merely the tattered flag that signalled deeper ruination. When it came to the rest, the real big fish, such was the devastated state in 2011 of the forces of political cronyism, of crony capitalism, of the Ceausescu-style edifice built by the social partner cronies, of the hollowed out kings and captains of the mandarin master class of secretary generals and regulators, anything could have been attempted and much could have been achieved. Instead, on the Coalition's first day, it had been Joe Higgins with his poorly received comparison of our new democratic revolutionary apprentices to the Irish Parliamentary Party of 1914, fit only to appease imperial masters, who had gotten it right.

Perhaps any attempt to reform poor Paddy would have been unworkable. But when it came to the no man's land of the Democratic Revolution, the Cartel had evaded the razor wire of reform, sped into the trenches and stayed there. Nothing more dangerous than axing a couple of town councils or allowing carefully whipped government TDs to talk for longer had been attempted. All the great enemies, the NAMA secret society, the bankers and builders had, after a brief period of almost apologetic exile, been allowed to first tiptoe and then march proudly back into government buildings. And then the Cartel came tripping on to the political stage looking for applause and roses. It was too late on that front. When it came to the Great Betrayal of the Democratic Revolution, the Cartel were like bold children who had been caught but, despite the chocolate stains on their mouth, would not admit to the crime. But was this the wisest course to take? Did the territory not exist for the admission that honest errors, sparked by the difficulties of the times, had been made? Like mysterious Magi, the Coalition could have declared that a long and arduous journey had been made, with snow eternally in their eyes and the tribespeople icy in their approach. A Great Betrayal had been committed, but, the Coalition could have said, it was of the accidental variant. It had not been committed with malicious aforethought. And now that a little light was shining upon everyone's faces, the Coalition could have directed us to a better roadmap from now. The Democratic Revolution might be deceased, but the congealing mix of fur, feathers, spit and sawdust left behind could still be regenerated. The phoenix could rise again from the brimming spittoon.

In a different time, Dear Leader Enda would have been the man for that particular task. What was needed was some of the empathy and regeneration stuff, tales of how my grandfather was a lighthouse keeper, pledges to shine a new light of hope upon the radiant future of our children – you know the drill. Sadly, when the Spring Statement arrived, it was abundantly clear the remaining Grumpy Old Men and their newer cabinet compatriots were too out of puff for that kind of stuff. The Spring Statement included many lists, as one of the grand features of the new age of 'more for less' is the prevalence of lists. Another 'more for less' feature, namely many fine projections and numbers, was in the Statement too. That, unfortunately, was where it ended. And while the figures themselves might have been pretty, there was neither heart nor sparkle attached to the event. It had, in short, disintegrated into another 'to do' list, which was all too reminiscent of the beginning of the Grumpy Old Men's reign via the whimper of Michael Noonan's anti-budget. Now, the Coalition was apparently intent on repeating the trick as a conclusion to their period in power.

The reign of the Coalition is all but over now anyway. We may have some time to go, but when it comes to the major political powers and the forthcoming election, despite its unofficial status as the Definitely Maybe 2016 vote, the only uncertainties about the big powers are when the roadshow will commence and who will live or die. We are closing in on the territories of the great *Rubáiyát of Omar Khayyám* and its warning about the infamous Moving Finger that 'writes; and, having writ, / Moves on: nor all thy Piety nor Wit / Shall lure it back to cancel half a Line, / Nor all thy Tears wash out a Word of it'. The Moving Finger has not yet quite finished writing about the Coalition. But after the Spring Statement, it was blowing on the ink.

The battle line-up is surprisingly clear. On the one side, the Coalition has finally fully embraced the Noonan–Kenny doctrine of cautious conservatism, where all we should aspire to is restoration rather than revolution. The growing acceptability of this philosophy provides us with a profound example of how nothing changes, no matter what happens, in Irish politics, for after all of the drama of the preceding years, we appear to be set for a reprise of the 1997 election. After that election, an overly strong Fianna Fáil and a dangerously weak PD coalition governed with the help of four of the oddest country and western-style Independents seen in the country. Now, under Bertie-Lite, the Coalition seems to be setting its hat no higher.

Mind you, at least Bertie faced a challenge. By contrast, while it is never unusual to say the opposition are the worst in the history of the state (TWOITHOTS), this lot are definitely special in terms of TWOITHOTS Syndrome. There is, of course, a reason why every opposition is dreadful. The vast boggy centre of Irish politics means that oppositions, or rather the big opposition parties, rarely have anything interesting or different to say to their government doppelgangers. That said, on this occasion, it really is the worst opposition ever. The metaphysical conjoining of the Sinn Féin Scientologists and the Fianna Fáil Embalmed Radicals is not accidental either. Whether they like it or not – and on this occasion they most assuredly do not – the alternative government being presented to the electorate consists of the dominant forces in the opposition benches. While Fine Gael and Labour snuggling up to each other may inspire similar emotions in the electorate as in teenage children watching their parents kiss, it has, more importantly, imposed an iron strategic bind upon the opposition. Whether Sinn Féin and Fianna Fáil like it or not – and again, they don't – the Fine Gael–Labour *entente non-cordiale* has forced these two very different political ghouls into each other's arms. It is, alas, a marriage made in hell, consisting as it does of a Fianna Fáil party that, like Fine Gael in the past, has responded to the attempt by the Coalition to it them by attempting to murder each other, and Sinn Féin, a party that stands for nothing except being the political equivalent of one of those Ponzi schemes in which naive fellows end up buying an apartment block in Bulgaria and wondering when the rent is going to start arriving from the locals.

There is, at least, the prospect of something new via Renua and the Ross Alliance. But these are terribly frail armies to be putting into the field against the feather-bedded Venetian doges of the old guard, fortified as they are by a treasure trove of taxpayers' money and a system devised to keep outsiders away from that cash. The new parties, one of which, to complicate things further, apparently isn't a party, would, after their lengthy gestation had concluded, discover that the Cartel had continued the fine work done by its Fianna Fáil predecessors, in squaring the Irish political pitch off. All wars are won by resources, and in a strange way Irish democracy has conspired to ensure that new parties are generally strangled at birth courtesy of a series of rules that make it almost impossible to raise funds from Irish citizens. Given that the same rules appear to be applicable to the big parties, the pitch might appear to be level. But the pitch is, in fact, subtly slanted. In a classic case study of Bertie Socialism at its best, all funding now comes to parties through the taxpayer, and new parties do not qualify for the odd €15 million a year trousered by the current Cartel. The transformation of Irish political funding into something that operates under the Ali Baba principle in *Aladdin* that them who have got the gold keep the gold is as fine an example of political reform under the Cartel as one could find. The unknowing taxpayer is supporting the dynastic principle in politics, and helping to preserve all of the old parties in aspic.

The new political fawns are hog-tied by other key weaknesses. When they entered the political fray, the PDs were already grizzled old veterans along the lines of Napoleon's old guard. By contrast, Renua's ranks are surrounded by the scented air of a children's crusade. There is, of course, no shortage of grizzled veterans in the ranks of the Ross–Fitzmaurice Alliance. However, the competing ambitions of members dividing out ministries before seats are secured means that they are in danger of being hoisted by the petard of their unjustified ambitions. And that is even prior to any damage the Coalition is planning to secure via their Machiavellian intrigues. There is also a slight element of the politics of the makettiup cake about the Ross experiment, which threatens to compromise its future. If you are wondering, the makettiup cake is a piece of confectionary thrifty bakers make when the larder is full of almost finished bags of sugar, flour, cocoa and other odds and ends. Rather than binning the produce, it is all mixed in the bowl in a cook's frolic crossed with a hopeful shot to nothing; if something that is actually edible comes out of the oven, we are in bonus country. When it came to the great Tullamore declaration, where the party that is not a party but – sigh – a loose alliance was delivered, the hopeful ethic of the makettiup cake surrounded the divergent crew that gathered. Shane, Finian and John Halligan were certainly birds of a similar feather. But new additions such as Brian Cowen's former running mate John Foley and former Green Party enfant terrible Paul Gogarty certainly spanned every shade of the political rainbow. Mind you, it was a measure of how the political world had changed that Gogarty's famous 'fuck you, Deputy Stagg' outburst, which had gathered such attention in the dying days of Biffo's regime, would these days appear to be an entirely normal intervention. Renua's launch, by contrast with Shane Ross's Alliance, was more than slightly hampered by the persistent question as to whether there were any ingredients in their cupboard at all.

All this meant that despite the milk-and-water nature of the Spring Statement, the Coalition is justified in looking forward to election 2016 with at least a smidgen of optimism. Such is the rediscovered strength of the Coalition Cartel, if only by comparison with their insipid opponents, the only question that appears to be left to answer is how much will they win by. Mind you, the insecurities left by the disasters of 2014 mean that even innocent queries of 'what could possibly go wrong?' are sufficient to put a wobble in the step of the brightest Coalition spin-doctor. Secretly, you see, they know that the Banquo's ghost of the Great Betrayal is still haunting them. It is the broken stirrup, the free-floating landmine. If the Coalition is lucky, the mine will float by and blow up nothing more important than sea-weed. But who can depend on luck in this world? Fianna Fáil were, after all, the last lot to try that game, and look how that turned out.

CHAPTER 18

THE STRANGE POLITICS OF LOVE

Yes, Paddy has a soul. No, really – it's just hard to find it

'*That new day is here, a bright new day where there is no gap, where the people and its government are one again, a day when our people are united in cause.*'

ENDA KENNY, 9 March 2011

T hough we have, as befits a book about the Great Betrayal, been somewhat cantankerous on occasion, it is now safe to indulge in a modicum of nostalgia as we enter the final quatrain of the 31st Dáil. This was a Dáil with flaws and often the cast of characters has irritated us to the very edge of reason. Some have compared the 31st Dáil to the early days of the First World War, where long periods of boredom were interspersed with brief outbreaks of terror. When it comes to the Coalition Cartel, the division is balanced somewhat more in favour of the terror than the boredom department. It is a Dáil that also introduced us, after the vast unchanging calm of the Ahern-era personnel, to an intriguing kaleidoscope of new political deities. Many indeed are the strange, sometimes wonderful, sometimes terrible political phenomena who rose like mushrooms in the night during the first four years of the reign of the Grumpy Old Men. Chief among these are the Grumpy Old Men themselves, whose belated triumph appeared to almost reverse Darwin's theories on progressive evolution. In the end, gravity did triumph as the more elderly members of the Coalition Cartel were replaced by a new generation of ministers such as Labour TDs Alan Kelly and the somewhat less youthful but still new Alex White. It remains to be seen whether they too will follow the fate of Larkin's parents and replicate the errors of the Grumpy Old Men fools in frock coats, but our hopes are not high.

Over the course of their time in government, Fine Gael split itself between the cawing backbench rooks of the Enda wing of the party and the Frappuccino Kids. The latter briefly appeared to pose a greater threat to Dear Leader Enda's future than the icy Sinn Féin Scientologists who gathered so comfortably around the melting feet of that clay icon Gerry Adams and his prototypical Superquinn Mum alternative Mary Lou. Ultimately, the Scientologists proved themselves as somewhat tougher than the Kids who melted away like accidental frost in high summer once the heat of the incipient election said hello.

As Enda morphed from a cheery *Playboy of the Western World*-style bachelor into Haughey crossed with a North Korean-style Dear Leader, Fine Gael's 'best of times, worst of times' political world contained much to create a furrowed brow. This was the first Dáil where the women question was challenged, if even more by accident than out of any predetermined purpose. But the increasing volume of wails that trailed after Cute Old Phil's revolutionary 'gender quotas' findings, which suggested the sky would not fall in if 30% of Dáil candidates were women, was not entirely edifying. Meanwhile, the Embalmed Radicals of Fianna Fáil performed in such a manner as to suggest they were incapable of reforming themselves, let alone the state. Instead, the party had reduced itself to such a state of supplication that elements of the once great national movement were reduced to hoping coalition as junior partners of Fine Gael might preserve some semblance of the old order of things. It was the political equivalent of 19th-century Germany seeking protection from the old ramshackle Austro-Hungarian duopoly, though some lightness of being was at least provided by Fianna Fáil's pedigree dogs wing, who were still snoozing and trotting around the Dáil with the airy insouciance of fellows on a day trip from the local working men's club. Mind you, they weren't the only ones displaying a lackadaisical attitude. While a great intensity of purpose radiated from the Richard Boyd Barrett wing of the Independents, the general mood of motley in their original ranks was more accurately set by the frolics of the 'Mick and Ming Show', starring Mick Wallace and Luke 'Ming' Flanagan.

As Fine Gael decided its version of reform would consist of evolving into Fianna Fáil-Lite, the state of Labour was reminiscent of the plight of Michael Lowry who, in the wake of the somewhat expletive-filled Phelan tapes controversy, was misfortunate enough to bump into a South Co. Dublin bejewelled dowager who made the famous Hyacinth Bucket look like a wall-flower. The dowager drew herself up to her full height, looked down a nose as long as a town bypass and grandly declared, 'Oh, it's yourself, Michael – the man with all the fucks'. Labour's status was summarised equally dismissively by the citizenry with a similar single transferable statement of 'Ah Labour – the party that broke all yer promises'. It was a Sadducees grave that poor Mrs Doubtfire – apologies, Mr Gilmore – and St Joan of Dublin West found remarkably hard to climb out of.

In fairness, there were studies in determination and a grim sort of courage to be found in the ranks of the Coalition Cartel and the John McGuinness–Éamon Ó Cuív wing of Fianna Fáil. But amidst this, and all of the comic soap-operas too, the one thing that was missing, as we moved past mere survival as an ambition, was any sense of uplift. Interestingly, one explanation for this absence can be found in the most dramatic post-millennium sex scandal of them all. During the Bill Clinton–Monica Lewinsky furore, Irish writer Colm Tóibín characterised their encounter, involving cigars, that dress and the DNA, as essentially representing an 'act of love'. The notion that desire, or love for that matter, could follow so a different path to orthodox convention was ignored in the usual panicky sort of a fashion by the arbitrators of public morality. Yet Tóibín's position captured much human – and political – truth. Desire for youth, for sex and even just for intimacy is ultimately, no matter what form it takes, an act of love.

Of course, one of the great sources of unease that informed the condemnation of the libidinous tales of Clinton was that it was a politician who was engaging in such love acts. One of the features of the modern state is the excision of any concept of love or humanity from political discourse beyond the sex scandal. Instead, in today's strangely frigid political amphitheatre, love, or any form of human passion beyond cantankerous complaint, is the emotion that dare not speak its name. The consequence of this, alas, is the creation of a new Puritan class of politicians who neither imagine nor feel nor emote, except in a false, pre-arranged sort of way.

It was not always this way. That grey icon of the Irish Republic Seán Lemass, who was a child of grit and strife rather than soft delights, famously claimed that the best of politics was informed by the love of people, of community and of country. However, the rise of the focus group means love and sometimes, outwardly at least, desire itself has been replaced by science crossed with fear. This means real Clinton- and Lemass-style humans have been replaced in the non-beating of modern politics with Labour robots, the Fine Gael Puritans and the harmless, interchangeable nodding pedigree dogs of the Fine Gael – apologies, Fianna Fáil opposition bench. Politics is now the changeling child under the tyranny of the focus group. But curiously, just like the Tin Man in *The Wizard of Oz* who cannot be happy or redeemed until he gets a real heart, the excision of the beating heart of humanity from politics has created unhappy politicians and even more miserable voters.

When it came to life under the sphinx without a riddle otherwise known as our Dear Leader Enda, love was particularly conspicuous in its absence from the politics of the Coalition. There was a brief wedding night-style consummation on election night 2011, when hope appeared to be intent on rhyming with history courtesy of the dramatic Democratic Revolution *démarche*. That moment and the passionate vigour of Enda Kenny's accession speech suggested that a new politics centred on the revolutionary concept of love might occur. The consummation was almost as brief, alas, as one of Henry VIII's marriages and no issue emerged from Enda's brief, loving knee-trembler with the Democratic Revolution. Instead, rather like Henry VIII, Enda and the rest of the league of Grumpy Old Men spent most of their subsequent time in office trying to place that unruly Democratic Revolution damsel into an appropriate care home. The Coalition Cartel never specifically denied that the democratic revolutionary flirtation had occurred. But psychologically they developed an intense sense of separation from the project. Such was the extent of the distance, it was as though another administration from a different age had spoken the words which ushered the people's revolutionary aspirations through the political door.

This distance, of course, is the Great Betrayal that has dogged the Coalition Cartel in a similar manner to the albatross haunting the Ancient Mariner. In economic terms, no-one can doubt the restoration they have forged has been a modest success and has brought with it an even more modest degree of prosperity. But the Great Betrayal has been a psychological and a moral one. In a beaten-down Republic full of troubled citizens, who looked at the scrapheap of their lives and hoped there could be a better way to do things, the 2011 election marked their definitive declaration that they were thirsting for reform. Instead of delivering on the electorate's hopes, the Coalition Cartel looked at the poisoned waters of the Irish political well and threw a few more bags of sand into it in the hope that filling it up might hide the smell of decomposition.

All of this led to an awesome sense of alienation as Irish citizens turned their face from every school of politics. Their response was understandable as, once again, politics had failed in a manner that suggested success was almost impossible. But though it might seem that way, politics does not always have to fail. Or it can at least try to fail more efficiently. For that, admittedly limited, aspiration to be met though, politics and politicians do have to try to evolve. That was not at all easy for our lot of Grumpy Old Men, who were used to doing things in a certain way. One of the little habits they had picked up over their many years in Leinster House was an understandable mistrust of Paddy's enthusiasm for reform. In fairness, the Coalition's suspicion that the Irish voter is a capricious, amoral opportunist who will always, if given the choice, slink over to a winking Berlusconi rather than a reforming Savonarola was justified, for even Paddy had difficulties with the notion of self-improvement. It does not, of course, help in that regard that one of the integral parts of Irish nature, thanks to our colonial past, is that Paddy is excessively hard upon himself. This problem with self-esteem means Paddy engages in self-flagellation beyond a point that is reasonable since, like any proper masochist, Paddy is only happy when he is confessing to a general state of base worthlessness. This means that when politicians tell him he cannot be improved, Paddy is often all too willing to be convinced of the correctness of this for his own good.

Paddy's complex relationship with reform is not at all helped by the cruel reality that Paddy has rarely been spoilt for choice when it comes finding a political party that might inspire him to improve himself. Paddy's unease with the reform thing is also not helped by the fallout from previous experimentation. The drowning of the poor Green puppies, the evolution of the PDs into the downtown office of Fianna Fáil and the even more unfortunate transformation of the Workers Party into Labour – or did that occur the other way round? – are all too familiar tales. Still though, every now and again Paddy gets a notion and goes cantering down the thorny old reform road. You see, despite all of the evidence, Paddy really does have a soul. His problem is just that it is not easy to find it. Indeed, occasionally even Paddy himself has quite the struggle in this regard. But sometimes, just sometimes, the weight of public expectation like that which existed in 2011 means the political classes feel obliged to have a run at the reform thing – on paper at least.

On his accession to the Taoiseach's office, Enda Kenny concluded an emotional speech by suggesting that it was now time 'for Ireland and each other, let us lift up our heads, turn our faces to the sun and ... hang out our brightest colours'. The colours are well washed out now. However, although the cynics are smiling, was it always destined to end this way? It might be entertaining in a grim reductive sort of way to suggest our not-so-bright new government of the Grumpy Old Men were always bound embrace the narrative of *Animal Farm* and that such will be the fate of their successors. But although amorality is rife in Irish politics, waving the white flag to the imperatives of the cynical impulse is an equally amoral act. It also makes life far too easy for our much disparaged political elite, since if we declare our expectation is that they will do and achieve nothing, then where is the impulse for them to challenge this?

We cannot, of course, evade the reality that the Grumpy Old Men contributed mightily, and with a rare enthusiasm, to their defenestration. The problem, you see, was that they charged in to attempt to tackle the symptoms of the Irish disease without pausing to first discover what the sickness actually was. The new Coalition simply decided the sickness was Fianna Fáil and that happily had been sorted out by the electorate. But we all know the Irish illness is far more complex than that. A proper recognition of this would have given the Coalition Cartel a compass to chart a route out of the morass our society had fallen into with eyes that were far more open than we pretend. Instead, turning Fianna Fáil into Guy Fawkes had the ironic consequence of allowing our Pious Protestors – or at least the Fine Gael wing of them – to turn into Cute Hoors at such a lick they were in danger of getting a collective speeding ticket.

It is, even after all that has happened, possible to sympathise with the travails which followed the Coalition. We should be careful, mind, for Paddy is a sucker for sympathy, even as she is picking his wallet. However, our grey heroes do have a defence for their cynical devolution to the default stance of self-pity so swiftly after gaining power. All governments tend to operate in distinct phases, which could be summarised as a four-quatrain poem. Normally, unless they are on their third ride on the not-so-merry-go-roundabout, the first quatrain is a period of green shoots and spring cleaning. During this time, the political world smells of fresh paint. All is optimistic, yet tremulous too, for you never know when unexpected frosts will chill the precious green shoots of ministers' new policies.

The uncertainties of spring, if survived, are usually followed by a brief summer quatrain, in which the government confidently basks in the warmth of the people's approval. Whether this is real or they are confusing self-approval with the views of the citizens is immaterial. If all goes well in summer, the next quatrain tells of how a government might, after a period of autumnal mellow fruitfulness, be re-elected. Sadly, for all administrations, the final quatrain always arrives, either at the end of their first, second or third terms, when the descent of a thin frost inevitably signals the incipient arrival of their political death. The government will attempt at such points to defy the evidence of their eyes, but there is no point. The inevitable cycle of life means that their acts are futile. There is no such thing as a happy ending in politics.

In the case of our Coalition of Pious Protestors, however, that particular quatrain cycle was out of sync from the start. When the various wise men and one difficult lady entered the Department of Finance, triumphantly brandishing their medals and trophies, they hoped for the song of an Irish spring. Instead, this administration inherited a nuclear winter where the only sound to be heard was the sardonic whistling of tumbleweed rolling down deserted icy streets. The moment the new administration found it would have to climb a glacier without boots or gloves, things changed utterly. Though they did not turn and flee, our Grumpy Old Men turned from revolutionaries into functionaries before they even began the real business of governing. Unusually, despite the Coalition's appalling start, spring actually did make an appearance, as Dear Leader Enda took to office with aplomb. In fairness, as in post-war Weimar Germany, some amount of dignity and national respect were restored in those initial Coalition years. And these were hard-won achievements. The problem, alas, is that Weimar Germany is not the best star to be setting your political course by in the long run. And in Irish politics, particularly during the ice age of austerity, the run is always long.

For a time, the political climate remained kind to the Coalition, and they experienced a sort of high summer where all things appeared possible. Labour, alas, was still the fretful child that was failing to thrive, but the continued weakness of their enemies meant the Coalition, it appeared, had little to fear. They resembled thrifty mail-clad Normans in a hill-top fort looking down upon the boggy marsh-lands where, like the old naked Irish savages, the massed ranks of Fianna Fáil, Sinn Féin and the Independents appeared to be as intent on fighting each other as their Coalition enemies. Rather like the Normans firing arrows and boiling oil upon their enemies from behind the ramparts, the Coalition were technically under pressure, but their fundamental position was secure.

The author of this particular cautious but cunning theory was our Finance Minister Noonan, whose somewhat mechanistic doctrine declared that all Fine Gael needed was to secure the support of a sixth of the voters, preferably the insider classes, in order to rule in a similar perpetual manner to Fianna Fáil. These numbers were cutting things a bit fine, to put it mildly, and they indicated that we had moved a long way on from those dreamy initial days when we were told this would be a national government of moral renewal. Instead, we got the cautious always-backwards-looking age of King Enda and his footstool of a Tánaiste. Mind you, looking at his scattered enemies, who could blame the Dear Leader for feeling nicely comfortable? But while the Coalition was triumphant amongst the saloon knife fight in Leinster House, the far more diffuse field of the outside world and the growing disenchantment of that five-sixths of the electorate who felt their interests were not being catered for meant they were actually in an uncertain place.

Ultimately, the saddest thing about summer is that autumn can arrive so quickly. Balanced beside the gristly season of winter, this is a time of equivocation. It can be the season of misty fruitfulness, in which the labour of the serious farmer receives its just reward. But, if our farmer has been improvident, if our crofter has slept rather than sweated his way through summer days, it can be a palace of incipient death. As the newly refurbished Grumpy Old Men reached the early autumn of their first administration, it became increasingly clear they were approaching the bad type of fall. The

Coalition was supposed to be the equivalent of that Reich that would last a thousand years. Then, mostly by their own hand, by the end of their third year it looked as though little more than a thousand days would be their lot. And there was worse to come. Strange apparitions such as Renua and the Ross Alliance were appearing in the political ether, while Sinn Féin looked on with sleek greedy eyes at the great harvest of votes that lay waiting for the kindness of any passing stranger. Surely, we thought, the Coalition would not replicate the vast error of their Rainbow predecessors in 1997 and lose an election that should have been impossible to lose. We shall have to wait and see.

Surprisingly, given the supposedly base nature of our natural instincts, the issue that continued to cause the greatest unease between the governors and the governed was that Democratic Revolution business. It was, in many ways, inevitable that when the recriminations and the dust-ups with our passive-aggressive Coalition rulers began that they would blame us. The Coalition maintained that it was simply that Paddy had got the story wrong, as is his wont. Paddy had believed the nice story that the Democratic Revolution would be coming after the election. However, the more familiar the government became with the soft settees of office, the more Paddy was told he had leapt to revolutionary conclusions far too quickly. Paddy, you see, had been so bedazzled by the capital letters being fired at him by Fine Gael and Labour that he had failed to read the small print. Apparently the 'democratic revolution' Enda was referring to had already occurred when the Taoiseach announced it. The case was closed!

This was, unfortunately for our Coalition, an analysis that failed to secure much traction. The voters, for once, had thought the Democratic Revolution was a very good idea when it was mentioned and were not at all impressed at being treated like the polite victims of timeshare salesmen. It soon became clear we were witnessing a dialogue of the deaf, for the government were equally confused and annoyed by the fury of an electorate whose prior commitment to revolutions of any sort, particularly during the Bertie Ahern era, had been timorous. Generally, the cautious Irish Cute Hoor electorate had held that the central article of faith when it comes to modern politics is that it really is always about 'the economy, stupid', rather than democratic revolution and reform. However, entirely accidentally, a phrase casually thrown out to fill a moment of media space became the defining phrase of this government.

We shall never know whether the voters were genuinely committed to this strange notion or whether they were simply using it as a convenient Aunt Sally to berate the government for doing things to them they did not like. Though he is an enigmatic fellow, Paddy, often being strapped for time, confines his ideological concepts in politics to the single sentence. This can vary from 'sound man, Bertie' to 'Bertie the bollix' to 'Ah Labour – the party that broke all yer promises'. And in the case of the Coalition, the measure Paddy chose for the pilgrim's progress of our Coalition was the 'democratic revolution' crossed with venomous snarls about 'broken promises'. The consequences of the public's perception that the Coalition had reneged on the Democratic Revolution were, to put it mildly, surprising. Suddenly, and ironically, just as everything calmed down on the economic front, Ireland began to experience an accelerating existential crisis of being.

In looking at the nature of this crisis, and the growing chasm between the Coalition Cartel and the citizens of Ireland, it is worth noting one of the essential signifiers of a fascist state is the distortion of language and of meaning – not, of course, that the Coalition created a fascist state. Issues such as language are often seen by the hardy Cute Old Phils who proliferate in Irish politics as the political equivalent of 'women's things'. But the arteries of a healthy democratic politics consist of communication and the creation of a shared narrative about what society's goals are. By contrast, in a fascist state, words never mean what they are supposed to mean, because the state always lies to its citizens. Ironically, this often evolves into a relationship of mutual lying, for citizens, if they are not loyal but wish to live, must be as deceitful as their masters. This inevitably means a subversive language of wink and nod emerges, in which the grandiose pronouncements of the current Dear Leader are acclaimed and disbelieved in a sentence and politicians receive declarations from the voters about their desire for revolution with a positive nod and then act as if they had never heard them. Such was the tragic fate of our poor Democratic Revolution as the voters responded to Enda's Bertie-Lite-style winking and nodding with an even more elliptical series of winks, nods and slaps on the back for Dear Leader Enda – until they reached the sanctuary of the ballot box in 2014. Once safely contained within the darkness of the confessional, they gave the Dear Leader the most substantial kick in his vulnerable nether regions possible before scuttling outside to meet their limping leader with a further series of equally false winks, nods and expressions of concern over this terrible assault upon his sacred persona.

It should be noted, in fairness to Enda, that Ireland is not a fascist state – or, to put it more accurately, we are no more of a fascist state than we were under Bertie. Ireland is still a democracy with all of the democratic bells and whistles of elections and parties. The problem with democracy, and the source of the great surge of alienation that sparked the Independent rise, is that all the elections, despite their differing results, appear to create a set of politicians who serve the same classes, no matter who is in power. The critical question thrown up by the great alienation of Ireland's voters, which was sparked by the Great Disruption under Fianna Fáil and grew into a huge blaze under the Coalition Cartel's Great Betrayal, is whether a new political dispensation can be developed out of this.

It is all very well to cluck at Paddy and say he has the free will not to elect another bunch of *Animal Farm*-style politicians, but we have been somewhat lacking in the choice department up until now. In good news for Paddy, the selection box is improving as the Definitely Maybe 2016 monster approaches. However, while Paddy is fairly fed up of the eternal repetition of Orwell's famous denouement, he needs to be careful too. In particular, alienated Paddy would do well to consider what *Lord of the Flies*-style world the accelerating forces of Sinn Féin would plunge us into.

But a change in the electorate is occurring. Paddy knows that the old ways are dated and that in a country where reform has been an alien for twenty years, someone somewhere must chart a better way. It is now up to some fine body of souls to find a way to seduce Paddy's better impulses. The responsibility of our political class is to now go find it.

The reward, you ask?

Well, that's called power.

NEVER AGAIN SUCH INNOCENCE?

Betrayal is a funny sort of fellow.

It rarely is the black and white thing the tabloids like it to be. More often than not, as was the case with Philip Larkin's careless parents, it is the entirely unintentional child of forces that are no worse than a fatal absence of imagination.

Convention will, of course, insist on profiling betrayal as an active art involving infidelity or murder or preferably both. But often the worst and longest reaching betrayal of all is that born of indolence crossed with cowardice. It is the dream not acted upon, the fear not confronted, the task of work evaded.

Betrayal in Irish politics has its own unique aspect. It is the dragon's teeth of the colonial stain we have never quite washed away. Paddy, and, worse still, Ireland's politicians, are never inclined to overly extend themselves to protect a state that is the enemy. The latest and greatest betrayal of Paddy by the politicians he elected was the evolution of a Coalition elected on the tide of hope for a democratic revolution into a cautious cartel that once again left Irish citizens behind in their rush to embrace carefully selected insiders.

Given that we started with him, we shall end with Philip Larkin, the poet laureate of the Great Betrayal, and 'MCMXIV', his elegy on the dead of the First World War. In the poem, he describes young soldiers leaving tidy gardens and marriages behind them on their way to their deaths on the front; we would never see 'such innocence, / Never before or since … / Never such innocence again'.

It would be somewhat excessive to say we were in the same state of idyllic innocence when the Grumpy Old Men tottered on to save the country. But never before had a country been so open to reform. Never before had there been such a trust that change would come. And never before had there been such a willing disposition among the people of Ireland to fundamentally change how we do business as a people.

Instead, though our Coalition's intentions were not cruel, Irish voters, the working poor and the squeezed middle, the young caught in a cleft stick of responsibilities and the collapse of opportunity, experienced the Great Betrayal of their expectations.

The country had been destroyed by the politics of cronyism and insider political trading. Then astonishingly, a government elected to end this devoted their full attention to a loving restoration of that edifice to such an extent that even the dry rot was preserved.

So when it comes to hope, is it a case of 'never again'?

All one can say to that is: hopefully not.